PRAISE FOR TECH LEADERSHIP

"In *Tech Leadership*, Andrew Swerdlow lays out a pragmatic set of principles for leading teams to achieve outstanding results while nurturing a positive team culture and ethical values. His approach is backed up with lots of compelling examples from his experience working for the leaders in the tech world. Highly recommend."

—Matthew Stepka, venture investor and former vice president of business operations and strategy, Google

"*Tech Leadership* is a testament to Swerdlow's dedication and passion for helping others achieve their goals and maximize their impact in the tech industry. He understands the challenges that come with being a leader in this field, and his insights and strategies are invaluable for anyone looking to level up in their career. His writing is clear, concise, and actionable, making it easy for readers to implement his advice and see results. If you're looking for a secret weapon on your journey in the tech industry, this book is it."

—Yan Budman, chief strategy officer and partner, Meaningful Works

"Andrew Swerdlow's blueprint for tech leaders is invaluable as they navigate uncharted waters in this age of generative AI. His ability to extract the most salient lessons and examples provides a practical and inspirational resource for authentic leadership that anyone can use. This book both challenges tech leaders to ask hard questions, and equips them with the knowledge and emotional framework to make lasting change."

—Georgeta Dragoiu, former White House Presidential Innovation Fellow, U.S. Department of Health and Human Services

"Andrew Swerdlow's impressive leadership track record comes to life in every chapter of this pragmatic guide for effective tech leadership. He shares valuable insights on how to lead productive teams through daunting situations, while cultivating positivity and productivity and empowering individual contributors to reach their full potential. *Tech Leadership* offers a rare peek into the mind of a one-of-a-kind tech leader. This book should be required reading for emerging leaders in Big Tech and beyond."

—Laura Klelnman Malhotra, associate general counsel, Instagram, former Amazon, former big law

"For those looking to transition from individual contributor to tech leader, *Tech Leadership* will give you a practical framework to unlock your full potential. With years of experience in the tech industry and a proven track record of developing successful teams, Andrew Swerdlow provides valuable insights and practical advice for those seeking to take their career to the next level."

—Lee Maliniak, head of product management, Matic

"I was lucky to work with Andrew Swerdlow at Google. He tackled some of the hardest problems for tech companies and built diverse, highly skilled teams with different viewpoints and skill sets who stayed passionate and motivated despite a fair amount of swimming upstream. The cohesiveness of Andrew's teams is a testament to his leadership talents."

—Jessica Staddon, managing director, JPMorgan Chase, and former research scientist, Google

"Andrew Swerdlow has created an amazing resource for individuals looking to grow themselves and advance their professional careers. In *Tech Leadership*, he combines his real-world experience with deep analysis of the many nuanced aspects of leadership. Actionable insights and developmental lessons are presented to the reader with real-world context and relatable examples. Anyone working within the technology space will benefit from the mentorship and guidance this book offers."

—Thomas Knych, senior technical director, Roblox, and former principal engineer, Google and Coinbase

"In *Tech Leadership,* Andrew Swerdlow presents a fresh perspective on the challenges faced by both new and seasoned leaders in the technology industry. His personal, introspective, and relatable writing style is sure to resonate with leaders at any stage of their journey. Swerdlow's pragmatic guidance spans a wide range of topics, including leading through change, integrating DEI into the journey, and emphasizing the significance of organizational culture. His insights are grounded in real-world examples and well-researched background information, making his work highly relevant for the post-pandemic era."

—Emmanuel Saint-Loubert-Bié, senior engineering director, YouTube

"What an incredibly valuable collection of wisdom! Andrew Swerdlow distills his key insights and learnings from over two decades of experience into a series of practical frameworks and inspiring lessons that are highly applicable for leaders in tech. I strongly recommend this book to anyone looking to transition into a leadership role or grow their craft as a tech leader."

—Francis Ma, senior director of product and engineering, Google

"What sets *Tech Leadership* apart is its authenticity. Andrew Swerdlow draws on his own wide-ranging experiences to distill career growth and team management principles into clear, practical advice and lessons that anyone can use, regardless of role or industry. He writes honestly and knowledgeably about everything from the criticality of vision and communication to the importance of motivating and inspiring others, because he's faced these challenges himself. I'll be sharing this book with my entire team."

—Caitlin Pantos, director of program management, privacy, security and safety, Google

"Andrew Swerdlow was there at the start one—of the original people who helped build the foundations of Google's privacy program. In this incredibly useful view of leadership in data protection, he brings his rich experience and perspective to the topic in a way that will be useful for anyone interested in privacy —whether you are just getting started or have called it your profession for years."

—Troy Sauro, global lead, privacy legal, Nike

"*Tech Leadership* is an indispensable guide for anyone eager to scale the ladder of success in the tech industry. With an exceptional ability to distill complex ideas into practical wisdom,

Swerdlow's book is more than a guide—it's a transformative journey from being an individual contributor to becoming an influential leader and mentor. If you're passionate about propelling your career, empowering others, and learning from today's tech visionaries, then *Tech Leadership* should be your next read."

—Ed Roman, managing director, Hack VC, and former CEO, Ghostfire Games

"Andrew Swerdlow provides an in-depth guide to leading technical teams. His natural curiosity creates a spectacular story that takes the reader around the world and through the history of some of Google's best-known products. Swerdlow teaches lessons learned from his own experience and expands upon those with anecdotes from other tech titans. This book will help you think critically about your leadership style and push your organizational thinking to the next level."

—Cy Khormaee, director of product management, Google

"In *Tech Leadership*, Andrew Swerdlow takes us beyond the tools and domain knowledge we are typically told will lead to advancement, and helps the reader learn the mindset and interpersonal skills that are critical to solving technology's most challenging problems. From fostering a learning mindset to creating an environment of psychological safety for your team, Swerdlow walks you through the qualities that will help both you and your organization remain energized and innovative in a world of ever-increasing complexity."

—Kathryn Campbell, research and insights leader, Meta, Live Nation/Ticketmaster, and Razorfish

"Andrew Swerdlow and I have worked together for over a decade at Google and Meta. He personally helped me transition into product management and then rapidly advance in a way that would not have been possible without his insights and guidance. I'm excited that Andrew is sharing his leadership playbook with the world. I know *Tech Leadership* will help people uplevel their careers—and raise the leadership bar for the entire industry."

—Brian Kemler, senior product manager, Meta, and former Google employee

"Andrew Swerdlow is a pragmatic leader who carefully listened, understood, and sponsored the development of a foundational team for trust and safety at Instagram. He was a champion for many, and inspired the company to fund, hire, and develop high-functioning teams in critical roles. I'm thrilled Swerdlow is sharing his leadership blueprint in this book, and look forward to seeing the tech industry's bar raised."

—Andrew Jeon, director of product, Coupang, and former Meta employee

TECH LEADERSHIP

TECH
LEADERSHIP

The Blueprint for Evolving from
INDIVIDUAL CONTRIBUTOR
TO TECH LEADER

ANDREW SWERDLOW

BASETWO
PUBLISHING

Tech Leadership:
The Blueprint for Evolving from Individual Contributor to Tech Leader

Disclaimer: This book reflects the author's recollections and experiences. Some names have been changed or details limited or modified to protect privacy. Other events were omitted or compressed.

ISBN (hardcover): 979-8-9889849-0-0
ISBN (paperback): 979-8-9889849-1-7
ISBN (e-book): 979-8-9889849-2-4

Library of Congress Control Number: 2023916581

Edited by Scott and Jocelyn Carbonara of Spiritus Communications
Cover Design by George Stevens
Interior Design by Jenny Lisk

Published by Base Two Publishing, San Francisco, California

CONTENTS

Foreword   xiii
Alana Karen

Introduction   1

SECTION I
PERSONAL LEADERSHIP

1. Keep Growing   9
2. Embrace Change   21
3. Challenge the Status Quo   35

SECTION II
PEOPLE LEADERSHIP

4. Show Deep Care   55
5. Connect the Dots   73
6. Fuel Engagement   95
7. Lead as a Coach   113

SECTION III
COLLABORATIVE LEADERSHIP

8. Collaborate, Collaborate, Collaborate   143
9. Create Cross-Functional Teams   161
10. Foster Diversity, Equity, & Inclusion (DEI)   185

SECTION IV
STRATEGIC LEADERSHIP

11. Take Ownership, Initiative, & Accountability   211
12. Becoming a Cultural Steward   231

SECTION V
EXECUTIONAL LEADERSHIP

13. Focus on Top Goals   261
14. Build Capabilities to Drive Results   279
15. Offer (and Receive) Ongoing Feedback   301

Afterword   319
Acknowledgments   321
References   323
About the Author   339

FOREWORD
ALANA KAREN

Oddly enough, as soon as I heard that Andrew was writing a book on transitioning from independent contributor to leader, I wanted to write the foreword. He could have recommended sitting with cats for five hours a day to learn how they rule the world, and I would have been just as excited to be part of his book.

Why?

First, I've seen Andrew in action during his time as an engineering leader at Google, and I know he deeply cares about leadership. Having watched him demonstrate firsthand the skills he talks about in this book, like stepping up to own problems for the betterment of the company, I know that Andrew models leadership. He also can speak difficult truths to collaborate even (or especially) when situations are cross-functional and ambiguous.

Second, I'm a sucker for any engineer who figures out how to lead. Leadership is not an easy or intuitive road for everyone, nor is it for the faint of heart. The engineering discipline doesn't always translate to a strong belief in fellow humans, and many times engineers fall back on the relatively straightforward nature of machines. As Andrew outlines, one must truly have the passion for leadership, and dare I say, a faith in humanity.

After I read the book, it was easy to see why I'd had such trust. Andrew isn't just a successful engineering leader with a career full of experience at Google, Instagram, Facebook, and YouTube. He's also an artist-turned-technical-leader, a founder, a mountain climber, and a parent of an inquisitive toddler. He has been a leader in various unique areas like translation and privacy, initiated the Seven Wonders effort for Google Street View, is a patent owner, and expanded equity at Instagram.

From all that experience, he has collected his own research and that of others to write a manual for how to become a strong and well-rounded leader. His approach is thorough, starting from mindset to how you build relationships, engage with your team, and manage performance. The book is full of personal anecdotes, stories, and experiences from other companies and leaders, and research examples. Most importantly, Andrew provides exercises for you and your team.

Now I'll turn this over to Andrew on how you can join the leadership journey, as he says, "One step at a time."

Alana Karen
Twenty-plus-year director at Google
Author of *The Adventures of Women in Tech: How We Got Here and Why Stay* and *The Adventures of Women in Tech Handbook*

INTRODUCTION

"Stone Age. Bronze Age. Iron Age. We define entire
epics of humanity by the technology they use."
—Reed Hastings, CEO of Netflix

When Charles Babbage developed the first mechanical computing device in 1822, humankind had no idea that the world had just entered the Technological Age (Encyclopedia Britannica 2022). Today, more than five billion people across the globe use the internet regularly. Beyond laptop internet connections, mobile phones are used by 92 percent of internet users to access that technology. Researchers estimate that more than two-thirds of the world's population will be online by the end of 2023 (DataReportal 2022).

As more people gain access to technology, the need for skilled tech workers keeps accelerating. The tech sector currently makes up nearly 8 percent of the US workforce and is the second largest industry, with more than half a million tech companies (Flynn 2022).

Tech's ongoing growth presents both a challenge and an opportunity. *Forbes* recently asked multiple tech leaders about the challenges facing the industry. Tech leaders expressed these concerns, wondering how they could—

- Keep up with the pace of digital transformation.
- Upskill and retain current tech workers.
- Cope with staff shortages.
- Engage remote team members.
- Differentiate themselves in the marketplace.
- Develop the next generation of workers.
- Combat team-member burnout.
- Retain and recruit the next generation of tech workers.
- Implement meaningful diversity, equity, and inclusion initiatives (Forbes 2022).

Having worked in tech for two decades—mostly in leadership at companies like Google, YouTube, Facebook, and Instagram—I would add one more challenge and opportunity: *equipping tech leaders to lead*. And that's why I wrote this book. While mentoring hundreds of individual contributors through the years, I never found a written resource that served as a blueprint for moving from *contributor* to *tech leader*.

Sadly, the tech sector has a deficit of qualified leaders.

- Typical MBA programs focus on the block-and-tackle of traditional management, the same theories and processes used in old-school assembly-line manufacturing jobs. These programs don't sufficiently address the challenges of leading in the fast-paced tech world.
- Tech companies already struggle with finding qualified, diverse tech workers, but the bigger challenge is developing diverse leaders. Tech workers, especially those in traditionally

underrepresented groups, need a resource that contains the *tribal knowledge* required for breaking into leadership roles.

- Tech companies often promote "top engineers" into leadership roles. This removes high-performing engineers from their teams, leaving a void in engineering expertise. Even worse, these promotions frequently turn the best engineers into mediocre leaders. Without specific training, these newly-promoted leaders revert to acting like individual contributors, more comfortable *doing the work* instead of *leading the best work* in their teams.

Are you wondering if this book is for you? Consider:

- Are you a high performer in your current role?
- Are you willing to develop a leader's mindset?
- Do you have an insatiable desire to learn new things?
- Do colleagues come to you for help, because they see you as both knowledgeable and eager to share what you know?
- Do you believe you can create a deeper, more positive impact by leading others rather than being a sole knowledge worker?

If you answered yes to those questions, this book will teach you the most critical leadership areas to develop to become a well-respected tech leader.

Andrew Swerdlow

SECTION I

PERSONAL LEADERSHIP

Most universities require prerequisite courses such as calculus, statistics, and linear algebra before pursuing a degree in computer science. Which is why I had to retake many of my high school math and science classes. I knew (and the university I applied to reinforced) that if I lacked the fundamentals, I'd struggle with the computer science coursework.

Leading others also has some prerequisites. For example, leaders must possess the right reasons to lead. If you'd be happy doing anything besides leading others, do that instead. If you get into leadership for the wrong reasons, you'll be miserable, your team will be miserable, and you'll never achieve great results.

Answer this question honestly: *why do you want to become a leader?* If it's because you're bored with your current role, stay out of leadership. Boredom indicates that you lack a fire burning inside of you. Earning the title of leader won't ignite that void. If you want to lead because you long for the "trappings" of leadership—like title, money, or power—your team will know it. You could make an outstanding solopreneur, but pass on leadership. Professionals are too savvy to support your ego quest.

Not just anyone should lead. Leadership is a calling. If you're hard-wired to achieve greatness, you can accomplish that as a knowledge worker and subject-matter expert. Leadership, though, isn't about personal greatness; it's about bringing out greatness in others.

Every great leader I've worked with felt a burning desire to serve others—driven by what they could give, not get. Whatever they learned, they shared.

The best leaders care for those around them, and as a result, build positive, collaborative teams. Instead of micromanaging or being "the smartest person in the room," great leaders empower others and surrounded themselves with brilliant team members. They love coaching and supporting.

If that sounds like you, you're my ideal reader. Because you can become a phenomenal leader.

But possessing the right purpose is only one prerequisite. The first three chapters outline the other prerequisites for evolving into a valued leader:

- Keep growing.
- Embrace change.
- Challenge the status quo.

CHAPTER 1
KEEP GROWING

A TALE OF TWO TEAM MEMBERS

Tracy and Jamal (all names in this book have been changed) were individually assigned with completing different tasks, ones unlike anything they'd done in the past.

I don't even know where to begin. I'm at a loss, Tracy told herself once she started. After a couple of hours of online research and asking her coworkers for their ideas, Tracy concluded, "I can't do this. I don't know why I thought I'd be any good in programming."

On the other side of the office, Jamal sat with his own nearly impossible bug and had some similar thoughts. *I don't even know where to begin*, he thought as he organized the task. *This is completely beyond my experience.* But after a couple of hours of researching online and asking his coworkers for their ideas, Jamal unblocked himself and came to a different conclusion: *I can do this. I can find a way.*

Who was right, Tracy or Jamal? It turns out, they both were.

This saying commonly attributed to Henry Ford is right: "Whether you think you can, or you think you can't, you're right."

FIXED VERSUS GROWTH MINDSETS

In her 2006 groundbreaking book, *Mindset: The New Psychology of Success*, psychologist Carol Dweck shared her research about *fixed* or *growth mindsets*. She concluded that people with a growth mindset are more able to persevere despite challenges to succeed. But what is a fixed or growth mindset?

Dweck defines people with a *fixed mindset* as those who embrace the belief that their abilities are fixed and can't expand. Individuals with a fixed mindset view talent and intelligence as something you either have or don't. Justifying their inability to learn, grow, and succeed, adherents to a fixed mindset embrace the misconception that says, "There's no sense in trying if I'm just going to fail."

Dweck describes those with a *growth mindset* as individuals who believe that learning is a lifelong endeavor, and these individuals have nearly infinite learning abilities. People with a *growth mindset* find ways to learn, grow, and succeed despite their challenges (Dweck 2016). That's because they live with a different reality: *what I don't already know, I can learn.*

Fixed Mindset Beliefs	Growth Mindset Beliefs
My skills and abilities are set. I either know something, or I don't. I can't change that.	My skills and abilities grow over time based on what I choose to learn. There's no limit to what I can learn and apply. It changes throughout my life.
Feedback is code for criticism.	Feedback is fodder for growth.
I'm really bad at ____.	I'm not great at ____ today, but with effort I can improve.
I wasn't born smart.	I was born with endless potential.
Your success makes me feel like a failure.	Your success shows me that I, too, can be successful.
Repeated failure tells me I should quit trying.	Repeated failure means I'm closer to success! I've already eliminated things I know that don't work.

Think back to the story of Tracy and Jamal. Tracy believed she had limited capabilities, that the work she'd been assigned fell beyond her abilities. That belief, not her lack of intelligence, prevented her from completing her task. Jamal—a coworker with the same formal education, experience, and intelligence as Tracy —believed that he could learn and succeed, leading him to push himself, start his task, try new things, implement various ideas, and succeed.

YOU BELIEVE WHAT YOU TELL YOURSELF

I had no background in tech. I wanted to be an artist. After entering the UK to make just enough money to continue travelling across Europe, I discovered that I enjoyed the varied roles in my new job at a telecommunications company. I answered phones, made sales calls, and helped customers—all responsibilities that I enjoyed more than I expected. I didn't have to stretch myself in that job to succeed. I already knew how to use a phone, say hello, and talk in a polite, engaging manner. My leader didn't need to teach me those skills.

After a short time, I reached a defining moment in my career when I could choose either a fixed or growth mindset. If I chose a fixed mindset, I would have told myself, *I'm an artist, not a Techie. I don't know anything about engineering. Only "technical" people can figure out that stuff.* Then I never would have tried to learn anything about tech beyond using the telephone.

"That's my opinion and I'm sticking to it" is a self-limiting way to live. People who never let go of their views never evolve.

Growth isn't just about embracing new ideas. It's also about rethinking old ones.

Refusing to change your mind is making a decision to stop learning.

—Adam Grant, number-one *New York Times* best-seller of *Think Again* (Grant 2022)

Instead, I chose a growth mindset, which led me to believe, *I don't know anything about technology today. But I bet I can learn.* And that's when I taught myself how to do basic scripting, programming, and systems administration.

I didn't learn engineering skills because I'm "smart"; I learned technical skills because I told myself that *I could learn technical skills.* I applied that same growth mindset when I decided that I could learn how to lead.

BUILDING A GROWTH MINDSET

Think back to when you learned something new, like how to ride a bike, drive a car, or write a basic computer program. You weren't born knowing how to do any of those things. You had to learn. But you did.

The same is true with leadership skills. You can learn to lead.

Start the day saying this to yourself: *I can learn whatever is required to be a successful leader.*

Tell yourself you *can,* and you're half-way there; tell yourself you *can't,* and you've failed already.

If your goal is to move from the frontline into a leadership role, know that *leadership skills can be learned* the same way as engineering, finance, interpersonal skills, accounting, and every other body of knowledge—through reading, observation, education, apprenticeship, and trial-and-error, which I consider the most significant method. No one is born knowing how to lead. Real leadership doesn't come with a checklist but rather from life experiences. Making mistakes builds the scar tissue that leads to eventual success.

Fixed and growth mindsets are neither simply binary nor magical. For example, I choose a growth mindset when learning a new skill, such as playing hockey—something I did briefly in my childhood. I learned the rules and various components of the sport, like how to ice skate, hold a stick, and shoot the puck. But I never had the right combination of desire, talent, or physical makeup to be recruited into the NHL—growth mindset or not!

When moving from the frontline to leadership, a growth mindset is the first requirement. In addition to reading Carol

Dweck's book, *Mindset: The New Psychology of Success,* following are ways to foster a growth mindset to accelerate your learning and leadership skills.

Create and Use a Growth Mindset Mantra

I'm a big believer in the power of mantras. They started in Hinduism and Buddhism as a meditation aid. Today, we think of a mantra as a short, simple slogan or statement that we repeat to inspire ourselves and others.

About halfway through a climb to the Mount Everest Base Camp in a tiny village called Namche Bazaar, I started feeling the effects of altitude sickness. As if stomach upset, dizziness, and a headache weren't bad enough, the prolonged exposure to the damp cold chilled my bones, and fatigue permeated me.

My inner dialogue grew incessant. *I should just turn around and go back. No one would think I'm weak. I've climbed higher mountains than the Everest Base Camp. I can come up with a plausible excuse for quitting...*

Then another part of my mind argued to press on. I kept seeing prayer wheels along the path, which are cylindrical wheels on spindles made from various materials, often carved with mantras. Then I spotted locals who not only hiked up sheer ice trails like they were walking on city sidewalks, but they also carried heavy burdens. I heard them muttering something to themselves as they passed.

"What are they saying?" I asked my climbing companion. "Do you know?"

"Yes," he replied, "they're saying mantras to themselves. You know, a few words they repeat while climbing to give them strength and focus."

"Can you understand their words?" I asked, fascinated.

"Yes," he nodded. "I think it would translate to 'one step at a time, one step at a time, one step at a time...'"

I made that mantra my own. The next day, I remained cold, wet, and exhausted. But this time, I faced my hardships by saying silently as I climbed, *One step at a time*. And it really helped. When my body said, *Go back!*, my mind repeated, *One step at a time*. I knew that each step forward got me one step closer to Namche Bazaar. After I lifted my leg, pointed it uphill, and stepped down again, I repeated, *One step at a time*. Before I knew it, I'd reached 12,000 feet above sea level at Namche Bazaar. The journey couldn't be done in one giant leap; it required thousands of small steps, each "one step at a time." That very short, simple mantra propelled me to complete my goal.

Since I'd found a mantra that kept me from quitting ahead of my goal, I'll offer suggestions of mantras that might help you internalize the concepts in each chapter. Following are some examples to get you started on using your own growth mindset mantra:

- *I am not defined by what I know today but by the limitless things I can learn tomorrow.*
- *I am smart and capable enough to learn anything that's important to me.*
- *I can learn whatever is required to be a successful leader.*

Set High Goals for Yourself, and Be Willing to Fail

It's impossible to think about famous inventors without remembering Thomas Edison. The "Wizard of Menlo Park" held more than a thousand patents that included the alkaline storage battery, phonograph, and long-burning lightbulb (Kiger 2020). Few people would argue that Edison was an expert in pioneering new inventions or reimagining existing ones.

But not each of Edison's attempted inventions succeeded.

One of Edison's more epic failures happened when he combined two existing commodities: his wax cylinder phonograph player with a children's doll, which he sold as Edison's Talking Doll. His invention cost what amounted to a working man's weekly paycheck. Children quickly lost the crank to power the phonograph. The wax cylinder recordings that recited well-known nursery rhymes like "Mary Had a Little Lamb" and "Hickory Dickory Dock" were prone to breakage. The cylinders that didn't break grew distorted by heat, turning the once sweet-sounding, female recorded voices into demonic utterances (Dawson 2015). A commercial failure, Edison took his talking doll off the market within a few weeks.

Edison had an interesting and often-quoted perspective on the times his inventions didn't work out as planned: "I have not failed. I've just found a thousand ways that won't work."

If you wish to lead others, expect to make mistakes. When something doesn't work as you hoped or intended, call it a *learning experience*. Instead of trying to avoid errors, learn from them. Make different mistakes next time. Try a new approach. Value what you learn along the way, not just the result.

I embrace the *fail fast* idea of mistakes.

Who doesn't want to develop and deliver a product that customers love—quickly and affordably? We all do! But sometimes even the best ideas take too long or cost too much. If you're going to fail, fail before investing too many resources into a disaster. And then learn from your mistake.

Give yourself and your team members permission to fail. What you learn in the process can help you succeed next time.

Monitor Your Self-Talk When You Face a New Task

Check yourself to see how often you entertain fixed mindset thoughts such as—

- *I'm in over my head.*
- *I need to get out of this.*
- *I must find someone to do this for me.*
- *I can already hear the criticism from my upcoming failure.*
- *This isn't my job.*
- *I can't do this.*

Don't think you're guilty of negative self-talk? The National Science Foundation estimates that 80 percent of our thoughts are negative, including those dwelling on our past failures. The same research suggests that 95 percent of people's negative thoughts are the same ones they had the day before.

Leaders can't allow their minds to trick them into embracing a sense of impending doom before they've even started. Instead, they must challenge self-defeating thoughts at their first appearance.

When self-defeating thoughts enter your mind, replace them with growth mindset mantras like—

- *I haven't seen anything like this before. I can't wait to learn something new.*
- *I love a new challenge.*
- *I've seen others do even harder things, so I know I can step up to this challenge.*
- *I need to find some experts to critique my work, so I can benefit from their feedback.*
- *Failure gets me one step closer to getting it right.*
- *I will make it my job to answer the questions I don't yet have answers to.*

Observe Others Demonstrating a Growth Mindset

Reading about the necessary mindset is a start to acquiring knowledge, but some lessons stick with us longer when we experience them in real life.

Learn from others around you who approach challenges with a growth mindset. Here are some telltale signs that the person you're observing demonstrates a growth mindset:

What They Do	What They Say
Actively seek feedback.	"What can I improve? What am I missing?
Congratulate others for their successes and promotions.	"I didn't get promoted this time, but I will be more ready next time."
Stay discontent with the status quo.	"What if we were to...?"
Volunteer for new opportunities.	"I'm willing to head this up."

The second mindset of leadership relates closely to *growth mindset,* but it's especially critical in times of change and opportunity. Read on to learn more.

CHAPTER 2
EMBRACE CHANGE

SAME WORDS, DIFFERENT MEANING

When Uma and Samuel read the email that they would be getting a new boss, the same thought popped into their heads: *Really?* But that simple word meant very different things to each of them.

When Uma heard the news that a new boss was relocating to Uma's office from the corporate headquarters, she reflected over her nine months of working with her current boss. That boss had taught Uma so much in a short time, and Uma became her boss's go-to person. In fact, Uma grew so quickly that she wondered what else she might learn. So when Uma got word that she'd be reporting to a new boss who had been with the organization for a decade, she was thrilled. When she thought, *Really?,* she felt only positive anticipation of what her new boss might teach her.

On the other side of the office, Samuel's response to the email echoed Uma's: *Really?* Samuel had worked for his current boss for nearly two years, and he'd learned how to stay off her radar. Samuel did enough to receive good performance reviews, and he got his assignments done on time. Even while Samuel's performance was steady, he'd developed a bit of a reputation for buttering up his boss and heaping lavish praise on her every decision. When he finished reading the email about getting a new boss, Samuel's first thought was also, *Really?* But the conversation in his head added: *I've spent time building a great relationship with my leader. Now I have to start all over again with someone new?*

Do you view change as a growth opportunity or a crisis?

Former IBM CEO Ginni Rometty said, "Growth and comfort do not coexist" (Nusca 2014).

LEADERS VIEW CHANGE AS GROWTH OPPORTUNITIES

Ongoing change happens in every part of our lives. Our cells die and get replaced. Ideologies come and go. The stock market rises and falls. Each season passes into a new one. And when it comes to tech, the pace of change continues to accelerate. New products and advancements launched on a Monday are copied, improved, and approach obsolescence by the next Friday.

While working at Google, its name changed to Alphabet; while working at Facebook, its name changed to Meta. Beyond new names, many other things have changed since I began my tenure with large tech companies. On my first day with Google in 2005, my leader handed me a Blackberry phone and a Windows laptop running installed software like Outlook, an Oracle Calendar, and Internet Explorer. Within five years, the entire world shifted to smartphones like the Android or iPhone, and software got replaced with cloud operating systems like ChromeOS, running services like Gmail, GCal, and Chrome.

When it comes to changes in the tech sector, each blink

ushers in a new era. We can't stop or even slow the pace. Nor should we try. But change isn't always easy, especially when it threatens our motivation.

Three factors impact our motivation to embrace—or reject—change: autonomy, relatedness, and competence (Deci and Ryan 2005). Especially in times of change, we consider the ways in which our self-determination will be enhanced or reduced by asking ourselves certain questions:

- Autonomy. *How will this situation impact my ability to make choices for myself?*
- Relatedness. *How will this situation impact my ability to feel connected and viewed by those around me?*
- Competence. *How will this situation impact my ability to experience mastery and be effective in my work?*

Situations that increase the likelihood we'll lose autonomy, relatedness, or competence feel threatening, and we resist them. However, we welcome changes that we believe will enhance our autonomy, relatedness, or competence.

In the story of Uma and Samuel, Uma viewed a change in leadership as an opportunity to accelerate her growth and development. Samuel, however, felt threatened by the same news, fearing he might lose his close relationship with his leader. Samuel could worry that a new leader might take away some of his earned autonomy, or that he might fail to meet his new leader's expectations.

You can't embrace change without a *growth mindset*. But I've known some who demonstrated a growth mindset except when it came to change and uncertainty.

Those who feel threatened by change will struggle to survive in the fast-paced tech industry. That's even more true of those leading in the tech space. Tech leaders must not only survive change, but they must be the catalysts, visionaries, and champions for change.

If you wish to lead, learn to love change. Leaders drive change, whether it's scaling a product to meet rising demand, rapidly iterating in a growing space, or pivoting a product or company to meet a changing market. Leaders must hunger to seek difficulty, challenges, and change. If you're not pushing a rock up a hill, you're either missing the problems or an opportunity.

FINDING THE OPPORTUNITY IN CHANGE

How do you view change? When something changes, do you see an obstacle or an opportunity?

Embrace a Change Mindset

I mentioned earlier that I didn't start in tech with a strong background in mathematics. But I didn't mention I was even held back in grade two because I didn't catch on quickly enough to the materials covered ! I would never be confused with mathematical genius of Einstein, and I had the heart of an artist; yet I still grew into a tech leader. Instead of seeing my limitations as insurmountable obstacles, I took them as opportunities and made my non-traditional entry into the tech space.

And I'm not alone. Some of the best engineers and engineering leaders I've worked with came from non-traditional backgrounds. One of my managers took a job with Google, because she faced a barrier: she ran out of money to pay for her PhD in art history. She joined the company just as Google hired its one-hundredth Googler. Google saw her as a creative genius and eagerly tapped into how she saw the world. And her team members turned to her for guidance because of her unique take. She grew to be a highly-successful leader. An obstacle didn't kill her dreams; it redirected them and permitted her reinvention.

Another engineering manager I worked for wanted to be an actress, but she also wanted to work part-time in any job that offered an air-conditioned environment for half of each day! Her inability to afford air conditioning brought her to a tech job where she stayed on, earned her PhD in computer science, and served as a phenomenal leader.

Some people seek new careers when their circumstances (like a layoff, family emergency, financial crunch, or shift in passion) change. Others seek new careers for a love of learning and desire to push themselves.

Sadly, most people resist change. In his 2007 book, *Change or Die: The Three Keys to Change at Work and in Life,* author Alan Deutschman points to studies that show nearly nine out of ten people don't change their lifestyles and behaviors *even when their lives depend upon it* (Deutschman 2007). For example, most people refuse the make changes in their diets, smoking habits, and exercise even after a heart attack.

A leader isn't simply the *one person in ten* with willingness to change or die. They change even when the status quo seems comfortable, or at least familiar. Leaders throw themselves into change with such passion that others willingly come along for the adventure.

Lead Others to a Change Mindset

As hard as it can be to accept and embrace change in our own lives, the role of a leader is twice as complicated. They must work through their own feelings about change until they get excited about the next chapter. Then they must bring their team along with them.

When things change, many people get stuck in what's known as "the valley of despair," a place characterized by grief for the loss of the familiar and old way of doing things (Croucher 2022).

No leader has the magic power to eliminate the valley of despair that some team members will experience. However, your goal is to minimize the distraction of the valley as you encourage forward progress. Ultimately, you want them to experiment with the change, decide to accept it, and integrate and socialize it into their new way of doing business.

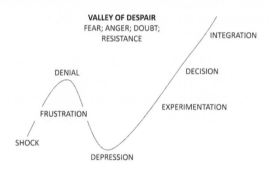

Following are some things to focus on while people are in the valley:

- Focus on the *what* and not the *how*. You will all work together to figure out the *how* at the right time.
- Focus on creating hope. The best leaders sell hope even in difficult times.
- Focus on your people. If you've worked with your team for a while, you've been through changes before. Remind them of other challenges you've faced and how you got through them together.

CHANGE EXPANDS, NOT SHRINKS, YOUR ORIGINAL DREAMS

Remember when I shared that I wanted to be an artist? Theft and financial constraints changed my direction. Did I give up my goal of becoming an artist? Never. Instead, I redefined the meaning of artist, broadened my definition of the concept, and applied the same artistic thinking I used in photography and pencils to engineering. If I had a fixed idea, I would have to consider myself a *failed* artist. I don't. My medium and focus changed but not my creative output.

Today, I live in San Francisco, a city with huge real estate prices. The expansion of tech companies and jobs in the area helped drive up costs. Only the most financially successful artists can afford to live in this city.

How can we bring the arts back to the city? I wondered. Over time, I developed the idea of creating a space for artists, musicians, immersive theater, poetry readings, and other crazy events. I reasoned that if San Francisco had such a space, the city could showcase unknown yet talented artists as they perfected their crafts.

With that line of thinking, I started The Laundry about a decade ago. The Laundry serves as an art gallery in the daytime and rental space for events in the evening. The Laundry has hosted elections for various countries and given local and statewide politicians a venue to share their vision with the audience. It's become a civic center for creative and visionary people.

Yes, I'm still an artist at heart. But instead of creating and selling artwork, I expanded my vision to give a platform to hundreds of artists and their thousands of patrons. The Laundry filled a hole in San Francisco by making art once again accessible—serving the arts community in a way that I couldn't have achieved as a solo artist with my camera and pencils.

Be ready to embrace change. Don't let a fear of the unknown keep you from taking a different route than you envisioned. When a leader dons a change-ready mindset, any goal becomes obtainable. And a leader who can motivate others in times of change will always be in high demand.

HOW TO FOSTER CHANGE-READINESS

"Going through change can feel like grief," leadership trainer and author Scott Carbonara told me on a recent call. "Both change and grief feel final, putting us in a state of free-fall where we are removed from the familiar and standing on the fissure between what known and unknown."

Carbonara said that the commonly-used Kübler-Ross model outlining the five stages of grief—denial, anger, bargaining, depression, and acceptance—doesn't go far enough when it comes to times of change. "Acceptance isn't enough when facing change," Carbonara shared. "Acceptance is the furthest point from the security of yesterday and the hope for tomorrow. Leaders don't accept change; they drive it at all levels of their organizations."

Create and Use a Change Mantra

As you know, I'm a big believer in mantras. As you step into the role of leader, consider developing and repeating a mantra that helps you accept, embrace, and move others forward during change. You can use one of these, or you can use these as starting points to creating your own change manta:

- *I thrive in times of change.*
- *Beyond the status quo lies something better.*

- *My team will embrace change to the extent that I do.*
- *I am ready to embrace and lead change.*
- *I will face change with excitement, passion, and enthusiasm.*

Reframe Your Self-Talk

What words come to mind when you hear the word *change?* What words come out of your mouth when you communicate to others that change is coming? Look at the following list. The column on the left includes words that make change feel threatening. The column on the right uses words that put change in a positive and more helpful context.

Threatening Words	Positive/Hope-Filled Words
Uncertainty Fear Risk Impossibility	Unlimited possibilities Excitement Reward Challenge A blank-canvas opportunity Ground-floor Unscripted Innovative

If you tell yourself and your team that an upcoming change will be difficult, don't be surprised to see a *this-is-going-to-be-difficult* mindset brought to the challenge. If you remind yourself of the benefits of the change, you'll tap into your motivation as well as that of your team members.

Business owner Ingvar Kamprad—born on Elmtaryd farm near the village of Agunnaryd, Sweden—had a problem. As a furniture maker since 1948, Kamprad got hit with two unprecedented obstacles: the cost of his furniture deliveries rose at the same time he saw an increase in the number of damaged products returned to the warehouse.

Kamprad refused to give up. In 1953, he launched an idea that addressed both the cost of shipping and quality of delivered goods. Instead of shipping furniture the way he'd always done it, he shipped it in flat-packs, unassembled, allowing his trucks to transport more goods while the flat-packs kept the products ding-free in transport.

If you're a fan of Swedish meatballs, high-end Scandinavian design, and assembling your own furniture, you probably recognize the story of IKEA, named after the two initials of the founder's name along with the initial of his farm and local village (IKEA 1999).

Kamprad saw change as an opportunity. Today, IKEA runs 471 stores in sixty-four markets (IKEA 2022).

In a perfect world, your first response to change would be "YAY!" But the world isn't perfect, and some changes take time to process.

The next time you hear about an unanticipated change at work or in your personal life, think about your thought. If your first thought isn't excitement as you see the opportunity, challenge your thinking. Then reframe your thoughts, while still being honest and hopeful, until you uncover the embedded opportunity. Finally, replace any threatening thoughts with ones of hope and potential.

Replace Threats	With Opportunity
I'm going to lose something in this change.	I stand to grow as a result of this change.
This change threatens my autonomy, relatedness, or competence.	This change can enhance my autonomy, relatedness, or competence.
If it ain't broke, don't fix it.	If something can be made more efficient, user-friendly, or less expensive, I must try it.

Talk Through Your Feelings and Encourage Those You Lead to Do the Same

Psychologists have long known that putting our feelings into words helps reduce feelings of sadness, anger, and pain (Lieberman et al 2007). Dr. Dan Siegel later coined the phrase "name it to tame it" when explaining how labeling our emotions helps prevent these emotions from controlling us (Freeman 2021).

As a leader, you'll face times when you aren't 100 percent in agreement with a change that you've been asked to spearhead, like an effort you believe is doomed to fail. Do you have concerns? Are you afraid of a bad outcome? Does the task—and its potential failure—feel career-ending?

What if you disagree with a decision made by your leadership? Then it's time to practice the principle of "Disagree and Commit."

One of Amazon's leadership principles says this:

Have backbone; disagree and commit. Leaders are obligated to respectfully challenge decisions when they disagree, even when doing so is uncomfortable or exhausting. Leaders have conviction and are tenacious. They do not compromise for the sake of social cohesion. Once a decision is determined, they commit wholly (Amazon 2022).

Former CEO of Intel, Andy Grove, explained why: "If you disagree with an idea, you should work especially hard to implement it well because that way when it fails, you'll know it was a bad idea. Not bad execution" (Muñoz 2019).

Share your feelings with someone you trust, preferably outside your organization or at least your department. If you don't have anyone available, talk with yourself, playing both the interviewer and the interviewee. Ask yourself, *What am I feeling? Why do I feel this way? How might that feeling change if I get behind this idea as if it were my own?*

Take time to label your feelings. Let's say you feel "mad." Go deeper. Ask yourself, *Why am I mad? Do I think I'm set up to fail? Do I think I don't have the resources to succeed? Do I think I'm being given this task as "punishment" for something?* Go as deep as you can with your response, until you get to the source of your feelings.

After labeling your feelings, you'll find the negative feelings begin losing their power over you. As a bonus, this process gives you insight into how your team members team likely feel— allowing you to talk with them individually to let them share their feelings.

As a leader, it's perfectly acceptable to disagree. But once a decision has been made, it's time to commit everything you've got to making that decision pay off. Disagree, certainly, but commit. Why? Ask yourself this: *What happens if I agree initially but then waffle on getting behind it? Or disagree without really committing?* Your role as a leader isn't just to lead the way, but to follow the way. And if you can't get behind a decision made by your leader, you're probably not in the right role.

If you assume the role of sounding-board for your team members, embrace these guidelines:

- You're not duct tape. You can't "fix" anyone. You're not a magician. You can't make people's problems disappear.
- You don't have to agree with other people's feelings, but you can still offer empathy for how they feel.
- You're not there to debate. Instead of trying to talk people out of their feelings, diffuse their emotions by showing them that they're heard. Say, "I hear you."
- Don't leave people raw or worked up. Listening to others express negative feelings can potentially escalate their negativity. Before ending your discussion, offer them a few words of hope from the positive perspective you're embracing.

The best leaders I've worked with modeled the importance of the concepts of *keep growing* and *embrace change*. But there's one more critical mindset a strong leader must possess as a prerequisite to leading others: *challenge the status quo*. Read on to learn more.

CHAPTER 3
CHALLENGE THE STATUS QUO

THE SPAGHETTI MARSHMALLOW CHALLENGE

Here's the task. The facilitator creates small teams, giving each twenty pieces of dry spaghetti, a yard of tape, a yard of string, and one marshmallow. Then the facilitator issues instructions like, "You have eighteen minutes to plan and build the tallest freestanding structure using the items I've given you, with one stipulation: the marshmallow must be placed at the top the structure. Go!"

Peter Skillman, the creator of the challenge, has overseen hundreds of groups, ranging from kindergarteners to CEOs, tasked with the same assignment. The results are astounding.

Do you know which group typically performs the worst? Business school students. Why? Because MBAs waste time discussing who will lead the team, how decisions will be made, and various other topics unrelated to building their structure. They spend most of their time planning how to build their structure instead of just building it.

The MBAs' approach mirrors the status quo for how many business teams operate.

Kindergartners outperform MBAs. Why? Their natural curiosity leads them to start touching and interacting with their building materials immediately. Within moments, a kindergartner will stick a piece of spaghetti into their marshmallow and understand how it wobbles when held upright by the noodle. Each time their attempted structure topples, they learn from their mistakes and start over, undeterred. They don't view failure as a risk; instead, they consider failure a given. They don't suffer from fragile egos, care who gets credit, or worry about who's boss—conditions considered "high risk" that hinder the other groups (Skillman 2019). The simple *curiosity* and *daring* of kindergartners give them an advantage over groups with more life experience and education.

When Steve Jobs delivered the 2005 commencement speech at Stanford University, he quoted the famous words from the back cover of the 1974 *Whole Earth Catalog*: "Stay hungry. Stay foolish" (Jobs 2005). Jobs could have been describing how kindergarteners approach challenges: with curiosity and daring.

Warren Bennis, the godfather of modern leadership studies, said this: "Curiosity and daring are two basic ingredients of leadership. Leaders wonder about everything, want to learn as much as they can, are willing to take risks, experiment, try new things. They do not worry about failure, but embrace errors, knowing they will learn from them" (Nassira 2021).

THE ONLY WAY TO SATIATE CURIOSITY IS TO ASK MORE QUESTIONS

I got my master's in engineering management because I found the more I learned, the more questions I had. When you're curious, you're never satisfied with simple, surface answers. Your insatiable appetite to discover keeps you asking more questions.

My four-year-old son reminds me of this all the time. Each time I answer his questions, he comes back with the same response: "Why?" Even if my answer would have earned a 100 percent mark on any college essay, my son will ask a predictable follow-up question: "But *why?*"

Strong leaders are like toddlers in that they keep asking *why* questions. Known as the Five Whys technique, this method of asking ever-deeper questions originated in the 1930s with Sakichi Toyoda, the founder of Toyota Industries. Toyota still uses this approach to find the root of any challenges (MindTools 2021).

But the power of the Five Whys is two-fold. First, as Toyoda found, the answer to each *why* question reveals a deeper, more profound level of information. Second, the exchange of questions and answers between two people demonstrates interest, understanding, and engagement in the topic—all keys to making deeper connections with others. I'll share more about care and engagement later in the book, but for now, know that sincere questions—those coming from a place of curiosity—not only increase your understanding of a topic, but they also build your relationship with the person to whom you're speaking.

If you don't relish the idea of sounding like a toddler, then act like an investigative journalist. Add to your *why* other questions like *who, what, where, when,* and *how*? Curious leaders ask questions to understand—

At the Onset of a Task	After Completing a Task
"Who must be involved?"	"Who helped with this effort?"
"Under what circumstances does this bug occur?"	"Under what circumstances does this address the bug?"
"Where do we see the problem most often?"	"Where does the problem go away?"
"What do we want to see happen?"	"What happened?"
"What might happen if we do x?"	"What caused x to happen?"
"How will we know when we've been successful?"	"What is the meaning behind what just happened?"

Curious leaders have an insatiable desire to know more, but that doesn't mean they suffer from *analysis paralysis*. Rather, like kindergartners in the Stillman Challenge, they have a *bias for action*.

"Analysis paralysis is an inability to make a decision due to over-thinking a problem. An individual or a group can have too much data. The result is endless wrangling over the upsides and downsides of each option, and an inability to pick one," says James Chen, CMT, author of *Essentials of Technical Analysis for Financial Markets* (Chen 2022).

Jeff Bezos—founder, executive chair, and former president and CEO of Amazon—created leadership principles for running Amazon. One of these demonstrates the balance between analysis paralysis and being daring (having a bias for action): "Speed matters in business. Many decisions and actions are reversible and do not need extensive study. We value calculated risk-taking" (Amazon 2022).

Risk meets speed; courage meets curiosity. Those natural traits of kindergartners once again exemplify the phrase Steve Jobs used at the commencement speech: "Stay hungry, stay foolish."

WHEN I GOT CURIOUS AND TOOK RISKS

When I worked on internationalization and traveled to places like India and Brazil, I met some fascinating people. Desiring to stay in touch, I added them to my social networks.

But I quickly discovered that they often posted in their native languages, ones that I didn't speak or read. I started wondering, *Is it possible to integrate a translator, so I can understand what they're sharing?* That led me to ask other questions, mainly: *Why not?*

What started as a pet project of mine took off. Others who shared my passion stepped forward. Eventually, we created a new open-source extension for Google's Chrome browser that translated social network posts using Google Translate, a feature that is now common on most social media platforms.

"But what risk did you take?" you might ask. Raise your hand if you like failing. No? How about embarrassment. Do you enjoy the thought of saying you're going to do something, finding out you can't, and then wondering if people are making fun of you behind your back? Curiosity got the ball rolling, but once I'd announced my idea, I felt the pressure of making it work.

Leaders can't afford to *not* take risks.

When Street View started growing more popular, I thought how awesome it would be to see places I'd never visited. But I didn't want to just see areas of the world with streets; I wondered if we could do the same thing with areas far off the grid. Then I got excited about the idea of capturing images of the Seven Wonders of the Natural World.

My excitement became contagious. I attracted other people who had the same curiosity. Together, we came up with the idea of photographing the Seven Summits of the world so we could share mountain views.

Normally, Street View technology relies on a car equipped with cameras driving around to record images. That wouldn't work with the highest summits, which had no roads. The idea kept morphing, until I realized that we could blend three of our passions together: technology, photography, and mountain-climbing.

So that's what we did. Loading up our packs with digital SLR cameras, we climbed and photographed mountains like Kilimanjaro, the Everest Base Camp, and other summits across the globe. We placed out cameras on tripods and took 360-degree shots. Using software and borrowing expertise from the Google Maps team, we stitched together the photos to create a Street-View-like experience for the Seven Summits.

Curiosity drove the work. As far as risks, well, if you haven't climbed a mountain with a heavy pack, you'll just have to trust me that the risks went beyond potential embarrassment. A dear friend and coworker of mine died a couple of years later (unrelated to our Street View project) climbing Everest. The risks are real.

Not only did expansion of Street View allow non-climbers to see the world from near the top, but it also gained its share of positive press, which few organizations will turn down (Headlee and Swerdlow 2013).

DEVELOPING CURIOSITY AND TAKING RISKS: A CASE STUDY

Think of curiosity like a muscle that grows stronger with use.

Ed Roberts and Robert Mims founded MITS (Micro Instrumentation and Telemetry Systems) in 1969. In 1975, the company sold their Altair 8800, the world's first minicomputer kit, in *Popular Electronics* magazine. While the Altair 8800 was considered more user-friendly than other personal computers of its day, most customers were engineers and hobbyists (History-Computer.com 2021).

The same year Roberts and Mims launched their Altair 8800, two friends, Steve Jobs and Steve Wozniak, determined to piggyback on the success of the Altair 8800. Working from Jobs' parents' garage, they created a prototype of the Apple I (Brownlee 2011).

But Jobs's curiosity wasn't satiated by merely imitating the Altair 8800. He longed to build something that could be used by beginners instead of engineers, or as he called it, a "computer for the rest of us." Two years later, Jobs and Wozniak launched the Apple II prototype, a user-friendly personal computer that included color graphics and a keyboard.

Curiosity paid off. First-year sales of Apple II reached $3 million. Two years later, sales hit $200 million.

But what risks did Jobs and Wozniak take to reach $200 million? They started their business by selling the two things they owned with monetary value. Jobs sold his Volkswagen microbus, and Wozniak sold his HP calculator. While the $1,350 the two Steves used as working capital to start Apple may seem like a pittance, ask yourself if you would risk 100 percent of your assets to build your own company. Probably not. The Steves knew if they failed, they'd have nothing. By betting on their own success, they started a product revolution called Apple, which has led creativity in the tech industry ever since (Entrepreneur 2022).

The CEO of Uber, Dara Khosrowshahi, understood what drove the two Steves to invest everything to make their business successful, as referenced in this statement attributed to him, "Desperation sometimes drives innovation."

Incurious leaders often look to the quick and easy, which can overlook both problems and opportunities. Sometimes they jump to conclusions, assuming they know more than they do. Curious, risk-taking leaders don't think and act in a vacuum. They seek out other curious people as partners. They then make careful observations as they learn, typically watching and asking questions of those closest to the work as well as the end-user.

One tech writer wrote this about the genius of Jobs: "[F]or Steve Jobs, consumers weren't just consumers, they were people. People with dreams, hopes, and ambitions and he got Apple to create products to help them achieve their dreams and goals" (Villafañe 2018).

Instead of making assumptions, curious leaders enter inquiry and research as if they were novices in the field, gathering multiple data points as they learn new perspectives and challenge old ones. Curious leaders ask; lazy leaders assume. Here are some questions to ask yourself to foster your own curiosity as a leader:

- *If I were the team lead, how would I proceed?*
- *If I were the team lead, what would I need to know before taking action?*

- *If I were the team lead, what questions must I answer?*
- *If I were the team lead, what would happen if I were to...? If I were the team lead, what similar situations could I study?*
- *If I were the team lead, what must I learn?*
- *If I were the team lead, what's the worst that could happen if I were to choose option X? What's the best that could happen?*

HOW TO FOSTER COURAGEOUS CURIOSITY

Curiosity is a leadership mindset. The most curious leaders never stop asking questions. Sir Isaac Newton's curiosity about what made an apple fall from a tree instead of hovering in the air or floating away gave way to his theory of gravity. But we don't need to be scientists to develop great curiosity. Try the following tips to unleash your curiosity.

Create and Use a Curious, Risk-Taking Mantra

Some curious, risk-taking behaviors are dangerous. Toddlers are often inexplicably drawn to the small, covered boxes with little round and semi-circular holes in them on the walls throughout their home. That's why parents put plastic covers over electrical outlets. Curiosity must be paired with an understanding of potential risk; otherwise, people can make bad decisions.

But leaders can use a mantra to help them balance curiosity with the inherent risks. I've included some examples to stimulate you to create your own curious, risk-taking mantra:

- *I will ask questions to gain insight and use intelligence to determine if a risk is worth taking.*
- *My first name is But. My middle name is Why. My last name is Not.*
- *I will encourage my team to be forever curious, and I will take full accountability for the risks they take.*

Maintain a Childlike Fascination

Look at the following picture, and then answer: "Which way is the bus heading?"

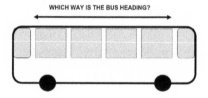

WHICH WAY IS THE BUS HEADING?

1. To the right
2. To the left
3. Insufficient information

After studying the picture, many adults determine the correct answer is C. School children, though, would hardly glance at the photo before answering, "B." It turns out, they are correct. Since children are much more likely to ride a bus to and from school, they know that to board a bus, it must have a door!

Remember the Peter Skillman challenge? Children possess no preconceived notions of their intellectual superiority or life experience, so they often perform better than educated "experts." Few children view failure or embarrassment as risks. Instead, they see a game as a challenge, and the fun comes from experimenting.

A quote which has attributed to Carl Sagan states: "You go talk to kindergartners or first-grade kids, and you find a class full of science enthusiasts. And they ask deep questions! They ask: 'What is a dream, why do we have toes, why is the moon round, what is the birthday of the world, why is the grass green?' These are profound, important questions! They just bubble right out of them."

There's an old proverb that says, "Little pitchers have big ears," meaning children often absorb more than adults might imagine. My small child is a natural observer of everything around him. Given his limited life experience, he gets fascinated by even seemingly trivial things he sees and hears.

Curiosity grows when it's fed. Nurture your curiosity intentionally by practicing simple actions in your job. Following are some examples that apply to professionals both inside and outside tech roles.

- Look closely at a process in your company that you find cumbersome, redundant, or primed for improvement or automation. Ask others what they know about how the process:
- "Who initiated it?"
- "When was the process launched? When was the last time it was updated?"
- "What problem was the process intended to solve, or what opportunity was the process designed to optimize?"

- "Who still uses the process?"
- Start with a blank canvas to "build a better mousetrap," one that makes the current process less cumbersome and redundant, or automated.
- "What would it cost to improve the process?"
- "How would you approach changing the process?"
- "Who would you need to involve for the change to be successful?"
- "What would be the risks in changing the process?"
- "How would your solution represent an improvement?"

Outside of work, you can push your curiosity in additional ways:

- Pick an area of study that interests you, but about which you don't currently know much.
- Read fifteen minutes each day on the subject for a week.
- Make notes of what you learn, taking careful considerations of how it can help you in your personal or work life.
- Pick a topic on which you have a strong opinion.
- List the contrary opinions others might have about the same topic.
- Interview people with contrary viewpoints to learn why they hold their positions. (Note: interview out of curiosity, not to interrogate to disprove.)
- If you're not working in tech, research website features and designs that could support your side hustle or a business you'd like to start.
- Review several websites connected to your area of interest.

- Take notes of the features, look, and functionality of the ones you like and dislike.
- List the must-haves based on what you've seen.
- Finally, think about ideas you haven't seen on a website but would love to see on yours.

These simple, no-cost ideas foster your creativity and tap into your curiosity, while also helping you evaluate potential risks along the way.

Question Everything

It's easy to conflate questioning everything with playing the "devil's advocate" or showing downright skepticism or cynicism. Just like investigative journalists care only about the facts of a matter, a curious mind hungers to go deeper, know more, and get to the bottom of situations. It's all in how you ask the questions. Make people feel threatened, and they stop talking. Keep the conversation engaging, and they willingly open up.

Instead of comparing curious leaders to naysayers, think of them as scientists using a time-tested process—the scientific method—to deepen their discovery process.

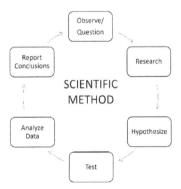

Curious leaders use the scientific method to innovate or reimagine new ideas and products. Note that the scientific method starts with observations and/or questions, a sign of curiosity, as opposed to merely analyzing data that reinforces preconceived beliefs.

Scratch Your Curiosity Itch

Professor George Loewenstein's research suggests that the source of curiosity is the information gap between what we know and what we'd like to know. The information gap is what inspires us to discover, learn, grow, and scratch the curiosity itch (Loewenstein 1994).

"If knowledge is power, then curiosity is the muscle."
—attributed to Danielle LaPorte, bestselling author and entrepreneur

---

You chose this book because you wanted to move from a subject-matter expert to a leader. That's a sign of curiosity and a hunger to learn.

What made this teenage wannabe artist explore working in tech? The change in my financial circumstances led me to an opportunity. What told me I *could* learn tech? A growth mindset assured me that I could learn just as quickly as anyone else. Of course, I didn't know that at the time! Back then, I just wanted a job to make some money. But the more I learned, the deeper my curiosity grew. What made me dig deeper still, eventually pursuing multiple degrees in tech? A curiosity that grew each time I learned something new and realized just how much I could still learn.

Those who will one day lead possess different mindsets than average team members—recognizing that the opposition to moving from the frontline to leadership is only in their own heads. Their growth-and-change-ready, curious mindsets serve as the foundation for their future leadership challenges.

If you have the prerequisite skills to lead, you're ready to step into the next challenge: people leadership.

SECTION II

PEOPLE LEADERSHIP

A day in the life of a tech manager is never boring—with budgets, staffing, vacation approvals, meeting agendas and schedules, compliance, project oversight, quality control and assurance, technical standards, code requirements, product requirements and design, processes and workflows, goal-setting, testing, reporting, technical guidance, project management, and more.

I listed those tasks to contrast *management* with *leadership*. Managers have no shortage of tasks that must be completed. But leadership requires focusing on something more critical to running a successful team or organization.

When writing about where leaders must focus to create successful teams, Eric Schmidt and Jonathon Rosenberg, authors of *Trillion Dollar Coach: The Leadership Playbook of Silicon Valley's Bill Campbell*, didn't mention checking boxes on the necessary managerial tasks; instead, they wrote this: "IT'S THE PEOPLE. People are the foundation of any company's success" (Schmidt and Rosenberg 2020).

Leadership requires focusing on your people. Unless you care for your team members, communicate effectively with them, engage them, and coach them to achieve greater things than they thought possible, you can't become a great leader.

The concept of people and the human factor required in

organizational success is relatively new. Years ago, companies created *tables of organization* (T/Os) to place worker names in an org-chart box to show where they reported within a department and corporate structure. Would you rather be known as a placeholder in a T/O, or a person? If you've ever used the term *RIF,* you're familiar with similarly dehumanizing words. When a company has a *RIF,* it just means they are undergoing a "reduction in force"—a non-human euphemism that means some people no longer have jobs.

To me, words like *employee* and *worker* are still dehumanizing, suggesting that there are leaders, and then others who are less-than. You'll see throughout this book that I frequently use the words *team* and *team member* to remind leaders that they exist in service of people, not nameless, faceless T/Os or members of the workforce. (When I cite research and share stories that use the word *employee,* I've kept the researchers' original words.)

Why am I telling you this? Because in this section, I'll share how to develop your *people leadership* skills so you can lead a successful team. If you have the privilege of leading *people*, then I don't want you to lose sight of their value.

CHAPTER 4
SHOW DEEP CARE

I PAY THEM TO DO A JOB! ISN'T THAT ENOUGH?

Tony got promoted to a leadership role and then transferred to a new work area to assume responsibility for a different team. While the personal belongings he took with him were few enough to fit into a small box, the baggage he brought filled up the entire work area. That baggage came from the era of manufacturing, a time when bosses roamed the factory floor looking for people who were "screwing up" or "screwing around."

On his first day, he ran production reports on every team member, so he knew how they performed. After looking through a half-dozen, he shook his head and dropped the reports on his desk. Next, he sent out an email to his team announcing a huddle at 8:00 a.m. the next day.

"Good morning," he told the team gathered around the work area the next day. "I don't know most of your names yet. I suppose that will come with time. But I know how you're all performing, and the numbers are disappointing."

Some of his team members looked down. A few shuffled their feet.

"Since you don't know me, let me start by telling you what I expect. You see the productivity chart on the wall? I expect you to look at it before each shift to learn how you're performing. Then I want to see each of you fall at or above peer norm."

A few more looked away.

"Let me be clear," Tony added sternly. "I'm not your mother or your friend. I'm your boss. Don't confuse me with someone who will listen to any sob stories or excuses about why you're not hitting your numbers. I pay you to do a job and do it well. If you aren't performing, you don't need to be here. Any questions?"

No one had any questions. But three of Tony's twenty-seven team members gave their two-weeks' notice before his first week ended.

Leadership speaker and author John Maxwell is attributed as saying, "People quit people, not companies" (Maxwell 2008). And that's why Tony's team left. They quit Tony, the boss, who didn't understand what it meant to be a *leader*.

As a knowledge worker, you're responsible for your own attitude, behavior, well-being, and performance. When you become a leader, your responsibility still includes managing your own thoughts, well-being, and performance, but you also hold accountability for your people and team.

According to *Harvard Business Review*, once you're in a leadership role, you have a "duty of care" that extends to every member of your team (Moore 2022). "[I]f a leader doesn't care about their team members, their team members won't care about them or the organization," says tech leader Anthony Boyd (Boyd 2022).

HOW DOES A LEADER SHOW CARE?

If you wish to lead others, it's imperative that you build a relationship with each team member. And when I say relationship, I mean that you *develop a productive, positive connection* that includes the following qualities.

Time

If you love golf, you spend time golfing. If you love video games, you put in as many hours as possible to reach the next level. And if you love your family, you crave to be with them. If you want to know what someone values, watch where they spend their time.

One of the simplest ways to show your team that you care is with your time. Spending quality, one-on-one time with each member allows you to get to know them personally. I frequently spend my own holiday time and money to visit with team members, taking them out for dinner or drinks so I can experience and learn about their lives outside of work. The cost of a meal is nothing compared to the ROI I receive by taking a little effort to show them that I care.

Attention

Everyone thinks they excel in multitasking. How many job descriptions have you seen which include verbiage like "must possess the ability to work in a fast-paced environment while managing multiple concurrent priorities"? The problem comes when you are multitasking while talking with a team member. In situations like that, your multitasking can look like disrespect.

When my son talks to me, he wants my eyes and ears on him completely without a hint of distraction. When you're building a relationship with a team member, keep in mind that your eyes and ears signal your focus. Nothing demonstrates care like putting other work aside when you're talking to someone. In fact, one of our team norms is to have no open laptops or phones out in meetings. I bring a notebook and pen only. When we meet, I want 100 percent of my focus on my team members and our discussion.

Questions

We don't learn about other people by making statements. We learn about them through asking questions and listening.

Think about college dating. You ask questions because you're curious and want to get to know someone. Yet doing so comes with risks. Ask a question too soon or at the wrong moment, and you could come across as nosy instead of curious. Ask a question when you're not open to their response, and you could end your date before it begins.

While work isn't Match.com, the questions people ask when dating give them insight about the other person. The listener can then demonstrate care by turning those insights into actions.

You Ask	They Answer	You Show You Care
"Favorite food?"	"Italian"	Take to dinner at Olive Garden.
"Favorite band?"	"Maroon 5"	Check for local tour dates.
"Major?"	"Biology"	Ask, "What got you interested?"
"Vacation?"	"Belize"	Ask, "What was the best part?"
"Favorite downtime activity?"	"Hiking"	Ask, "Do you want to go hiking with me on Saturday?"

Answers to such simple questions indicate what the other person likes and values, so you can better connect. But more than that, questions show that you care enough to ask.

When it comes to your team members, the act of asking questions like, "What do you think?" and, "How would you approach this challenge?" goes beyond small-talk and getting-to-know-you niceties. These open-ended questions show that you value their opinions and desire their thoughts.

Making simple observations can also tell you what a team member enjoys. For example, if you see photos of children on their desk, that gives you an opening to make a personal connection beyond work. Note: Being curious isn't the same as being nosy. *Curious* shows you *want* to learn more; *nosy* says you *need* to know more to form an opinion.

Mike, a former employee of a prominent health insurance company, described how the president would regularly walk the floors to talk with employees.

Seeing a photo on Mike's desk, the president asked, "Who are these gorgeous kids?"

"That's my oldest daughter, Diana, in the middle,"

Mike answered. "And my son, David, is on the left of her, and my youngest boy, Jeffrey, is on her right."

Months later, the president entered the same elevator with Mike.

"Hi Mike," the president greeted his employee warmly. "How are Diana, David, and Jeffrey doing? Have they started school yet?"

Perhaps the president used a mnemonic device to remember the names. But to Mike, that brief elevator ride made him say to himself, *The president of the company cares about me and my family.*

Empathy

In my early days at Google, the company grew quickly and added so many engineers that leaders had as many as fifty direct reports. A meme circulated that managers didn't add much value, so having a flat hierarchy made practical and financial sense.

That perception changed when Google conducted an internal survey and learned that Googlers very much valued managers. But the survey findings came with a caveat: those managers couldn't be just "bosses"; they had to be great leaders too.

Next, Google undertook a deeper analysis called Project Oxygen, aimed at figuring out the qualities of great leaders. In the process, Google took special care in selecting leaders with the right characteristics. Then they reduced manager span-of-control so that leaders would have five to ten direct reports.

Armed with new insights from Project Oxygen, Google conducted Project Aristotle to determine what factors contributed to the best teams.

Empathy: /ˈempəTHē/
Noun: "the ability to sense other people's emotions, coupled with the ability to imagine what someone else might be thinking or feeling" (Greater Good 2022).

I'll share more about Project Aristotle in a later section, but here I want to relate a key finding around the concept of *team member care*. Google found that effective teams offered members something known as *psychological safety*, which involves building a relationship where people feel safe to share their opinions without fear of being judged. Google learned that top performing teams created a safe environment, a place where no one viewed anyone else as "ignorant, incompetent, negative, or disruptive… They feel confident that no one on the team will embarrass or punish anyone else for admitting a mistake, asking a question, or offering a new idea" (Google 2022).

Satya Nadella, the executive chair and CEO of Microsoft, understands that empathy unleashes innovation. He says, "Empathy makes you a better innovator. If I look at the most successful products we [at Microsoft] have created, it comes with that ability to meet the unmet, unarticulated needs of customers" (Lev-Ram 2017).

Empathy fuels innovation just like it fuels team relationships. When team members feel supported and understood by their peers and leaders, instead of wasting energy feeling insecure, they contribute their best efforts.

Empathy is "the gateway to trust and psychological safety," says leadership consulting practice CEO Melissa Majors (Majors 2022). Majors spent time rebuilding trust within Uber after the company suffered "from a series of deep, self-inflicted wounds" (Frei and Morriss 2021). As a leader, how you respond to team members is imperative to building their trust and fostering psychological safety. If you react with negatively to the opinions or feelings expressed by a team member, you don't just hurt one person. You make the entire team feel unsafe. However, if you respond with curiosity, ask follow-up questions, and allow team members to express their feelings, your empathy creates the kind of safe environment where your team will offer you their trust and best efforts.

PUTTING IT ALL TOGETHER

How do you show your team that you care about them? Give them your time and full attention, ask questions, and feel *with* them by offering empathy.

When I first started managing managers, a phenomenal leader reported to me who had built an amazing team from the ground up. Her team always performed at the highest level, and I respected her style and consistency.

But after some time, I watched the performance of her team grow spotty. I noticed that she seemed distracted. She forgot some deadlines and made simple mistakes. Then her own team started noticing. And they started telling me about it.

Since I was newish in my job, I didn't know if I should say anything. I mean, she had a stellar track record prior to this, from what I could tell, and I wondered if I should just cut her some slack and say nothing. Instead of conducting a formal performance review to discuss this, I tried to make myself seen, approachable, and available should she want to talk with me. One way I did that—for her and all my team members—was to keep open blocks of time for them to pop in, like when I ate lunch at my desk.

She took me up on my open-door pop-in routine, paying me a visit. At first, we engaged in small talk. Eventually though, she started to share more.

"I'm not really sure that I should share this with you," she finally said, "but there's something going on in my personal life that I know is affecting my work."

"I'm here for you," I responded. "Can you tell me what's going on? And then maybe we can work together to find a solution."

After she shared the situation, I reassured her that I was glad she was willing to be vulnerable and honest with me.

"We don't just work together," I told her. "I also consider us friends. And friends support one another. I'm glad you told me what's been going on in your life."

Near the end of our conversation, I told her that I'd do anything possible to help her challenges. I offered her a more flexible schedule, so she could better balance her work and personal life. Then I told her about some corporate and community resources that she might contact.

I didn't have a single goal in our conversation. I had many. First, I wanted to assure her that I cared and wanted to help. Second, I wanted her to know she was safe. Finally, I wanted to help her find a solution so she could continue growing and contributing to the organization.

She took me up on changing her work hours and connected to additional resources. And even though she was in the office less, she became more focused and productive. After a few months, she sorted out her personal situation and returned to work stronger than ever.

Had I claimed to have an "open-door policy" and then closed my door, we wouldn't have had that conversation. Had I forced a performance review conversation on her, I might not have learned the barriers she faced and the solutions to work around them. And had I not been sending clear messages that any team member could see me during my open blocks, she might have lacked the wherewithal to pay me a visit.

During good times when performance and energy are high, it's easy to share in others' positive emotions and show how much you care about the team. But real care and empathy come out when someone is hurting, and you meet them where they are. Nothing shows care like sitting with someone in their struggles.

TEAM MEMBER CARE: YOUR ROLE AND PRIORITY

As many retail businesses replace people with self-service models, you might think self-service coupled with machine learning and other technology will soon make leaders obsolete. I don't see that happening. Organizations need leaders to provide the human touch, something that a machine can't replicate. Artificial intelligence (AI) and tech can offer suggestions based on algorithms, but they can't offer meaningful, heartfelt encouragement to someone who looks dispirited.

As a leader, you own the role of team care when you strive to improve people's jobs and lives. You're best positioned to influence and guide team members on the human side of work. Only a human leader can offer praise, empathy, direction, feedback, and, of course, care. The sole reason an organization put you in leadership is to inspire better results than people could achieve without your direction.

Make team care your priority. Famous leadership sage Peter Drucker has been credited as saying, "What gets measured gets managed." Think of all the tasks you're accountable for and measured against as a leader. Do you measure how much time you spend caring for your team? If you don't, you should start, if only to get a baseline.

Robert Greenleaf spent forty years researching management and development. From his years traveling as a manager for AT&T, Greenleaf concluded that most capable leaders served as supportive coaches who met both the needs of their people and companies.

"The organization exists for the person as much as the person exists for the organization," Greenleaf believed.

After nearly forty years with AT&T, Greenleaf took an early retirement to start the Greenleaf Center for Servant Leadership. His 1977 book, *Servant Leadership: A Journey into the Nature of Legitimate Power and Greatness*, put the concept of a leader as servant into the mainstream business culture.

If you're curious about what concepts Greenleaf included in his seminars and writings, he believed the top leaders listened, demonstrated empathy, promoted healing, practiced stewardship, nurtured growth in others, and built community.

"Good leaders must first become good servants," Greenleaf taught (Frick 2021).

The next time you hear that someone is a "boss," manager, or leader, transpose the word in your mind to *servant.* Then watch that person's behavior. You'll quickly discover if you're watching someone with just a title, or someone who knows how to lead by serving others.

THE CARING LEADER'S NON-CHECKLIST

I want to be a great father, and I've read books and articles on the subject. According to some sources, great dads take their kids camping at least a couple of times each year, enroll them in at least one team sport each season, and make at least two pilgrimages to Disney World in Florida before they turn twelve years old. In reality, I could do all of those things and not be a good dad. Conversely, I could be a great dad without doing any of them.

The same is true of leadership, a role that doesn't come with a checklist. Your goal is to be a great leader, not to check items off a list. And while leadership doesn't come with a checklist, I will distill some practical activities to practice as you start. If you desire to care for your team members sincerely, they will notice and appreciate your efforts.

Create and Use a Caring Mantra

Some leaders seem hardwired to achieve results. Their focus, words, and actions can come across as impatience for anything that doesn't accomplish results. Other leaders gravitate towards the people-side of leadership. They care about results, but they understand the value of connecting with people to get things done.

If you tend to be a results first/people second leader, see if any of these mantras resonate with you:

- *I get better results by caring for my people than by riding my people.*
- *Team achievement mirrors how much they believe I care about them.*

- *The best way to tap into my team's discretionary effort is by demonstrating that I care about them.*
- *I can achieve sustainable team results by practicing ongoing team care.*
- *Not every team member will reach a milestone each day, but each team member should feel cared for each day.*

Learn How Your Team Members Wish to Connect with You

As a teenager, I had two main ways to communicate with my friends outside of the classroom. I could meet them somewhere, or I could call them from a box connected to the kitchen wall, which joined via a wire to a box in their homes.

Communication is no longer tethered by wall mounts and wires. Even if you don't work in tech, you've used your smartphone, email, chat, Zoom-like technology, and a host of other tools to stay connected.

But do you know how your team members *like* to connect with you? In his bestselling book, *The Five Love Languages,* author Gary Chapman says that each person speaks a primary love language (Chapman 1992). To show love, you can speak your own love language, but when you speak the love language of the person you love, they *feel* your love as you intended.

The same holds true of how team members like to be contacted. Do you know how they want to hear from you? Do they prefer written communication or verbal? Face-to-face meetings or video? They will appreciate any contact from you, but when you know how they like to connect, and you use their preferred channel, you show that you care about even the little things. I will share more details on communication in Chapter 5.

Connect One-on-One Regularly

If you lead a geographically-deployed team, you likely know that face-to-face meetings with each of your team members is nearly impossible. While face-to-face meetings offer the quickest way to build relationships, other vehicles can help you maintain those relationships.

Technology has rewritten the script about how relationships begin.

Thirty-nine percent of romantic couples today met online instead of the once-common first meeting at church, through family or friends, or in a bar. All couples need today is a communication platform (Sheshkevich 2019).

Prior to the 1990s, employment for nearly every job required a physical location. By 1995, thanks to technology, companies like American Express, IBM, and AT&T ventured into remote work. Today, 60 percent of jobs in a tech-heavy city like Austin, Texas, went to remote workers; 30 percent of jobs in San Francisco went to remote workers (We Work Remotely 2022). Since COVID-19, most professional knowledge workers have been given the opportunity (or mandate) to work remotely.

Technology has forever changed the way both personal and professional relationships begin and grow. The practice of "managing by walking around" might still exist in manufacturing, but that approach is impossible given the widely deployed knowledge-worker of today.

To prioritize one-on-one time, first gather an idea of how much time you get with each team member. Of course, this is an easier task if you lead twenty team members instead of two hundred. Remember that time is simplest way to demonstrate your personal care.

Then document what you do when you meet one-on-one. I'm a firm believer in agenda-free check-ins with my team members. They might look and sound like small talk, but I want to see how they're doing and what's new in their lives. I invest this time as two fellow humans in a caring relationship.

Ask Caring Questions

"How are you doing?" and "How's it going?" come out of our mouths several times each day, yet most people understand that those are rote greetings and not real questions designed to be answered. When you want to demonstrate care, do more than scratch the surface by asking deeper, more meaningful questions such as:

- "I'd like to hear about the project you're working on. What are you learning from it?"
- "How are you enjoying your work on the team?"
- "Do you feel like we're challenging you enough? Are you growing?"
- "Is there anything that keeps you up at night in a good way? In a bad way?"
- "What one thing could I do for you that would make you love your work even more?"

Integrative medicine professor Rachel Naomi Remen has been attributed as saying: "The most basic and powerful way to connect to another person is to listen. Just listen. Perhaps the most important thing we ever give each other is our attention...A loving silence often has far more power to heal and to connect than the most well-intentioned words."

We build relationships with our attention, time, and ears, not with motivational posters on office walls or well-rehearsed platitudes.

Notice that each of the previous questions come from a work perspective. Don't get me wrong; they are great questions, and they're exactly the kind you must ask as a supportive leader. But don't be afraid to go further. For example, ask questions like, "Do you have any fun plans for the weekend?" This takes your connection beyond the current work task.

Then take it one step further. Let's say your team member says that they're attending a concert to watch Ghost play live. How do you think they would feel on Monday if you reached out to ask, "How was the Ghost show? I'd love to hear about it!" They'd likely feel that you cared about them.

Keep these two proverbs in mind. First, *a trouble shared is a trouble halved.* Be the leader who people feel comfortable sharing about the challenging parts of their lives. You'll not only lift their spirits, but you'll forge a deeper understanding of their lives. Second, *a joy shared is a joy doubled.* When you follow up with topics they revealed in your personal conversations, you'll let them relive a positive experience with you.

Note that none of these questions have right or wrong answers. They are conversation-starters and relationship-builders. They show team members that you're there for them, value their opinions, want to see them grow, and care for them individually.

Demonstrate Care Whenever Team Members Gather

If you have a hundred team members, you could spend every moment of your team meeting with them one-on-one and still not get to all of them. But you can still demonstrate care to your team in group settings.

Consider starting meetings with these two questions:

1. "Will a couple of people share a personal (non-work-related) achievement or joy you recently experienced?"
2. "Does anyone wish to share a personal (non-work-related) challenge you're facing, so we can send positive thoughts your way?"

Yes, these questions are personal. Sharing is completely voluntary. Remember that psychological safety starts with trust and empathy. You can't snap your fingers and command that people trust you and feel safe. But you can encourage team members to share parts of their lives. When they do, the entire group benefits from a sense of safety and closeness.

Knowing about a team member's challenges, like a sick family member or a car in the repair shop, also gives the leader information to follow up with. Imagine if you learn that a team member has a sick child at home. What would happen if you followed up after the meeting asking, "How's your son? Is there anything I can do? Do you need to take some time off to be with him?"

On a final note, *care* isn't about making a few grand

gestures. Sure, you could show how much you care by paying for team members to take a two-week holiday in Tahiti. Not only is that unnecessary, but that's also not the kind of care I'm talking about. Show care in your interpersonal, human outreach —like your smile, acknowledgment, questions, approachability, and time. Those actions demonstrate a servant's heart.

In the next chapter, I'll share thoughts on how a leader can become a highly effective communicator.

CHAPTER 5
CONNECT THE DOTS

COMMUNICATION GOES BEYOND SHARING INFORMATION

Professional, technical, administrative, and clerical people spend 50 to 80 percent of their workdays communicating, with most of that time spent talking (Klemmer and Snyder 1972). Leaders spend 70 to 90 percent of their time communicating each day (Dixon 2022). But what kind of communication tasks take up most of a leader's time?

The purpose of communication has three *I*s: inform, influence, and inspire. When you think about your daily communication, would it be fair to say that most of your time is spent *informing*? Leaders spend countless hours each week sharing and receiving information through the following:

- Providing status updates
- Reading reports
- Sending and responding to emails
- Sitting in meetings
- Sharing policy changes

- Updating their team on modified deliverables
- Scheduling meetings
- Answering technical questions

Exchanging information is critical to team and organizational success, but information is tactical and ever-changing, only as up-to-date as the last email.

Speaker, author, and digital analyst of disruptive technology at Altimeter Group, Brian Solis, says, "Information overload is a symptom of our desire to not focus on what's important" (Glowasz 2022).

Leaders—especially those working in tech—appreciate and value the plethora of information at their fingertips. Many tech leaders prefer looking at data, trends, spreadsheets, and project plans, because they've honed those skills.

Leaders need to stretch beyond mere information exchange to focus on what's even more meaningful, dynamic, and transformational: communication that influences and inspires team members.

As a kid, I drew in coloring books. I especially loved connect-the-dots activities. If you don't remember these puzzles, each dot had a number beside it. A random-looking array of dots, when connected in numerical order, took on the recognizable picture of a well-known cartoon character, animal, or landmark. The complicated puzzles were impossible to decipher until several dots were connected, and the picture would start to take shape.

Workers spend about 28 percent of their workweeks managing e-mail and almost 20 percent looking for internal information, which can involve finding the right person to answer a question about a task (Chui et al. 2019).

We don't have a problem with accessing information; we struggle with finding it when we need it.

Leaders and team members alike are overwhelmed with information, to the extent that it's often hard to know what's important. That's why organizations need leaders with effective communication skills to connect the most essential dots for their teams.

COMMUNICATION IS HARD

Leaders struggle communicating for four different reasons:

- They don't know *how* to communicate.
- They don't know *what* to communicate.
- They focus on *what does this mean to me?* instead of *what does this mean for my team?*
- They believe communication is someone else's job.

You Don't Know How to Communicate

Few leaders will admit that they don't know how to communicate. Insisting that their communication skills are perfectly fine, these leaders fall prey to the Dunning-Kruger effect—a cognitive bias where those with the least amount of knowledge or skills on a topic have the greatest tendency to overestimate their competence (Duignan 2019).

Not to worry. If you don't know how to communicate, this chapter will help you connect the dots for your team members.

You Don't Know What to Communicate

I've never heard of an organization suffering from a lack of communication. Just look at your email inbox. Unless you practice email hygiene—like "touch an email once and respond," organizing emails into files by topic or sender, or deleting emails at the end of each day—you likely have hundreds of emails you plan to read or respond to "someday."

Communication without *context* is unlikely to be retained. Context is the cement within communication. If you don't know the context of a message you've been asked to share, how can you pass it along to your team? You can't. Context is decisive. Leaders who understand the critical *why a particular message is vital* can more easily cull through reams of information to communicate the most important bits.

You Communicate What's Important to You Instead of What's Important to Your Team Members

You might remember reading the news back in July of 2022 that Microsoft announced its intention to lay off some workers as the organization realigned certain business groups and reevaluated its priorities (Bass 2022). If you were one of the 180,000 people working for Microsoft then, I'm sure you remember this announcement. And if you happened to be one of the 1 percent directly impacted by this layoff, you'll likely remember the announcement for months or even years to come.

What makes some messages stick? When they apply to you. When things like a layoff happen inside an organization, team members from the C-suite on down wonder the same thing: *What does this mean for me? What does this mean for my job?* It's human nature. Our first concern is about our own futures.

Author Scott Carbonara refers to the place that some leaders retreat to when they focus on themselves instead of those they lead as "Meville" (think "Me"-ville). When those leaders enter Meville, they don't think or care about others (Carbonara 2013, 191). They focus on themselves, asking questions like, "What's going to happen to me?"

The problem with leaders living in Meville, Carbonara says, is that team members are left to draw their own conclusion. Who's communicating the big picture to the team? No one. Left to connect their own dots, your team will feel abandoned, insecure, and alone.

As a leader, you're only human. You have feelings, and you'll need time to process them. But you also serve in the critical role of communicating to your team so that negative changes create as little disruption as possible.

When Better.com CEO and founder Vishal Garg laid off 900 people on a Zoom call on December 1, 2021, the story made headlines for: timing the layoffs just before the holidays, how he communicated the layoffs, the insults he made to those impacted, and his accusations that hundreds of employees had stolen from the company by not working as many hours as reported.

Garg was immediately put on a leave of absence for his actions. He then took leave of his role "to reflect on his leadership, reconnect with the values that make

Better great, and work closely with an executive coach." By January, Garg sent out an email to his employees, apologizing for his actions and the distraction they caused (Jeans 2022).

Leaders aren't perfect, nor is their communication. Garg reclaimed his role with Better.com, but his actions spotlighted why a leader must check their own emotions before undertaking high-stakes communication.

You Believe Communication Is Someone Else's Job

Companies, especially large ones, have departments dedicated to internal and external communications, and a host of human resource professionals who spend most of their time communicating company-wide. Communication *is* their job. But those groups aren't as credible as two other critical parties.

A team member's most credible, meaningful communication within every organization comes directly from their senior leaders and immediate supervisors. According to research conducted by Prosci, the global leader in change management solutions, messages shared by senior leadership and immediate supervisors are deemed more credible than any other communication source. And you might be surprised to know that between senior leaders and immediate supervisors, team members deem supervisors as the most credible (Creasey 2022).

So no, you're not off the hook for communication. Connecting the dots for teams is very much your job as a leader.

No leader likes delivering what could be viewed as bad news. But even massive, financially strong companies aren't immune from economic downturns. That includes Google.

In July of 2022, Google CEO Sundar Pichai sent a memo to Googlers informing them that Google would slow its hiring throughout the rest of the year. But Pichai didn't just use his communication to *inform* Googlers about bad news. Pichai took advantage of his message to provide context as well as to *influence* and *inspire* Googlers. He thanked them for their commitment and efforts up front. Then he built trust by being transparent about the future, expressing that he and other Google leaders had concerns about the state of the economy. Then he moved into the bad news, telling Googlers they must have even a "sharper focus" and work with "more hunger" under the current economic insecurities (Zetlin 2022).

Pichai's email went on the say, "Scarcity breeds clarity. [It] drives focus and creativity that ultimately leads to better products that help people all over the world. That's the opportunity in front of us today, and I'm excited for us to rise to the moment again."

Pichai didn't write, "I'm sorry. Things look grim right now." Instead, he praised Googlers, respected them as adults by being transparent in his message, provided context, informed them about the upcoming changes, and inspired them by letting Googlers know they were *in this together* and would ultimately be better equipped to serve consumers worldwide.

While immediate supervisors are considered the most credible to team members on the frontline, Pichai's message serves as a stellar example of how a

senior leader can influence and inspire by setting the
tone and leading the charge.

WHERE TO FIND THE DOTS

For a leader to connect the dots, they need access to the right
dots. As mentioned earlier, leaders sometimes retreat to Meville
instead of providing "big picture" answers to their teams. I
would add another destination where leaders get stuck:
"Teamville." In Teamville, the leader hyper-focuses on what's
going on within their team to the extent that they miss what's
going on across the organization.

The only way to see the big picture is to step back. If you
work for a large company, you know how information gets siloed
—sometimes creating blind spots even to the department next to
yours. How can you stay on top of what's going on? Put your
tentacles out, and talk to as many people as possible. Don't
expect information to find you. You must actively search.

I never eat alone. Instead, I try to take someone different to
lunch every day, meeting with people in an adjacent area or
across the company. I'm often rewarded by learning that the
person dining with me is working on something related to my
team's work.

I also schedule time with other leaders and make it my business to find out what they're working on. I scan posts and notes
saved (by others) to common drives, join groups, and read as
many documents as I can to see how the work of my team might
overlap with others. This social networking allows me to identify
possible duplications of efforts as well as adjacencies, where one
solution can fix multiple bugs. Additionally, by keeping my ears
open, I often find that my team can offer support to other teams.

Several times, I've found duplicate projects running from
multiple departments. More than once, I found three teams

looking at the same problem and developing similar solutions. Not only did this create team morale issues—feeling like they'd been wasting their time—but it wasted money. None of this happened due to malicious intent. It happened because some leaders got stuck in Teamville, and they stopped looking beyond their own shop.

Since that discovery, I've tried to join the meetings of other teams at their earliest stages, so I can understand the scope and scale of their work—ideally when people are still ideating, creating, designing, and planning. It's easy to change words in a planning document, but it's hard to change software running in production. When I find possible duplications, I talk with the other leaders to see which team should run the current project, and which should move on to other high-priority work.

When I started working on Android Developer Infrastructure, I quickly found that the organization had multiple teams building more of less the same set of tools and products. Once I discovered this, we decided to merge projects, which allowed us to improve our tooling, reduce the complexity of our codebase, and maximize our precious engineering time.

Successful leaders don't operate in a bubble. Instead, they work within a team while staying connected to what's happening around them. To connect the dots, they actively search for the dots that might be working in isolation.

BECOMING A BETTER DOT-CONNECTOR

Given how much time leaders spend communicating each day, they better get good at it. Following are some pointers for becoming a strong dot-connector.

Develop Your Own Communication Mantra

Create a communication mantra that you repeat daily. Following are some mantra ideas to get you started on building your own:

- "My team deserves a leader who is a transparent communicator."
- "I will be the most trusted communication source for my team."
- "Unless I'm told specifically that something I learn shouldn't be shared, I will pass it along to my team."
- "My communication builds trust, caring relationships, and empowerment."

Condition Your Team About What to Expect from You

If you blast out every message using voicemail, email, scrolling computer banners, company-wide meetings, team huddles, and face-to-face meetings, you'll condition your team to ignore every message, because they'd have to be on the summit of Everest to *not* get the message!

Instead, create your own guidelines and a list of the channels you use most frequently. Then consider what kinds of messages you will use for each of these communication channels, which may include the following:

- Email
- Video streaming
- Slack
- Text
- IM
- Team huddles

- One-on-ones
- Shared docs/Wikis

Next, let your team members know which channel you'll use most often for the various messages. Given the number of channels available, don't expect team members to keep up with all of them. Teach your team where they can find the most important messages from you.

Use Email as One Tool, Not Your Only Tool

In most organizations, email is still the primary communication channel. When I worked at Google, we all used Gmail as our primary communication method. At Instagram, we used WorkplaceChat.

Just because something is used doesn't mean it's effective. Email represents the largest area for improvement. Following are some ways to better use email communication.

Show a clear subject heading and call to action. Make the topic of the email clear. What do you want the reader to think or do because of your message? Let them know if they must retain the details or if there is a call to action. Mark FYIs as such so people can skip over them.

Share the fewest, most critical details. The image of five-pages is an email from a leader outlining the new office security protocols for their office. While some messages must be in writing to create a paper trail for compliance, do you really think any team member stopped and read this when they received it in their inbox? Longer documents like these should be shared using non-email communication technology.

When writing an email, resist the urge to write everything you can think of about a subject.

Effective emails, not to be confused with a master's thesis, often contain bulleted key points.

If you must pack an email with a lot of information, tell the reader upfront, saying something like, "This is a long and detailed message about ____." Or by putting TLDR (too long; didn't read) shorthand into the subject line, you let the reader know that the written materials may be too much to digest by a quick scan, suggesting, "If you don't have time to read it now, please come back to it when you have time." A warning allows team members to make the best use of their time instead of reading something that won't immediately impact their work.

Other helpful subject lines you can use in email are NNTR and WINFY:

NNTR = No Need To Respond

WINFY = What I Need From You

It's okay to use shorthand with your team or within your broader organization if its use has been institutional-ized as common.

Write professionally, respectfully, and cautiously. Your email communication with team members should comply with formal business writing standards. You can let your personality show, but business communication is different than an email you'd send to your college buddies.

Emails sent and received to your business email account shouldn't be considered private. Some companies monitor email communications, especially when they have concerns about potentially damaging exchanges such as harassment, bullying, illegal activities, or sharing information that is considered proprietary.

I won't share the name of the CEO or the company, but I will assure you that this email is real. This is what a CEO sent to his COO:

If our financials improve throughout the summer, I will consider letting you retain your position. I'm not trying to be a dick, but I think you're clueless when it comes to REAL NUMBERS and what it takes to RUN A COMPANY. I feel like I have to explain the same shit to you over and over, because you don't understand how math works. And now I'm getting pissed off. I just can't believe how bad [the numbers are] right now. How did it get like this???

Talk about a lawsuit waiting to happen! The CEO got lucky when his COO quit without suing; although, given how many similar emails the CEO sent his COO, the whole story would have made an interesting series on Netflix.

The CEO's message didn't demonstrate curiosity or problem-solving, nor was he trying to share information, influence, or inspire the COO. Instead, this CEO demonstrated an utter lack of emotional intelligence, emotional self-regulation, and emotional control.

Understand the Message Before Trying to "Sell" It

Think back to the connect-the-dots activity. What makes the puzzle less random is clear instructions with corresponding numbers next to each dot. That's how connecting the dots work: with a puzzle, dots, numbers, directions, and a pencil bringing order to chaos.

Effective leaders are those who bring order to what could become *communication chaos*. Leaders are like the puzzle maker: they must know the "picture" their communication will reveal before they can explain it to their team members.

The day after an operations director named Amy communicated with her managers about two new corporate priorities, using the corporate travel office for all air travel and cutting costs across the board, one of her managers approached with a question.

"I understand that all air travel needs to go through our travel office," the manager told Amy. "But I don't know how that saves money. The same flight from corporate travel costs $800 more than when I checked prices directly with the airline. Can you help me understand this?"

"No," Amy didn't try to bluff. "I don't understand it either. I had no idea booking with corporate travel would cost more. Let me check with my boss."

Amy asked her own boss, Feng, a senior vice president, about the two policies that seemed to have conflicting goals.

"Your question tells me that we missed the mark on how we communicated these two issues," Feng replied, then explaining how the two initiatives were related. Even though each individual corporate business traveler *could* save money from their own costs centers by booking their own travel directly, the travel office secured deep discounts, tallied at the end of the year based on the organization's total travel expenses.

"While your manager could save $800 from her cost center by booking her own flight, the corporate travel office could save the company $1,000 on that same flight when rebates are applied in the aggregate."

Equipped with that context and new understanding, Amy could now connect the dots for her team leaders.

Understand the message and anticipate the questions you'll get before you try to share it.

Don't Look Only Inside Your Team for Dots

As I've mentioned, the work of other areas and teams can greatly impact your work area. Schedule time to meet with your peers and share what you're working on. Look for opportunities to leverage work between areas or remove duplication of efforts. Stay informed on what other areas are working on by scanning updates and notes posted to common and shared drives.

Ask Yourself, How Will This Affect My Team?

Remember, Meville is where a leader thinks of themself and asks, "What does this mean for me?" But the better question focuses on the team, like, "What does this mean for them?"

At a director's meeting, the CEO announced a corporate merger. After making the business case for the merger and doing Q&A for an hour, the CEO urged the directors to share the same presentation with their managers and then hold group meetings with their team members.

Immediately after the directors left the meeting, most hurried back to their offices, closed their doors, and called their vice presidents to see what additional information they might learn. Here's the question they most wanted answered: "Will I still have a job?" The second question was, "Do you know who I might be reporting to?"

Guess what the vice presidents were doing at the same time. They were calling their senior vice presidents, asking, "Will I still have a job? Do you know who I might be reporting to?"

Employees across two large companies watched as management doors closed while their bosses held hushed, double-top-secret conversations. Employees knew that something big was happening, and the rumor mill churned out several stories, most of them not close to the truth.

Think of Meville like a vacation. You can visit there for a short time. You can spend a little time wondering, "How is this going to impact me?" But don't stay in that mindset too long. If you retreat to Meville, who's addressing the concerns of your team?

As a leader, take care of your team first. Communicate with them about the direction the organization is taking. If you don't check on the team's feelings and thoughts when they need you most, don't be surprised if good people start creating exit strategies due to insecurity.

When I need to communicate a message to my team members, I ask myself the following questions:

- *What channel should I use to communicate this message?*
- *What's the most positive way someone might interpret this message?*
- *What's the most negative way someone might interpret this message?*
- *What questions do I anticipate they'll have about this message?*
- *Does this message come with a subtext of potential reward, or loss?*
- *What do I expect my team to do after hearing this message?*
- *Where can team members and I get more information or additional questions answered?*
- *If the message involves difficult news, what inspiration can I offer?*

Communicate with Context

Whenever I ask my toddler to do something (pick up his toys, get ready for bed, and so on), he used to reply by asking, "Why?" Instead of getting frustrated with him, I've learned that he—and even most adults—learn better with rationales.

Context is especially critical when communicating about a change or shift in directions. Additionally, context saves you time, because you won't need to answer each team member who asks you *why?* if you provide the answer up front.

Anticipate the *whys* of your team. Realize that it's human nature to interpret new events based on whatever experiences are most recent and negative in people's minds. When I need to share a big announcement with my team, I first send a "Rude Questions" document to my leadership team—listing the potential rude questions I might get in response by my team members. Then I ask the leaders to add to the document any other concern, criticism, or rude question they think I may receive.

Go in prepared. If you don't anticipate potential responses, your communication might foster frustration and leave your team festering with negativity.

Following is a list of messages that require a well-thought-out context before jumping into the details or facts:

- New corporate leadership/ownership
- Mergers and acquisitions
- Reorgs (such as terminating, blending areas, creating new departments, etc.)
- Positive or negative media coverage
- Replacing obsolete systems
- Killing off a product
- Large scale outage or bug
- Changes to business strategy
- Sharing strategy and roadmaps

In 2018, a massive investment company purchased an international media company. Maybe the leaders of both companies got their wires crossed on the timing of the message. Perhaps leaders were busy working out the details. Whatever happened, no one took ownership of crafting a message delivered to the media company's employees or deciding who would communicate it.

How did employees of the media company learn that they had been purchased? They read about it on their own news service!

Imagine if you'd been a leader inside that company when a team member forwarded you the news service post asking, "What does this mean?" Obviously, you wouldn't have been prepared for a message that you knew nothing about. Making matters worse, your team likely would believe you knew more than you did—eroding their trust.

Leaders who have built trust with their team can weather storms. Your role as a leader is to communicate what you know when you know it, assuming it's not confidential, while providing the context behind key messages.

Don't Do "One-n-Done" Communication

Leaders sometimes confuse "I have communicated" with "my team knows enough to be productive and without distraction."

Famous Irish playwright George Bernard Shaw said it best: "The single biggest problem with communication is the illusion that it has taken place" (Kenny 2020).

"But I already told them," I've heard frustrated leaders say when their team seems uninformed. Yet when you consider how many times you've had to hear certain messages to grasp their intended messages, context, subtext, and next steps, you realize that what's clear to one person looks like a mud puddle to the next.

Just because you've said a few words, sent out an email, or distributed an update doesn't mean they "get it." And don't assume a lack of questions is a good sign, either. The real test of your communication is that your intended audience *heard* you, *understood* you, and *knows what to do* because of your communication. And then you can observe the effectiveness of your communication in your team's actions.

When I worked for YouTube, CEO Susan Wojcicki would repeat our annual goals at each large company meeting, because she wasn't convinced that team members internalized the messages she shared. She challenged several of her leaders to ask team members at random what they remembered of her messages. If we reported back to her that those we spoke with struggled to retain her main points, she would rework her message for the next meeting and find additional ways to socialize her message.

When you have a critical message, evaluate the best communication channel to deliver it, as discussed earlier. Refine your message after you know the key talking points, and make sure you know what you're talking about before you start. If you need to communicate without having all the details (as is often the case during rapid change), let your team know what to expect by answering questions like:

- When do you expect to know more? What's the timeline?
- How will you share the information once you have it?
- Where can team members go with questions?

> "Trust is a serious problem, we have to get to a new level of transparency—only through radical transparency will we get to radical new levels of trust" (Sanders 2015).
> —Marc R. Benioff, CEO of SalesForce

By now, you likely see that the sections and chapters in this book build sequentially like stairs, starting with what leaders must possess on the inside (mindset) and progressing into the strategies yielding concrete performance results. People leadership starts by demonstrating care for your people before tackling critical communication. Once you've built a strong relationship with your team members, they cut you some slack when you're imperfect. Likewise, practicing solid communication earns additional grace from your team.

The next chapter takes people leadership further as we explore ideas on how to build engagement with your team.

CHAPTER 6
FUEL ENGAGEMENT

WHAT IS ENGAGEMENT AND WHY DOES IT MATTER?

Ahmad and Lena began working at the same tech start-up during a hiring boom. They both had computer science degrees, and based on their resumes, their hiring manager had every reason to believe they would become stellar performers.

Lena's performance impressed her boss. She learned quickly, took on added responsibility, and earned her peers' respect. She brought "a little something extra" to every project she touched, according to her team lead.

Ahmad struggled to operate within the team, but they didn't leave him behind. They instructed Ahmad about their organizational culture and the importance of taking initiative and gave him opportunities to plug in. Yet he didn't step up; instead, he did what was asked of him—nothing more, and sometimes less.

Every leader I've known can name the Ahmad and Lena on their teams. Some team members shine, while others seem content doing just enough to get by. It's a matter of *engagement*. Engaged team members give more because they care more.

Gallup has studied engagement for years and created a helpful definition from their research: "the involvement and enthusiasm of employees in their work and workplace" (Gallup 2022).

Sadly, Gallup also reports that only 32 percent of full- and part-time employees are engaged. And 17 percent of employees are actively disengaged, which are those employees "who aren't just unhappy at work; they are busy acting out their unhappiness" (Harter 2022). "[Disengaged employees] undermine what their engaged coworkers accomplish" (Kahn 1990, 701).

Imagine what your team could accomplish if every member showed the same involvement and enthusiasm as Lena.

THE ENGAGEMENT ADVANTAGE

Engagement links directly to how you care for your team members (Chapter 4). In fact, Gallup makes a strong business case for *care* and *engagement*. In a 2022 study, Gallup reported that employees who agreed that "my employer cares about my overall well-being" were:

- 69 percent less likely to actively search for a new job
- 71 percent less likely to report experiencing burnout
- Five times more likely to strongly advocate for their company as a good place to work
- Five times more likely to trust the leadership of their organization
- Three times more likely to be engaged at work
- 36 percent more likely to thrive in their overall lives (Harter 2022).

These outcomes show that engagement brings more advantages than just making people "feel good." Engaged teams are an organization's key business differentiator.

While looking at the following list, think of your team members. Which category would you put each person in based on how they show up at work?

Disengaged Team Member	Engaged Team Member
If-I-have-to attitude	Can-do attitude
Excited only for certain tasks	Excited
Performs "at or below"	Performs "above and beyond"
Waits to be told	Takes initiative
Disinterested	Curious
Naysaying	Encouraging
Offers complaints	Offers praise
Discontent, and it shows	Happy, and it shows
Poor peer relationships	Collaborates with peers
Wastes time	Works efficiently
Bad-mouths team members and organization	Shows loyalty to team and organization

Would you rather do business with a company filled with team members on the left or right? Would you rather take on your biggest career challenge with a disengaged or engaged team? The answer may seem simple, but realize that engagement often gets overlooked.

Even beyond your team, consider the ROI of engagement for your organization. A Gallup meta-analysis found that organizations with employees scoring in the highest quartile for engagement experienced better business performance than other organizations, including a:

- 21 percent increase in profits
- 20 percent increase in sales
- 17 percent increase in productivity
- 10 percent increase in customer ratings.

At the same time that the most highly-engaged organizations found their key performance indicators (KPIs) increasing, they also saw a drop in undesirable indices, including a:

- 41 percent reduction in absenteeism
- 24 percent reduction in turnover (Harter et al. 2016).

If you're reading this book, at some point in your career, you most likely demonstrated the attitudes and behaviors of someone who loved their job, made positive contributions, worked with enthusiasm, and developed a reputation for getting things done. You were engaged.

It's also likely that you brought an attitude of engagement with you, and you worked for a leader who you found engaging.

Don't confuse employee engagement with employee satisfaction, happiness, or well-being. While the concepts are related, employee engagement alone moves the needle on performance.

Here's how satisfaction, happiness, and well-being aren't enough:

Satisfaction doesn't link to improved performance. Some employees find great satisfaction by putting in just enough hours to justify their salaries. Satisfaction can be fickle. In fact, you can define satisfaction as "not dissatisfied...*yet*."

Happiness is situation-based, a feeling that ebbs and flows with events. If the company announces a cash bonus after a highly profitable year, employees understandably become happier based on that positive turn of events. If a month later, that same company announces a reduction in the employer's contribution to healthcare, employees would feel unhappy. Happiness alone doesn't improve employee commitment to the organization or increase productivity.

Well-being efforts can certainly improve the lives of employees, making them happier, healthier, and more resilient. And well-being does positively impact engagement. But while well-being helps employees improve themselves, it doesn't drive their loyalty to a company.

Once you're a leader, it's vitally important that you remain engaged and model the best traits to your team. And it's just as important that you catalyze engagement within your team.

WHAT ENGAGEMENT LOOKS LIKE

As a leader, I make it my mission to connect my team members to work I believe they'll find interesting, rewarding, and engaging. Determining that takes more than guesswork. As I've shared, I spend enough time with each person to find their passions and interests.

While working on internationalization for Google Search, I met an engineer who was passionate about making search more robust and broadly available for less common languages and cultures. As an organization, we'd already mapped out all major languages, but he longed to expand into Haitian Creole and Cherokee. He started working on this as a hobby project while I sought opportunities for him to do this as part of his "day job." Before long, I found a way for him to apply his passion to help those cultural groups by expanding Google Search. His engagement skyrocketed while his work and the result empowered and aided members of those communities.

Beyond helping others, his determination set a new bar for the organization. We put more resources behind covering smaller cultural groups. This expansion gave other Googlers the opportunity to do work in cultural groups they were interested in assisting through tech.

This is what engagement looks like to me. People no longer just showed up for work. They invested their discretionary efforts in things that made them excited and ignited their passions. Because of their work, many team members received promotions, and Google offered better products to the world.

SETTING ENGAGEMENT ON FIRE

Quantum Workplace, a company with deep expertise in measuring and reporting employee engagement, identifies ten key drivers of employee engagement (Ryba 2021):

1. *My job allows me to utilize my strengths.*
2. I trust our senior leaders to lead the company to future success.
3. I believe this organization will be successful in the future.
4. *I find my job interesting and challenging.*
5. The senior leaders of this organization value people as their most important resource.
6. *My opinions seem to count at work.*
7. *If I contribute to the organization's success, I know I will be recognized.*

8. *I see professional growth and career development opportunities for myself here.*
9. The senior leaders of this organization demonstrate integrity.
10. *I have the information I need to do my job well.*

The *italicized* bullet points indicate statements that immediate leaders like supervisors own. Of the four remaining items, the immediate leader can greatly influence team member perception by connecting the dots (Chapter 5). In other words, immediate leaders directly impact team member perceptions, even about senior leaders and the organization.

EVALUATE HOW WELL YOU ENGAGE OTHERS

If you're already in a leadership role, rate yourself on a scale of 1 to 5 (1=lowest level, 5=highest level) for how strongly you agree with the following statements, related to the key engagement drivers:

Engagement Driver	#
I know the individual strengths of my team members and find ways for each to contribute their skills to the team's objectives.	
I provide interesting and challenging work for each team member.	
I seek out or act on team members' opinions or explain why I can't act on them.	
My team knows what it takes to receive praise, recognition, and social rewards.	
I know where each team member wishes to grow their careers, and I provide them with learning opportunities to pursue their dreams.	
I provide my team members with information and other resources they need to do their work well.	
Total	

This might sound like an impossible goal, but unless you scored a total of 30 on the six engagement drivers directly within your control, you have room for improvement.

It should make sense why the chapters on employee care (Chapter 4) and communication (Chapters 5) preceded this chapter on engagement: you must care for your team members and practice strong communication skills as part of engaging them.

If you're not currently a leader but aspire to move into leadership, rate yourself on a scale of 1 to 5 (1=lowest level, 5=highest level) for how strongly you agree with the following statements related to the key engagement drivers that you influence as a peer:

Peer Engagement Driver	#
I know the individual strengths of my team members and encourage them to apply their skills to the team's objectives.	
I point my teammates into interesting and challenging work that they enjoy.	
I seek out my peers' opinions, thanking them for sharing and acting on their ideas whenever I can.	
I regularly praise, recognize, and thank my peers.	
I encourage my peers to grow their careers and pursue their dreams.	
I share openly what I know with my peers and act as a resource in their work.	
Total	

You know that you're ready to take the next step into your leadership journey when you reach a total score of 25 or more. Those who don't engage others even while not holding a formal leadership title wouldn't be effective leaders if they held a title.

The first leadership role in tech is usually called tech lead. That title isn't tracked by HR, and it won't bring any changes in your paycheck. Other industries have similar roles, ones with additional responsibilities but not additional pay. But taking on the responsibility for lead is the first critical step into the leadership ranks. The lead role allows team member to practice what they know, assume greater responsibility, and take accountability for more than their own performance. It also lets management see how the lead handles themselves, their teams, and their results.

If you wish to grow from subject-matter expert into a leadership role, here's a short list of DON'Ts:

- Don't wait to engage your teammates until you get a promotion into the leadership ranks. Start engaging others now. Besides, in tech, promotions typically happen only after showing that you can effectively do the next-level job. Show the skills today to be seen as promotable tomorrow.

- Don't get so caught up in your own work that you don't connect with others. If you work in a self-imposed silo today, you'll bring that tendency into leadership.
- Don't ignore solid peer performance in your peers. Praise from a peer can be more meaningful than from a leader, because peers know the ins and outs of each job.
- Don't believe a title change will magically make you more engaging and caring. Leaders don't rely on titles to do the right thing.
- Don't think of your teammates as competition. View them as your fellow-collaborators and friends.

Keith Ferrazzi said in his 2019 TedTalk, "Leadership is not about the hero, and it certainly isn't about the individual. It's about the host who has the potential to convene a community that can build a movement" (Ferrazzi 2019).

If you can bring a community of people together, you can be a leader. If you can harness their talents and passions, you can build a movement.

THE LEADER AS CHIEF ENGAGEMENT OFFICER

Most people could match these companies with the leaders who served or still serve at the helm: Bill Gates, Microsoft; Mary Barra, General Motors; Jack Welch, General Electric; Steve Jobs,

Steve Wozniak, and Tim Cook, Apple; Jeff Bezos, Amazon; Sundar Pichai, Google; Mark Zuckerberg, Facebook; Safra Catz, Oracle Corporation; Tony Hsieh, Zappos.

Would anyone expect that Mary Barra could assemble a car? Did anyone ever see Jeff Bezos delivering packages? CEOs lead a handful of direct reports who are responsible for leading the organization. No one expects CEOs to have the skills to perform every job in the company. Frontline leaders, though, are expected to possess "know-how" and proficiency in the work performed by their team members.

That's especially true in technology. Most tech CEOs know more about technology than nearly everyone on the planet, yet no one would expect them to roll up their sleeves and start coding. Don't get me wrong, most of them code and could likely still do most jobs in the organization! But those skills are no longer part of their jobs. As CEOs, they had to learn a skill set to equip them for leading an entire organization.

If your goal is to lead a tech unit—or any specialized professional discipline— you must possess the same fundamental skills of those working for you. Then you need to engage others as you transition from "talent" to leadership. The following tips will help you get started.

Use an Engagement Mantra

Yes, another mantra. If you want to keep a thought and practice fresh in your mind, keep a list of your mantras with you to review and recite to yourself throughout the day. Choose one of the following mantras, or use these to prime your thinking as you develop your own:

- *Engagement starts with me. Today I will be engaged.*

- *Engagement is a prerequisite for high performance.*
- *When I see engagement in team members' behaviors, I will thank them for bringing me their best.*
- *People looking in from the outside of my team think every team member is the leader.*
- *My team members will engage no further than I am engaged.*

Model the Engagement You Want to See in Others

A leader can't pull the team into a meeting and say, "I need all of you to become engaged." That won't work for too many reasons to list. But a leader can and must lead engagement by living the best example of engagement at work. Passion and positivity increase team performance (Slack 2019).

Think of the words you use and the actions you show when you are 100 percent engaged. What do you *say*? What do you *do*? What can others see in you that communicates, "You look like you love your job!"? That's what your team must see in you to bring out their engagement. Model what you wish your team members to copy.

Work Alongside Your Team

The higher up you move in leadership in any organization, the less you're expected to know about the ins and outs of every job in the company. If you're the CEO, stay out of the way of the people doing their job. The CEO's time and skills are better invested elsewhere. But in tech and professional disciplines, team members will perceive you as a more credible and engaging leader if you work alongside your team. In other words, the work isn't *beneath* you. You're not *too good* to roll up your sleeves and work with your team members.

When I started at Facebook, I spent my first six weeks with new college graduates in Facebook Engineering Bootcamp. I hadn't been coding in years, and I knew nothing about the primary language used, called Hack. Facebook installed this bootcamp as part of its culture for engineers, where both new graduates as well as tenured engineers would work together, fixing bugs and learning from one another. This experience gave me invaluable insight into Facebook's culture, processes, and the talent they hired. As Vlad Fedorov, Facebook's engineering director, said of the bootcamp, "I would copy it if I were to start a company myself" (Feloni 2016), and I completely agree.

Leaders who are viewed as "one of us" by their team members demonstrate they are equally good followers. *Harvard Business Review* provided a concise summary of what it means to be a strong follower:

Leadership is a process that emerges from a relationship between leaders and followers. People [are] more effective leaders when their behaviors indicate that they are one of us, that they share our values, concerns, and experiences, and are working for us. Seen this way, perhaps the usual advice for aspiring leaders — "stand out from your peers" — is wrong. Perhaps aspiring leaders would be better served by ensuring that they are seen to be a good follower (Peters and Haslam 2018).

In ancient times, no king would order troops into battle while he sat in the palace sipping wine. Instead, the king would mount a horse and lead the charge. Similarly, leaders who are strong followers inspire team members with their willingness to get involved—working alongside the team to achieve a result.

Know the Unique Assets of Your Team Members

How well do you know your team members? Think of what you must see in your team, both in their work tasks and attitudes. On the left side, write a few tasks that must be performed for your team to be successful. On the right side, I've started a list of engaged attitudes that you'll likely want to see. You can also add your own. In the column next to each heading, write the initials of a team member who best performs the required task and has mastered the best attitude.

Work Task	In.	Work Attitude	In.
Example: Coding		Taking initiative	
		Peer coaching	
		Can-do attitude	
		Enthusiasm	
		Collaboration	
		Overdelivers	
		Consistency	

Many team leaders who have completed a similar exercise found that they used the same initials multiple times. Team members whose initials keep appearing on the list are likely the most engaged people on the team. Smart leaders use these members as role models for engagement to other team members.

If you struggled to come up with names (initials), that doesn't mean you have skill deficits within your team. But you must spend more time with team members individually to know where their strengths lie.

The director of strategic communications at a multibillion-dollar company "inherited" several employees after a reorganization. As he always did, he sent each new employee a survey so he could get to know them better. He also had them fill out something called The Achiever Pre-Employment Assessment, which evaluated both personality and mental acuity (Saterfiel & Associates 2020).

Looking through the assessment results, he was dismayed at how poorly one of his new employees performed on written communication. She struggled with English grammar across the board. As he continued reading, the report suggested that low scores in English grammar might indicate "an employee speaking English as a second language." But that wasn't the case. This employee had lived her entire life just twenty miles from the director's home. As the leader of strategic communications, he didn't know how to use her on his team.

A few days later, the director's executive vice president (EVP) asked if the strategic communication team had an employee skilled in data collection and reporting. The EVP wanted to discontinue using an expensive outside vendor who'd been crunching data for the organization's employee engagement surveys.

At first, the director couldn't think of anyone. After the meeting, he reviewed the assessment results from the employees he'd recently acquired, and he found one who had high aptitude with numbers. It was the same employee who struggled with English grammar.

He tasked this employee with learning from the vendor and evaluating if she could run the data the organization needed. She picked it up very quickly, and the director discharged the vendor after a month. He then assigned another team member with impeccable written communication skills to produce all outgoing written communications that the newly engaged employee generated with the data sets.

Had the director not gotten to know the skills of his new employees, he would have continued spending money on an outside consultant instead of cultivating in-house expertise. And his new employee would have failed, because her skillset didn't "fit the mold."

I've known leaders who think the best way to keep team performance high is by providing corrective feedback whenever they see something they don't like. Correction stops bad behaviors, but it doesn't maximize performance. Performance is directly related to how much team members perceive you care for them, invest in their successes, and allow them to do work that they love. Invest enough time with your team to know their strengths. When we use our strengths, we grow engaged in our work. And the time you invest in getting to know each person's strength not only demonstrates that you care for them, but it allows you to plug into their natural talents and passions (Llopis 2015).

Be Generous with Praise and Acknowledgement

In Chapter 4, I referenced the bestselling book *The Five Love Languages* by Gary Chapman. Chapman defines five primary ways that people show and receive love:

1. Acts of service

2. Receiving gifts
3. Quality time
4. Words of affirmation
5. Physical touch (Chapman 1995)

Let me be very clear about a couple of things before continuing. First, Chapman's book was written about personal relationships, not work ones. Second, I'm not suggesting that a leader should try to apply all five "languages" with their team members...especially the last one!

Sir Richard Branson, founder of Virgin Group and business magnate, reportedly put it this way: "I have always believed that the way you treat your employees is the way they will treat your customers...[P]eople flourish when they are praised."

However, the concept of love languages is relevant to leaders. Leaders, like all people, tend to give others what they most wish to receive. That's why two leaders might see the same positive behavior, and one might offer praise and recognition while the other says nothing. The leader who offers praise probably likes to receive praise; a leader who doesn't offer much praise probably wouldn't consider words of affirmation as their primary "love language."

Even if words of affirmation are your "native tongue," praise is the cheapest, most readily available engagement tool at a leader's disposal. Positive reinforcement, which includes praise, increases the functioning of a team and its members. According to positive psychology researcher Barbara Fredrickson, 3:1 is the ideal positivity ratio for all high-functioning relationships (Frederickson 2009).

When team members' feedback falls below the 3:1 ratio, they languish (Faulk et al. 2013, 378-390). Languishing is defined as the "absence of mental health, characterized by ennui, apathy, listlessness, and loss of interest in life" (APA 2022).

Do you see signs that some of your team members are languishing? Read the symptoms:

- Disconnection or dissociation from coworkers
- Irritability, sadness, confusion
- An inability to get excited about upcoming projects
- Difficulty focusing or remembering
- Cynicism about leaders, colleagues, or career
- Procrastination or lack of motivation to complete assignments
- Experiencing increasing stress or the "Sunday scaries" more frequently (Cooks-Campbell 2021)

But when team members receive 3:1 positive to negative reinforcement at work, they flourish. Flourishing is "good mental and physical health: the state of being free from illness and distress but, more important, of being filled with vitality and functioning well in one's personal and social life" (APA 2022).

Something as simple as checking in, thanking a team member for an update, or praising them for "expected" behaviors like timeliness, creativity, or completing a mundane task increases your positivity ratio, making it more likely that they will have boosted vitality for the day.

People leadership requires care, communication, and engagement. Read on to the final chapter in this section on coaching, where all the concepts in people leadership work together.

CHAPTER 7
LEAD AS A COACH

COACHING FAILURE

Hakeem attended a coaching seminar for new managers where the facilitator suggested meeting with team members one-on-one each month to review their performance. After the session, Hakeem scheduled thirty-minute sessions for individual coaching.

"Hello, come on in," Hakeem greeted Jada when she appeared at his door. He scheduled Jada as his first coaching session, because he had a list of topics he wanted to cover.

"Have a seat," he gestured to the chair across from him while gathering the notes he'd prepared for their meeting. "How are things for you?"

"Good," Jada said with a shrug. "Busy."

"That's great." Hakeem shifted positions in his chair. "Let me say up front that you're not in any trouble. Over the next month, I'll be meeting with each team member about their individual performance. Let me start by giving you a copy of your job description, because I'm going to refer to it through our time."

Jada wasn't sure why her boss handed her a copy of the job description she'd applied for nearly three years earlier, but she didn't have long to wait before learning out how it played into the meeting.

"First, I want to talk to you about..."

Jada lost track of how many points followed Hakeem's first one. For the next twenty-eight minutes, Hakeem went line-by-line through Jada's job description and pointed out the few things she did well, while spending most of the time sharing specific examples of how she hadn't yet reached his expected competency level for different items. Between each point, he'd ask, "Does that make sense?" before going on, without pausing.

"So next time we meet, I'd like you to tell me what you've been doing to address the areas where you need more work," he said minutes before the meeting ended. "Now, what do you need from me to be successful in the areas we've discussed?"

Over lunch, one of Jada's coworkers asked how the meeting went with Hakeem.

"Brutal," Jada said with a shake of her head. "I walked in there feeling great about myself and my work. But it's time for me to update my resume."

Before you say, "No one would 'coach' like that," let me assure you that some do. Metattude organization cites coaching to job descriptions as a leading coaching failure from managers (Mettatude 2014).

Author of *The Master Coach,* Gregg Thompson shared the ten most common coaching failures he's seen as a professional business coach (Thompson 2021). Of the ten, Hakeem made five errors in his attempt to coach Jada. They include:

1. *Doggedly following a coaching system.* In the coaching workshop, Hakeem heard something about connecting feedback to the team member's job description and

performance; unfortunately, Hakeem didn't apply the rest of the workshop that suggested "coaching to the person, not a static, dated piece of paper."

2. *Assuming the other person needs to be fixed.* Hakeem spent most of his time trying to "fix" Jada. The "fix" came by way of critiquing the "many ways" Jada failed to meet expectations, which long ago had lost relevance to her daily work.

3. *Talking too much.* Hakeem didn't allow space for dialogue. He monologued, and the only questions he asked were rhetorical.

4. *Giving lots of advice.* After pointing out an area where Jada's performance didn't match her job description, Hakeem offered tons of suggestions like "you should try" and "here's what I would do."

5. *Finishing without a commitment.* Hakeem ended by letting Jada know that they would revisit her progress at their next "coaching" session. But he didn't secure a commitment from Jada about how she'd bridge the "performance gaps" that Hakeem spent twenty-eight minutes detailing.

Gartner research indicates that manager-coaches fall into one of four types:

Always-on managers provide regular coaching feedback and drive employee development.

Teacher managers offer advice-based feedback and direct employee development.

Cheerleader managers offer plenty of positive feedback but little constructive criticism while encouraging employees to own their development.

Connector managers create a positive work environment, offer targeted feedback, and connect employees to others for development.

The same report says that only connector managers provide consistently high-quality coaching results. Connectors triple the likelihood that their team members become high performers. Connectors unleash team discretionary effort by 38 percent and boost engagement by up to 40 percent (Wiles 2019).

Not all coaching approaches and styles create the same results. When you see the word *coaching* in this chapter, I'm referring to connector managers.

Feedback is a critical component of coaching, but coaching goes beyond feedback. In Chapter 15, I'll discuss the extremely effective FAST Feedback Method.

WHAT DOES IT MEAN TO BE A COACH?

Coaches guide their teams to learn and achieve beyond what they would without support. *Coaching is the ongoing process of helping others stay motivated to achieve goals.* The best coaches turn poor performers into solid performers and solid performers into superstars.

The "secret sauce" of coaching requires several ingredients with one simple yet complex objective: to *create successful team members.*

The book *Trillion Dollar Coach: The Leadership Playbook of Silicon Valley's Bill Campbell* shares the coaching lessons of Bill Campbell. Campbell served in executive positions for companies such as Apple, Claris, and Intuit, and he served as the executive coach of Google's leaders Larry Page, Sergey Brin, Eric Schmidt as well as Amazon's Jeff Bezos and Facebook's Sheryl Sandberg (Schmidt et al. 2020).

Here's some insight the authors of *Trillion Dollar Coach* shared about the coaching heart of Bill Campbell:

"Coaching is no longer a specialty; you cannot be a good [leader] without being a good coach."

"[Campbell] only coached the coachable."

"When [Campbell yells] at you, it's because he loves you and cares and wants you to succeed" (Stanuch 2020).

Campbell believed that coaching served as a fundamental skill for good leadership, yet he also recognized that not every individual *wanted to be* or *could be* coached. And while yelling isn't a coaching core competency, the passion to see others succeed is critical.

I've never met a leader who didn't intellectually embrace the importance of coaching to improving performance. And yet I've worked with several leaders who viewed coaching as a low priority. In my experience, I've come across five excuses leaders make to themselves about why coaching isn't a higher priority:

1. *I don't have time.* When a leader says they don't have time to coach, that means they aren't convinced of the benefits. If they believed that one hour of coaching could generate two hours of improved productivity, they would see coaching as an investment with rich returns.
2. *I have too many people.* I've known general managers with five hundred team members. But those

managers have supervisors. Their actual span-of-control is much smaller. The number of coachable direct reports is likely smaller still.

3. *I did it already.* Coaching is an ongoing process. Would you turn down food today because you ate yesterday? Coaching isn't one-and-done; nor is every coaching session a formal, hour-long sit-down meeting.

4. *I must focus on getting real things done.* When you move into the leadership ranks, you're no longer compensated for how many lines of code you write or how many widgets you produce. Leadership is about maximizing performance while creating additional leaders. Coaching increases individual performance by 70 percent, team performance by 50 percent, and organizational performance by 48 percent (American University 2022). Those performance gains are the "real things" that leaders must accomplish.

5. *I don't know how.* Teams don't want another parent at work. They don't want someone looking over their shoulders to catch them doing something wrong, and they don't want a boss. When leaders don't know how to coach, they instead micromanage, believing that correcting people is like coaching. Wrong. Teams want a coach who knows the job, asks questions designed to improve their thinking, and leads them to getting results in meaningful, relevant work.

Psychotherapist Amy Morin wrote "The Ten Fears That Hold People Back in Life" (Morin 2019). Here's the list of the ten most common fears that clients shared with her:

1. Change
2. Something bad happening

3. Loneliness
4. Getting hurt/Pain
5. Failure
6. Being judged
7. Rejection
8. Inadequacy
9. Uncertainty
10. Loss of freedom or autonomy

How many items on that list pertain to fears team members face at work? All of them, although the risk of getting hurt or experiencing pain in tech is minimal.

How does that help you become an effective coach? Think about how much impact you'd have with your coaching if you minimized your team's fears by helping them achieve the opposite. Consider how effective you'd be as a leader if you could replace fears with something positive, like the items on this list:

Replace Their Fear of...	By Helping Them Experience...
Change	Excitement about the possibilities
Loneliness	A feeling of belonging
Failure	Success and achievement
Rejection	Acceptance
Uncertainty	Certainty around the right things
Something bad happening	Proactive planning
Being judged	Being celebrated
Inadequacy	Mastery
Loss of freedom or autonomy	Earned autonomy

I HAD TO LEARN HOW TO BE AN EFFECTIVE COACH

When I started my career at Google in 2006, managers were seen as "overhead." They had from twenty to fifty direct reports, since the prevailing belief was that engineers could self-organize without direction. I should mention that this was before Project Oxygen discovered the value of top managers.

But in my own experience, I quickly found that people really did value support and coaching. Without really knowing what it was called at the time, I coached my peers regularly. Google started growing rapidly, and the only way to orient and train new Googlers was through coaching. In the process, I learned that I loved coaching and mentoring others. I played the role of the supportive buddy who worked alongside new hires to show them the ropes and guide them to success.

After assuming the informal role of mentor to my peers, I started wondering, *Is this what it's like to be a manager? Because if it is, I want to be one!*

I set out to discover what I needed to learn to move into management. I couldn't find any internal training program that spelled out how to move from individual contributor to leader. After finding a couple of mentors who had made the transition, I asked them to show me what they did and learned along the way. What they taught me seemed like tribal knowledge. The problem was the organization had no repository to hold this knowledge.

Finally, I started a master's degree in engineering management at Drexel. I figured if nothing else, an advanced degree with the word "management" in the title would give me some credibility. After the nearly four years it took to complete that degree, I must say that I didn't find much practical help on how to be a great manager. Don't get me wrong. I value education, and I'm glad I got that degree. But as far as teaching me what I needed, I didn't walk away with what I'd consider leadership skills.

By the time I finished graduate school, I'd pieced together enough from some tidbits in classes, my mentors, and on-the-job experience as a mentor to create my own plan for transitioning from individual contributor to leader. Then I volunteered for every work opportunity that would give me practice in leading a team. I expressed my intention of moving into leadership, and I shifted my interest from knowledge worker to leader.

Once I was given the opportunity to lead a team of my own, I took it and applied everything I'd learned along the way. I found that I enjoyed coaching more than nearly any other leadership role. But at first, I believed that coaching was giving team members the answers to their questions. Whenever an engineer would come to me with a problem, I thought my job involved giving them the answer quickly and accurately.

Fortunately, I've had the benefit of some phenomenal coaches through the years, and they taught me a better way to coach. Coaching, I learned, isn't about "giving a person a fish." Instead, as the adage says, it's "teaching a person to fish." The best coaches teach you to think, grow, and expand the big picture. Answers are relatively easy to come by. But when you teach someone to think deeply, you've given them a tool with a limitless shelf life.

One of my coaches challenged me to consider if I had a gap in my skill set. "I've seen you working with your engineers," he said. "You're always quick to solve their problems. What would happen if instead of telling them what to do, you asked them questions to inspire their own answers?"

I didn't have a good response.

"When people solve their own problems, they gain owner-ship of their problems and solutions," he continued.

I hadn't thought about that. My instinct was to give them the fastest, best solution I could come up with. But those were my solutions, not theirs. They likely wouldn't have the same passion about making the solution work as they would if they'd come up with it themselves.

I changed my approach to asking more questions and offering more advice.

Another coach gave me similar feedback from observing me in a brainstorming session with my team. Afterwards, he asked to talk with me for a few minutes.

"Andrew, you and your team are doing an amazing job," she said. "But can I offer some feedback?"

"Please," I responded immediately.

"I noticed that at the beginning of the brainstorming session, you spoke first. For the rest of the meeting, your team members anchored to it. After that, no one offered up additional suggestions or ideas on the topic. You might want to try waiting to give your ideas and opinions until the end, so you don't imprint your thinking on everyone else."

I had no idea that I was doing that. I talked first because of my passion for the topic. But I didn't realize that my talking first could shut down additional brainstorming.

That's when I started to ask and listen more than I spoke. And do you know what? She was right. When I gave space for team members to develop their own ideas, they had no problem sharing brilliant thoughts on their own. And once they were the ones coming up with the solutions, they felt ownership of the work and outcome.

In my experience, the best coaches ask the best questions. Instead of being directive and prescriptive, coaching gives teams space to create their own solutions. At times, leaders also point out team members' blind spots so they can become even more successful. When the leader and team share a strong, caring relationship, these conversations come from a place of love, not pettiness. Teams grow hungry to learn more, so they can continue to develop.

LEADING LIKE A COACH

In the world of sports, coaching takes place in the locker room, during practice, and at the game. Locker-room coaching inspires the entire team at once, painting a picture of what challenges lie ahead as well as what strengths the team will harness to achieve success. Coaching during practice takes place on the field, in the absence of any opponents. Coaching at practice happens between the coach and individuals, and the coach and smaller teams, to build skills. This type of coaching prepares the bodies, minds, and hearts of team members for game day by focusing on the fundamentals. On game day, though, coaching comes from the sidelines. At the game, feedback is targeted and brief.

In the winter of 1960, the Green Bay Packers blew their fourth-quarter lead and lost to the NFL Championship Game to the Philadelphia Eagles. In the last play, the Packers rushed towards the goal line with what should have been the touchdown that won the game. Instead, they came up a few yards short. In the locker room after the game, head coach Vince Lombardi told his team these words: "This will never happen again. You will never lose another championship" (Maraniss 1999, 265).

On the first day of training camp the next year, players assumed that Lombardi would acknowledge how much the team had improved in the last two seasons, remind them that the last season saw the franchise win the NFL Western Conference for the first time since 1944, and pick up where they left off months before.

"Gentlemen, this is a football," Lombardi said while holding a ball over his head at the first day of training in

July of 1961. He didn't want to focus on what had happened the previous season. He had no new strategies to turn losses like the one the Packers experienced against the Eagles into a win. Instead, Lombardi uttered those words as his way of telling the team they needed to get back to the fundamentals like passing, running, blocking, tackling, catching, and kicking (Crandall 2021).

Lombardi coached the Packers to win their next nine post-season games. Under Lombardi's coaching, the Packers never lost another playoff game.

The key to Lombardi's coaching success wasn't based on locker-room inspiration, practice-day drills, or game-day strategies of how to best tap into his players. His success relied on all the above.

Coaching isn't an item on your to-do list. It's an ongoing activity, not a single event. It happens in your dialogues and not your monologues. Your questions are often more instructive than your statements. Coaching is a mindset that says, "My job is to create a successful team."

What can you start doing immediately in your coaching that will make the biggest difference to your team? Start with the following tips.

Use a Coaching Mantra

Think of a short, simple, sticky statement you can tell yourself each day to keep the coaching mindset fresh in your spirit. Here are some ideas to get you started:

- *I will listen to understand my team member's perspectives.*
- *I will coach to individuals, not to checklists.*
- *I know where my team members want to grow, and I will help them get there.*
- *I will ask powerful questions.*
- *I measure my success as a coach by how many leaders I develop.*

Make the Price of Entry High

Chick-fil-A receives about sixty thousand applications annually from people wanting to open Chick-fil-A franchises while the corporation plans to open fewer than eighty restaurants each year. That's a 0.13 percent acceptance rate, meaning statistically, it's harder to own a Chick-fil-A franchise than to get into Harvard (3.2 percent acceptance rate) or even become a Navy SEAL (1.5 percent acceptance rate). The corporation found that their high price of entry doesn't detour potential owners (Murphy 2022).

Follow the same practice when you build or expand your team. Keep the standards high, and let potential candidates know of your high expectations. Doing so lets the team members you hire start with a sense of pride and accomplishment for being accepted into such an elite group.

Any child in the US can attend kindergarten through grade twelve via free public education, but a little more than 5 percent of students drop out before completing high school (NCES 2022). Of the students who complete high school, only 40 percent enroll in college

(NCES 2022). Of the 40 percent who attend college, only about one-third complete their degrees (O'Shaughnessy 2022). In the US, only 1.2 percent of the population completes a PhD (Hankel 2021). Anyone earning a PhD shares the rarified air with the most elite, highly educated people in the country.

Picture a funnel. All students enter the academic world at the broadest part. Anyone can attend school. Most do. Standards increase (the funnel narrows) as students progress in their academic pursuits. Some can attend college. Fewer complete their degrees. Fewer still go on for advanced degrees. Those who make it through their PhDs can be proud by the "doctor" title they earn.

Likewise at work, getting on your team should be a huge accomplishment. Those who demonstrate the right fit earn the pride of being part of something special.

As the saying goes, "Hire for fit, train for skills." You don't need someone with the deepest skills in tech or any other discipline. You want someone who knows the basics while demonstrating that they're highly coachable and trainable. For that reason, create an interview process that includes team interviews, behavioral interviews, and even role plays. Your ideal hires should love collaboration, challenging work, and learning new things. If they possess those traits and are coachable, they can accomplish anything you throw at them.

Consider How You Like to Be Coached

Nearly every team member and leader across all industries receive some sort of performance evaluation, assessment, or appraisal along with feedback. And in many companies, the performance review and feedback processes are documented and reported to ensure they happen.

While those processes serve as potential starting points for coaching conversations, many leaders view these checklist activities as coaching itself. But they're not! Coaching involves a relationship where a dialogue takes place, one that may clarify expectations, remove barriers, enhance current skills or thinking, improve results, and achieve short- and long-term goals.

For a more concrete example of what coaching looks and feels like, consider how you like to be coached. Or maybe think about the worst coach you've ever had, and consider how you DON'T want to be coached. Look the list, and circle the actions/statements you most want from your own coach:

1. Eye rolls	11. Smiles
2. "I like your thinking"	12. Silence
3. To-do lists	13. Micromanagement
4. Empowerment	14. Encouragement
5. Praise	15. Sarcasm
6. Challenging work	16. Big picture
7. Being an insider	17. Busywork
8. Questions	18. Yelling
9. Public criticism	19. Correction
10. Direction	20. "WTF?!"

Normally I'd say there are no right or wrong answers. But some of the options listed clearly don't exemplify someone who wants to be seen as a professional.

While the list isn't prescriptive and not all team members desire the same coaching behaviors, think of it like the "love languages" mentioned earlier. Your own leaders have likely said or done things that made you flourish. Likewise, your leader has probably said or done things that make you languish at times. In your interactions with your team, intend to bring out their best. Ask yourself, "What can I say or do in this conversation that will be positively remembered by this employee in the weeks and months to come?"

Schedule Coaching Meetings

If you don't already practice this, create a coaching schedule for your team members who are ready for coaching. You can define *ready* in several ways. Those who have asked for more regular meetings, coaching, and feedback have self-identified. They're eager to work with you. Other criteria might be that someone already performers well, and you believe they can assume more responsibility and greater challenges.

Create a simple agenda for your first formal coaching meeting, like this list:

- Review their current performance.
- Ask, "How you think you're doing?"
- Say, "Here's how I think you're doing…" Spend more time discussing the tasks the person excels in instead of their deficits.
- Find out where they wish to grow.
- Ask, "What more would you like to be doing?"
- Ask, "What skills and interest do you have that aren't tapped into today?"
- Ask, "What do you see as your next career move?"

- Ask, "How can I partner with you to give you more opportunities in these areas?"

By sending an agenda like this in advance, no team member will come into your meeting with fear or uncertainty about its purpose. Remember the ten fears listed earlier? Your role is to minimize those fears wherever possible, so people won't waste energy worrying about things that don't apply to them.

Find Relevant, Meaningful Opportunities for Your Team Members

Tara worked in a call center. Her job? Answering call after call, all day, Monday through Friday. She didn't love her job. She'd earned a degree in performance arts. Her boss, Michelle, didn't know what performance arts involved, but Michelle was fairly certain that Tara's passion didn't lie in answering phones.

After a coaching session, Michelle learned that the only reason Tara took the job was to pay the bills until she could find a better opportunity suited her passion, which Michelle learned involved writing scripts, performing one-woman shows, and playing music. Tara loved telling stories that touched people's lives.

Once Michelle learned this, she coached Tara in three areas. First, she encouraged Tara to maintain her performance, since that was the job she got paid to do. Second, she asked her to start taking extensive notes on the customers she helped—documenting why they called, how they felt when placing the call, what they needed, what they said, and how they felt after she helped them. At the end of each week, Michelle asked Tara to report back the best "story" of a customer she served. Finally, Michelle promised that she would look for opportunities for Tara to do more in her area of passion.

Six months later, Tara got the reward of her lifetime. Michelle learned that the senior vice president of customer service, Joanne—someone who started thirty years earlier answering the phone just like Tara—was retiring.

"Joanne's retiring," Michelle mentioned in a coaching session.

"Oh, no," Tara moaned. "I love her! She's an inspiration to all female associates. She broke through the glass ceiling and paved the way for other women in the company."

"That's right," her boss continued. "And I've been asked to coordinate her retirement send-off."

Michelle asked Tara if she would write a script based on the movie *It's a Wonderful Life,* telling the story about what the customer service organization and company would look like had Joanne never been born.

"Are you kidding me? I'd love to!" Tara screamed.

"And I want you to play the part of Joanne," Michelle added.

Tara couldn't have been more excited had she earned a raise.

Finally, Michelle asked for a copy of all the customer service "stories" that Tara had documented during the previous six months. Michelle used those to create short videos showing the many people helped by their customer service department.

At the retirement celebration, Tara put on her play in

front of five hundred company leaders. The audience laughed and cried, and that night started an annual event of celebrating the people behind customer service.

One of Michelle's other team members watched from the wings and whispered in Michelle's ears, "I'm so glad you didn't ask me to be part of this. I would do anything for you, but you couldn't pay me enough to get me up there on stage."

Michelle thought to herself, *And I couldn't have paid Tara enough to keep her off the stage. She's waited years for an opportunity like this.*

People don't possess the same skills, nor do they want the same things. But when you know where a team member wants to be, you can create a plan that allows them to use their unique skills and talents to the benefit of the team and organization.

Instead of trying to track and create opportunities for all team members at once, start with one or two. Meet with leaders to uncover unannounced opportunities that would fit your team member's desired career paths, skills, and passions. Tell your peers what each of your team members has to offer, and advocate for them to take an active role in projects that are good fit for their skillset.

Use Peer Coaches

The idea of hiring for fit and training for skills sounds great... unless you happen to be the one doing all the training for skills! First, it takes time to train others. Second, especially in tech, after you've spent a few months away from the frontline, as I've shared earlier in the book, you might not have the most current knowledge and skills. Those doing the job know it better. Tap into them. Most team members love serving as peer coaches. It validates that they have strong, relevant skills, and it gives them practice should they wish to pursue a formal leadership role in the future.

Google offers "Tech Talks" that Googlers can attend to learn from peer experts. They also offer G2G, Googler to Googler training to spread learning throughout the organization. When I worked for Google, I cotaught classes on privacy and offered a course called, "So You Want to Be a Tech Lead?"

Great leaders leverage existing learning opportunities, whether from internal resources or external ones like workshops or online learning. Instead of providing all the coaching and learning opportunities for their team, leaders serve as the facilitators for growth by tapping into others. The best coaches are likely within your own team and broader organization. When you connect coaches with mentees and mentees with coaches, everybody wins.

As mentioned earlier, Gartner identified four distinct manager approaches to employee development:

1. Teacher managers use their own experiences and expertise to develop their employees.

2. Always-On managers rely on never-ending coaching and feedback to develop employees.

3. Cheerleader managers encourage employees to take charge of their own development.

4. Connector managers partner their employees with the right experts to fuel their development.

The *connector manager* delivers top results in employee engagement, discretionary effort, and retention. You could do all the coaching yourself, but why would you want to?

It's one thing to post a word like COACHING on the wall, and it's another thing to facilitate coaching to elevate the skills of each team member.

Create a Safe Team Environment

Earlier I wrote about Project Aristotle and the concept of psychological safety. If you've hired a team with high standards for their ability to collaborate, accept challenges, and learn, you don't need to be "the boss" or micromanage their work. Your role involves creating a safe environment where each team member learns, grows, contributes, makes mistakes, tries new things, innovates, pushes the status quo, and finds novel ways of getting things done.

View yourself the facilitator of a safe environment but not the sole member. Team members mirror the attitudes and work values of their leader. Over time, members of the team groom, shape, and train new members on priorities and how to get things done within the team. The facilitator encourages and leads by example.

Actions of a Boss	Actions of a Coach-Leader
Critiques ideas shared in brainstorming	Encourages "crazy" ideas
Asks a few to share ideas	Gets contribution from all
Criticizes ideas	Builds on ideas
Focuses on tasks-at-hand exclusively	Encourages group bonding
Says, "No, because…"	Says, "Yes, and…"
Shuts down dissent	Fosters open discussion
Punishes mistakes	Teaches through mistakes

Coach Using Questions

When a team hits a wall in problem-solving, the leader has an opportunity to use coaching to reinforce organizational values while elevating team thinking.

Imagine you lead a team responsible for engineering a new technology for users. If you convene a team meeting to tell the answers, you're wasting everyone's time. Instead of telling or jumping into the immediate task, ask questions to tap into the skills, engagement, and expertise of your team members. Consider the following:

- "Based on what we know of the end user, what minimal enhancements must we develop?"
- "Based on how the end user uses the product, what enhancements could be left out?"
- "What current features add the least value to our users? Which features are the most valuable?"

Your questions serve as coaching opportunities. How you

respond allows every team member to benefit from your context (communication) and direction.

Questions unleash the possibilities of *what if?* while providing you with multiple coaching moments.

Ask Your Team Members Where They Wish to Grow

Fifteen years ago, Amy hired Rod to work in a corporate, strategic role. While Rod had worked in operations, he expressed an interest to get closer to the business strategy.

"If I hire you for my team, what do you envision as your next step from there?" Amy asked Rod.

"Honestly," Rod answered, "I eventually want to go back to operations. I already know how to get things done there, but I've never understood how decisions get made at the corporate level. I believe if I learned more 'big picture" thinking, I could have a great impact leading a team there."

Amy's management team argued that Rod shouldn't be hired. Since the learning curve to be successful in Amy's team was long, they didn't want to invest a couple of years in getting Rod up to speed so he could leave and grow his career elsewhere in the company.

"But that's precisely why we need to hire Rod," Amy countered. "The worst outcome is that we invest a couple of years developing Rod, and then we lose him back to operations. But he could decide to stay and add value in our work with operations. And even if he leaves, we'll have a permanent advocate and champion inside operations. The question is if we're willing to make a long-term investment for the good of the organization, or if we'd rather select a 'sure thing' who could hit the ground, helping our department today. What do you think?"

Amy's managers decided to invest in Rod, giving him the opportunity he wanted so he could grow his own career. Amy and her team mentored and coached Rod to get him up to speed on the department's work. Then they continued to coach and provide him with opportunities that helped the team while giving Rod broader influence and exposure.

This turned out to be a great move for the team and the organization. Rod stayed five years in Amy's department instead of two, and he ended up leading a small team within the department. After five years, Rod moved back to operations as a manager over a large office. Two years after that, Rod got promoted to director of marketing. In the years that Amy, her managers, and Rod worked for the same organization, they continued to offer loyalty to one another and use their influence to help three departments and the organization take performance to a higher level.

Do you know where each of your team members wishes to take their careers? If not, get good at asking probing questions like the following:

- "What do you like most about your role today?"
- "What do you like least about your current role?"
- "Where do you want to learn and grow for your current position?"

- "Where do you see your career taking you in three years? Seven years? Fifteen years? "
- "What else do you wish to learn today to help you reach your future career goals?"
- "What other enrichment opportunities and experiences can I provide you with today that will help you on that route?"

When a leader knows a team member's career aspirations and provides opportunities to help them reach those goals, how could that person not actively engage in the coaching process? Too often, though, leaders coach their teams about poor performance on tasks instead of each member's desired future path.

Which is more critical, coaching to team member's aspirations or correcting poor performance? Call it a tie.

Corrective feedback is just one small part of coaching. Corrective feedback is straightforward and tactical, and it can be as simple as this process (more on this in Chapter 15):

- *Observe the problem*: "I saw you did/didn't do ____."
- *State the problem:* "When you do/don't do ____ it hurts____... because it____..."
  - List the stakeholders impacted (such as customers, peers, personal reputations, the organization, etc.).
  - Provide negative consequence on stakeholder (how the problem behavior hurts stakeholder relations).
- *Offer a solution*: "What I need you to do is ____."
- *Ensure their understanding:*
  - "Do you know how to do ____?"
  - "Does anything stand in the way of you ____ consistently?"
- *Secure their commitment and schedule follow-up:*
  - "I need to see ____ from you moving forward."

> • "I'll follow up with you on _____ to see that you've taken care of it."

Corrective feedback is a quick way to stop an undesired behavior and jump-start a desired behavior. Yet while it's effective in improving performance, don't confuse giving feedback with coaching.

Corrective feedback feels more like a monologue than a dialogue. Coaching, on the other hand, requires getting behind where your team wants to go and pushing in the same direction. It's a mutual *if/then* relationship that promises, "*If* you perform well in your current duties, *then* I'll find you even greater opportunities to achieve your most meaningful goals."

Remember the lesson from Bill Campbell: invest your time in coaching the coachable. Not every team member is coachable. Not everyone wants the *if/then* promise of a coaching relationship. Coaching is your gift to your team that yields improved employee performance and career growth. Coach those who crave coaching. At the same time, give every team member feedback to redirect their performance and activities around the priorities of the team and organization.

Sadly, when some leaders think they're wearing their *coach* hat, the label facing team members might read *micromanager*, *storyteller*, *counselor*, or *dictator*. The same is true for words like *collaboration*. It's easier to slap the word *collaboration* into a core values statement than it is to practice, embrace, model, and foster it throughout your team. In Section III, I'll explore the leadership-critical role that collaborative leadership plays in creating a high-performing, integrated, committed team.

SECTION III

COLLABORATIVE LEADERSHIP

Command-and-control leadership reigned for many years and saw common use in manufacturing. Post-WWII created conditions for manufacturing jobs to flourish. First, former military personnel, trained in life-or-death leadership, returned to the workforce. Second, with the Japanese and European post-war economies in shambles, the US became the hub of manufacturing for the world. Finally, American prosperity meant that post-war families had the money to buy homes and fill them with new, modern appliances. And of course, many parked new cars in their garages.

Command-and-control leadership focused on productivity and "hitting the numbers." Laborers who regularly hit their quotas were often promoted to management without any formal leadership training other than military service, training that often had them yelling, "Take that hill," knowing lives would be lost.

You can see the problems coming, right? The Japanese and European economies didn't stay dormant for long. By the 1960s, they rebounded and offered the US competition in the manufacturing industry. Unions for the US manufacturing sector met these competitive pressures by demanding increasingly larger pay and benefits for their members, further raising the costs of US goods.

The command-and-control leadership style useful in life-and-death situations in combat didn't translate to a workforce comprised of non-military professionals working in the service sector. Educated knowledge workers didn't respond well to bosses yelling, "Go faster!" and, "Do more!" These knowledge industry professionals needed a different kind of leadership, one that didn't deal only with production numbers but also deep thinking, creativity, and innovation.

Enter *collaborative leadership*, a management style where leaders seek team member input around idea generation and the work of the team.

CHAPTER 8
COLLABORATE, COLLABORATE, COLLABORATE

THE NEW WAY TO LEAD

From post-WWII to the mid-1960s, manufacturing fueled the US economy, and command-and-control leadership styles oversaw its production. At the same time the country shifted from manufacturing jobs towards the service and professional sectors, more workers completed college. In 1960, less than 8 percent of the US population had graduated from college. As of 2020, nearly 38 percent of people over age twenty-five in the US had a college degree (Duffin 2022). As the workforce became more educated and obtained specialized knowledge, the way managers led others needed to evolve.

Look at the difference between command-and-control versus collaborative leadership (Vidojevic 2022):

	Command-and-Control	Collaborative Leadership
Structure	Top-down chain of command	Cross-organizational network
Information flow	Controlled by leadership; need-to-know basis	Free; transparent
Decision-making	Management	The team
Accountability	Management	Everyone
Leadership's role	Direction; control	Influence; facilitation
Team member's role	Passive compliance; obedience	Active engagement
Team dynamic	Power struggle	Mutual empowerment

If you've never worked under a command-and-control leader, could you imagine waiting for your immediate supervisor to tell you what to do? Could you be successful if the information you needed to do your job came through a filter based on your "need to know" the driver or desired outcome?

In 1994, Rosabeth Moss Kanter wrote that critical business relationships "cannot be controlled by formal systems but require [a] dense web of interpersonal connections" (Kanter 1997). Today, we call that "dense web of interpersonal connections" a team.

Collaborative leadership requires skills that are the opposite of those used in command-and-control organization. "Collaboration needs a different kind of leadership; it needs leaders who can safeguard the process, facilitate interaction, and patiently deal with high levels of frustration (Chrislip 2002).

Here are the ten commandments for being a collaborative leader instead of a traditional "boss":

1. *Share a vision.* Back in the 1950s in manufacturing, a command-and-control leader would make changes on the assembly line to increase productivity or quality. But since "time is money" and explaining the rationale behind decisions took time away from production, employees weren't given the *why* behind what they were asked to do. Collaborative leaders share the "big picture" and context, so their team members understand not just what must be accomplished but also the vision for it.

2. *Balance the demands of various stakeholders.* Stakeholders often have various agendas. *You* want to be seen as a solid, competent leader. Your *immediate supervisor* wants you to deliver a quick, viable product. Your *team members* want to be valued for their efforts and unique skills. Your *customers* want low cost and high value. It's all about balance. Collaborative leaders know how to meet the needs of each stakeholder to create stronger results.

3. *Build trust by giving trust.* Don't say, "I trust you to make the right decision," if you plan to stand behind someone's shoulder to ensure they do the exact things in the exact way that you'd do them. Trust means giving teams room to make decisions, even when they may fail. Failure provides more learning than success.

4. *Share decision-making.* It's rare that the CEO will ask a tech lead what goals the organization should pursue for the next cycle. In fact, I don't think that's ever happened. But I know that CEOs *do* ask their direct reports for their input before rolling out goals. You probably have goals you've been asked to accomplish,

but when it comes to how to get the work done, that's up to you. When you share decision-making with your team, you give them ownership. Giving them skin in the game cements their commitment to getting results.

5. *Motivate your team.* Think about the worst way you were treated at work and how that treatment diminished your contribution. A hostile work environment that ridicules failure and punishes "bad ideas" is the antithesis of motivation. Collaborative leaders motivate with encouragement, support, and praise, while removing barriers to keep team morale high and resistance low.

6. *Refuse to the be the communication hub.* If everyone feels the need to communicate their findings directly to you, you'll become the biggest communication barrier on your team. Foster open communications between team members, so you're not stuck in the middle.

7. *Delegate to build up team members.* When you ask a team member to lead a project, you're saying, "You have the skills and insights we need." Delegation reinforces people in their areas of expertise, while fueling their engagement and letting them lead and grow.

8. *Tap into collaboration tools to get the entire team involved.* In addition to face-to-face meetings, use things like:
- Shared files,
- Team communication channels,
- Project management software,
- Chat tools like Slack,
- Whiteboard and Post-it notes brainstorming,

• Video calls and meetings.

9. *Lead with empathy.* Conflicts will arise on the team, and you may be asked to referee. Instead of trusting your gut or deciding based on your own biases, listen carefully and with understanding to both sides of the issue. Nothing builds safety like disagreeing with the opinion of another person while upholding their confidence and self-esteem.

10. *Get out of people's way.* Once you've done the first nine things, move aside and let your team deliver and do their best work. And don't worry, they will find you when they need your guidance.

Google's Project Aristotle validated what *Harvard Business Review* found: 20 to 35 percent of value-added collaborations came from only 3 to 5 percent of employees (Cross et al. 2021). Do you know what stifles collaboration in most teams? The leader. In most teams, the leader speaks 80 percent of the time or more!

As mentioned in Chapter 4, Google found that the best teams created a social code that included psychological safety. Teams flourish in a safe, judgment-free zone.

Another attribute of social codes of top teams was the inclusion of "equal speaking." Top teams, even ones with no apparent leader, agreed to share the floor equally between all team members.

Google found that Googlers on teams with equal speaking—

• Were less likely to leave their jobs at Google,
• Were more likely to harness the power of diverse ideas,

- Brought in more revenue from their efforts (Berkovic 2017).

In my fifteen-plus years at Google, I saw firsthand the benefits of giving my team members equal time to share their thoughts. Having helped pilot many of the best practices in collaboration, it's not surprising that Google regularly makes the list of *Fortune*'s "100 Best Companies to Work For," receiving the number-one ranking in eight of the last eleven years.

From my own experience, I know that Google does at least the following four things differently in how they value collaboration that sets the organization apart from other companies (William 2014).

Google Embraces Differences

I found that working at Google felt like working at the United Nations, in that I experienced different cultures and heard more languages spoken than I knew existed. The real strength of that diversity shows in the various talents and backgrounds of people working at Google. Each project taps into well-rounded and unique team member perspectives.

When a team approaches a singular goal from a variety of vantage points, the challenge becomes picking the best approach, as opposed to generating a handful of viable options.

Google Encourages "Casual Collisions"

Google's Mountain View, California, campus was designed to maximize people running into each other outside of meetings. In fact, all Googlers at the 1.1-million-square-foot complex are within a two-and-a-half-minute walk from each other.

When Tony Hsieh, former CEO of Zappos, invited me to speak at his Downtown Project in Las Vegas, I spent time talking with him about how he used casual collisions and serendipitous encounters around town. He estimated that he spent a thousand hours each year talking and listening with the people he met in Las Vegas to gather ideas to foster urban renewal.

Hsieh didn't want collaboration to end with his team members. He saw collaboration as a tool to benefit his entire community—all of Las Vegas. Hsieh's vision for Zappos focused on three Cs: *clothing, customer service*, and culture, but he envisioned adding the word *community* to his list.

Hsieh had such a passion for casual collisions that he shut down the enclosed skywalk from the parking garage to the Zappos headquarters to prompt team members to walk through the neighborhood and hold casual collisions with the locals (Burke 2013).

At Google, I would frequently walk to lunch where I would see someone from another department who I knew was a subject-matter expert on something my team worked on.

"Hey, I know you worked on Search. I'm working on a project now where I think your insight would be invaluable. If I send you the details, could you pop into our next meeting?" I'd ask.

Those casual collisions improved and fast-tracked some of my key projects. Casual collisions made our campus of four thousand Googlers feel like a tightknit community. In fact, some of my creative ideas around new product features were inspired by a casual collision and lunch with a coworker, like my patent for increasing comment visibility.

Google Promotes Team Member Engagement

Google took Kanter's words to heart—stating that critical business relationships "cannot be controlled by formal systems but require [a] dense web of interpersonal connections." That inspired the founders to create an environment that included play in work, suggesting that socializing isn't a barrier to productivity; it's an accelerant for collaboration.

Google's perks boost morale, but they also increase opportunities for engagement. Instead of limiting creative thinking and brainstorming to meeting rooms, Google encourages Googlers to enjoy unrelated activities—which keeps people engaged and connected.

Google Practices an Open-Door Policy

I've heard of countless companies that promote their open-door policies, but once a leader announces their intentions, they go into their offices and close the door. Mixed message much?

Leaders at Google do more than talk about an open door. They mean it. Leaders are approachable, and they create an environment that serves as a living, breathing "ask me" button. You can talk to them in the cafeteria, via email, at weekly all-hands meetings, or by knocking on their doors.

I mentioned earlier that I often block off time over lunch to encourage pop-ins. I could tell my team regularly that "I'm there for you!" but unless I made myself visible and available, I'd miss multiple impromptu problem-solving and brainstorming sessions as well as interpersonal conversations and relationship-building moments.

COLLABORATION FOR THE WIN!

When my leader asked me to take over a project on privacy at Google around 2008, privacy was in its infancy. My first thought was something like, *I don't know anything about privacy. Privacy isn't in my wheelhouse. I'm an engineer.* But I brought a growth mindset with me and jumped in.

I got quick confirmation that privacy dealt more in legal policy than engineering. My background in tech wouldn't be of much use to the team, I figured. But surprisingly, some of the most interesting projects I'd had took me far out of my area of expertise and required me to lean on others and their areas of knowledge.

Enter collaboration. When you don't know how to do a job, you have no choice but to learn from others and tap into their expertise. Each member of our cross-functional team brought unique skills sets to their work. Given that we had no areas of overlap, we found that together we could think through the challenges in unique and novel ways.

Ultimately, we developed amazing solutions and turned privacy from an art form into an engineering discipline. Eventually, the project work led to me using my engineering skills. As a result of that collaboration, I received more than thirty patents approved by the USPTO on privacy related technologies, including the client-side user model, image search privacy protections, and crowdsourcing privacy settings. I quickly moved from wary about my role to excited when I found how rewarding it was for me to work with a cross-functional team full of diverse skill sets.

Think about working at a company the size of Google. You can't possibility meet everyone. The company employs people with various skill sets to develop broad products for unique markets. We needed those different skills when we sought a way to better integrate Google Assistant to play YouTube music.

Google, Assistant, and YouTube operate as different business units within one company, which makes collaboration more challenging. During our first few iterations of YouTube music on Assistant, we found several bugs and user-experience challenges. Looking at our offering from the user perspective, the experience felt disjointed, because we were "shipping our organizational structure" instead of a clean, unified user experience.

Google had a plan of action once these gaps were identified. Googlers intuitively formed a working group to address discontinuity. In this case, we pulled team members from both the Assistant and YouTube product teams, testing experts, and user researchers for brainstorming solutions on a whiteboard and ultimately found a shared solution to vastly improve the user experience.

In my experience, large-scale projects can't be managed successfully by one person or one team. Companies like Google know how to leverage talent across their organization through collaboration. By eliminating organizational boundaries, they consistently drive tech forward.

ARE YOU READY TO COLLABORATE?

Leadership styles can feel like the *flavor of the month*. Some leadership "experts" tout the virtues of autocratic, laissez-faire, transformational, charismatic, bureaucratic, visionary, or pacesetting leadership. And many leaders practice versions of these while labeling their leadership style as Situational Leadership, a theory first introduced in the late 1960s by Paul Hersey and Ken Blanchard (Hersey and Blanchard 1969). Situational Leadership suggest that the approach you use to lead a person is based on the current mastery level of the person you are coaching. Unfortunately, leaders often instead lead based on how they *feel* in a particular moment in time.

Collaborative leadership isn't a flavor. Rather, it's a philosophy rooted in the belief that once you hire diverse and talented people, set the vision, and turn them loose, they will deliver better results than if you owned every step of the process.

Think of your tech team as a publishing house. Instead of working with researchers, writers, developmental and copy editors, proofreaders, and graphic designers, you work with data scientists, coders, programmers, software engineers, and web designers. Whether you're developing and launching a book or a new software solution, you need team members possessing deep subject-matter expertise.

Following are tips for tapping into the benefits of collaboration and preventing it from being a fad.

Create and Use a Collaboration Mantra

I once asked a friend with a black belt in karate where he focuses his energy when he prepares to smash a stack of cement blocks with his fist.

"I focus on the spot beneath the floor," he said. Then he continued, "If I focus on the top block, I'll break my wrist, which I've done a couple of times. That's because my mind tells my body that it's not possible to break so many blocks, which causes me to hesitate in releasing all my energy. But when I focus my energy on the spot beneath the floor, I can strike through everything between the top brick and the ground." His mantra? *"I can."*

It's all about mindset. Our perceived limitations, as well as our superhuman efforts, come from what we tell ourselves. If you wish to be a collaborative leader, start your day reminding yourself of a simple mantra. Following are some examples to help you get started on your own collaboration mantra:

- *My team's thoughts, talents, and contributions are exponentially greater than mine alone.*
- *I can't, but we can.*
- *My efforts are no match for my team's collective efforts.*
- *Collaboration turns a good idea into a brilliant idea.*
- *I contribute best by asking questions and getting others to feel safe enough to participate.*

Create Your Team Social Code

Many times, we lead based on what we believe the situation calls for. But that's not the same as Situational Leadership, which is based on the competence and experience of the team member you're coaching. Tech organizations often have an *adhocracy* culture (more on this in Chapter 12). Leaders in an adhocracy culture make changes quickly to respond to problems and capitalize on opportunities.

Collaborative leadership, which can be used in any culture and opportunity, starts with creating a shared social code for how the team will operate. The following questions might help your team get started:

- "How do you want to be treated in team meetings?"
- "How do you want to feel after each team meeting?"
- "How do you want to be challenged in the team?"

- "What do you see as my role (as the leader) within the team?"

Once you've primed the pump by asking them to discuss their answers, you're ready to facilitate your team in creating shared social norms. Following are eight steps to follow.

Step One. Ask team members to think about and share the best team experience they've been part of.

Step Two. Have each team member write on individual Post-it notes specific words, attitudes, beliefs, and actions that made the team work well together. Once they're done, have them post their notes on a wall.

Step Three. Ask the team to meet in front of the posted words and identify similarities and clusters. Encourage them to discuss any nuances and add any new words that might emerge.

Step Four. Ask the team to create sub-teams to distill a social norm statement for each major cluster, including any details that make a behavior readily understandable to new team members.

Step Five. Ask each sub-team to read their statements aloud. Ask other sub-teams for input and validation.

Step Six. Debrief the team by asking, "If we practice these social norms, will this create the kind of team that generates top ideas, values each member, and makes this the best environment to work?" Tweak your social norm statements as needed until the team agrees that these are the right norms to follow.

Step Seven. Ask the team how they will hold one another accountable to adhering to the team norms. This isn't asking, "How will we punish those who don't follow the rules?" Instead, it's asking them to develop prompts and cues to use with one another should someone start to stray from the social norms. It's also asking them how to recognize those who reach the standards.

Step Eight. Post and circulate your team norms to each team member. Start each meeting with a reading of the shared team norms. Remind the team that these norms were created as a team to benefit the team.

Keep some of these statements handy as affirmations if your team struggles to develop team norms:

- *We should strive to give each team member equal time to share their thoughts, ask questions, and voice concerns.*

- *We will respect one another as if they were valued friends and colleagues.*

- *We will remain open-minded to ideas that don't conform with our own thinking.*

- *We will avoid playing office politics.*

- *We will have a meeting agenda available prior to each meeting, or we will share the agenda at the beginning of each meeting, so everyone understands the purpose and what's to be accomplished*

- *We will always make time to celebrate milestones and accomplishments.*

- *We will start meetings on time and end on time, unless the team chooses to stay longer.*

- *We will offer two suggestions for every complaint about how to solve problems or move forward.*

Ask Your Team to Hold You Accountable

Ask them to hold you accountable to leading in a collaborative way. As humans, we're more likely to hold ourselves accountable when we receive positive reinforcement and punishment. But a caution: you must already have built psychological safety in order for team members to hold you accountable. If they fear that you'll get defensive or retaliate against them, they certainly won't feel comfortable nudging you towards accountability.

A few years back, I entered a Tough Mudder competition in Lake Tahoe with some colleagues. We'd all competed in marathons, triathlons, and bike races—which are individualistic endeavors where you compete against everyone else on the field.

A Tough Mudder is different. Of course, you must carry your own weight by getting into shape for the event, but you only succeed if every member completes the race.

Enter the part of the event where we faced an enormously tall wall that must be scaled. Only Spider-Man could stick to the wall and scale it, but mere mortals aren't equipped with webs. Still, most teams complete the obstacle. The secret is collaboration. Working together, we got one team member over the top of the wall. That person than reached down and pulled up the next person. Eventually, every team member was holding onto another to get the last person over.

Tough Mudder, just like every project I've worked on, isn't about what one person can achieve; rather, it's about what the collective can accomplish.

You can ask your team to tell you when you do something that helps move the group forward, brings out shared participation, or any other behavior that maximizes collaboration.

Likewise, you can ask your team to give you feedback when you miss the mark. Their critique of your collaboration attempts will help you focus on the shared norms and your role in bringing out their best.

Again, this requires a high level of trust in your leadership. I've seen strong leaders who have built a collaborative environment receive extremely insightful, useful feedback from their team members. I've also seen trust destroyed when a leader believes they're ready to receive feedback, when what they were really hoping for was praise. Responding poorly to feedback from any team member will erase any trust you may have built.

Manager Ron loved to talk. People around him knew that even a simple question such as, "When do you need this by?" would prompt Ron to offer multiple tangents about the customer, competitive pressures, his bosses' expectations, how he would approach the work, and more.

Ron's organization hired an executive coach to help him rein in his longwinded, irrelevant monologues. Ron seemed eager for the help, and he asked his team to hold him accountable.

The coach worked with Ron on asking questions instead of sharing his random thoughts, as well as on letting his team share their ideas with no input from him. After attending several of Ron's team meetings, the coach saw that Ron had made no improvement. And the team was getting increasingly frustrated.

The coach offered a radical solution: negative reinforcement to stop his rambling.

"You've probably seen a bell like this one," the consultant told the team at the next meeting. "It's the kind they use in hotels to call for a bellhop. We're going to ring this bell to signal that a team member is grandstanding and holding the floor for too long. When someone goes on longer than they should, or if they start injecting irrelevant information, I'd like every member of the team to feel empowered to ring the bell. That's a signal to the person speaking to move on."

A few minutes into the meeting, Ron started talking. And talking. And talking.

Ding. The consultant reached to the center of the table and hit the bell.

Ron responded, "I hear the bell, but this is important." Ron continued talking.

Ding, ding, ding. The consultant hit the bell three more times.

"I'm almost done," Ron protested.

When he failed to finish, the consultant, along with three of Ron's team members, reached to ring the bell at the same time.

Ding. Ding-ding-ding-ding. They rang the bell one after another.

Ron said he wanted help, but the roots of his habits were deep. Fortunately, he laughed when he recognized that he seemed pathologically unable to stop himself!

The bell became a fixture in team meetings for nearly a year. Eventually, when a team member even looked at the bell, Ron stopped talking. The ringing of the bell punished Ron for rambling, and its presence in the meeting represented something Ron worked hard to avoid hearing! The bell allowed him to check his behavior and alter his actions.

Conditioning is a powerful tool, but it doesn't develop immediately. It takes time to build new habits. Ron did learn. Not quickly, but he did learn.

We've all heard It takes a village. When you're willing to ask your team to hold you accountable to being a collaborative leader, change happens more quickly (for many leaders, anyway!).

Know Your Team Member's Strengths

The best solutions don't come from individuals but by the collaborative efforts of people investing their unique talents to a common goal.

Former Yahoo! president and CEO Marissa Mayer has been attributed as saying, "When you need to innovate, you need collaboration."

Many people working in tech are highly creative. But even creative people need to be surrounded by those with other talents or creative skills. When you know the strengths of each team member, you can leverage their abilities for the collective good on a project.

Working collaboratively is a prerequisite before you can create cross-functional teams, the subject of the following chapter. To lead a cross-functional effort, a leader must already be collaborating as an automatic process.

CHAPTER 9
CREATE CROSS-FUNCTIONAL TEAMS

DON'T TRY TO CLIMB A MOUNTAIN ALONE

When my colleagues and I got excited about expanding Google Street View to include mountaintop views, we thought we knew enough to be successful. But in truth, we had a lot to learn.

Fortunately, we chose an "easy" mountain for our first climb: Mount Fuji. I'll share more about this trek later, but we quickly learned that each team member had two main responsibilities: take care of yourself, and take care of at least one shared team responsibility.

Having just one out-of-shape, unprepared, or injured climber doesn't risk just that person's life; they threaten the lives of others. As challenging as it is to trek up and down steep climbs safely, carrying someone else would strain even a strong team of climbers. And we weren't a strong team of climbers! Dedicated and excited, yes, but none of us had years of climbing experience. Each member had to train and condition on their own to prepare for the trek.

But none of us could have managed the Google Street View project solo. We had food, clothing, tents, cameras, and heavy equipment to haul and operate once we reached the top. Each of the five of us could haul around twenty extra pounds, but no one could have carried the hundred pounds needed to complete the work.

Every member of our team had a different role. While one carried the photography equipment, another navigated our trek with the map and compass. One carried our food supplies, as another hauled our tents. And a couple served as scouts—going in front of the group to make sure the path ahead was passable, then hustling back to give us the all-clear.

Before we started the climb, we didn't think through any of those roles. We embraced the challenge with a "we'll figure it out" mindset. But boy did we learn as we took to the climb! By using trial and error to figure out who would do what and for how long, we finally set up a rotation so no one person got over-burdened with the heaviest pack for too long. Along the way, we also learned our limitations and capabilities.

We came together with a shared objective: climb Mount Fuji to photograph the view and share it with the world. Everything else we learned as we went. Our collaboration required that we check our egos at the door, or in our case, back at the taxi that dropped us off at the base of the mountain. We listened to one another, cared for one another, helped when someone got behind, took turns leading, and shared the burdens we carried.

Our collaboration started with a shared vision—clarifying roles and responsibilities, and sharing credit for victories—but we grew to work as a cross-functional team as each member took on unique roles. As far as Mount Fuji, we knew that afterwards we would celebrate with high-fives while hoisting cold beer—or consoling one another while hoisting cold beer. Whatever the outcome, we'd do it together—and with cold beer. (While cold beer isn't always part of project debriefs, my Google-Street-View-turned-mountain-climbing team made it part of each challenge.)

WHAT ARE CROSS-FUNCTIONAL TEAMS?

Collaborative teams require shared goals, clear roles, shared responsibilities, established social norms, continual 360-degree communication between team members, and a full understanding of the parameters and scope of the project. The leader is nearly invisible, but when necessary, the leader knows when to step in if a conflict arises or the team hits a wall.

Cross-functional teams are comprised of members from various disciplines, departments, or divisions within the organization. Even if you were to play the "I'm the boss" card on the team instead of the leader role, some members would say (and more would think), "Yeah, but you're not *my* boss." Worse yet, if a cross-functional team member feels that the initiative spearheaded by the team poses a threat to their silo or department, they may sabotage.

A Midwestern B2B company had used their twenty-plus-year-old home-grown system to grow their business to nearly $1 billion in annual revenue. Given the complexity and number of custom modifications and the company's projected growth, senior leadership decided to invest in an enterprise resource planning (ERP) system. Developing and implementing the new system required a cross-functional team with members from finance, HR, sales, customer service, manufacturing, shipping, warehouse management, and of course, the tech group.

Problems started during the first cross-functional team meeting. The vice president of finance insisted that the new ERP provide her team with richer information and ease of use, even when doing so would require extensive configuring and customization. The list of demands from the warehouse and shipping departments were equally long. Finally, the sales and customer service team representatives believed that any ERP replacement tool be tailored to their needs, since they were the only "profit center" that mattered.

I'd like to say the project had a happy ending. It didn't. Six years and more than $8 million over budget later, the company abandoned the implementation and continued to rely on an obsolete system that they intended to retire years before.

Never underestimate the importance of including the right stakeholders and getting their buy-in at the onset of any cross-functional team. Otherwise, you run the risk of team members running to Meville, as author Carbonara wrote about, instead of a place I like to think of as Goalville, the destination where all team members share a common motivation.

Enter the world of leading a cross-functional teams, where success relies on your ability to tap into people outside your direct reporting relationship. While most team members in tech companies agree that collaboration yields better results, some still fight it, especially when they don't understand their role or feel empowered.

Successfully leading a cross-functional team requires collaboration. Following are some derailers to effectively leading cross-functional teams.

Lack of Clarity

Since your cross-functional team isn't a standing team comprised of your direct reports, it's imperative that you provide clear expectations about each member's role and responsibility. Hold one-on-one conversations with each team member about your expectations and their role *before* the first team meeting. Then at the first team meeting, ask each member to introduce themselves by stating their role and responsibilities to the larger group.

At the first meeting, it's also time to get clarity about the team's goals. No one enjoys entering a team with conflicting goals, but conflicting goals are less frustrating than joining a team with no clear goals.

Leadership author and consultant Marlene Chism is an expert on creating drama-free leaders and workplaces. She states, "The one with clarity navigates the ship" (Chism 2018).

Think about that ship metaphor for a moment. People working in the engine room generate power, but they can't see the horizon. Generalists in maintenance rarely come on deck. Cooks are more proficient with knives than compasses, electronic calculators, computers, and satellite navigation systems. Who has the clarity to navigate your project?

You. Or at least you better have more clarity than anyone else before starting. As discussed earlier, you can't communicate the direction if you don't know it. Clarity minimizes infighting and aligns members to one clear objective. As the leader, you also must navigate your stakeholders, various agendas, timelines, budgets, information overload and/or deficits, etc., all while ensuring that you keep your eyes on the goal: generate revenue, grow customers, fix a bug, or a launch a new product.

Lack of Awareness about Related Efforts

More than once, I've lead a cross-functional team around a new project and heard a team member say, "Did you know that ____ team is working on something similar?" In Chapter 5, I wrote about where I find *my* dots to connect. I continually meet with other area leaders, read project updates, and attend meetings so I have a better picture of the environment in which my team will operate. By making yourself aware of what's going on across your organization, you can prevent duplicating efforts while leveraging the knowledge the other team may have uncovered.

Once you're assigned to lead a project, you can get tunnel vision when you turn your mental spotlight to your project while filtering out everything else. Remember, I called this Teamville, the myopic belief that everything of importance is taking place in your own team. By adopting a Goalville mindset, you're always scanning for other "dots" that may impact your work.

Lack of Sponsorship (or Low Sponsorship Visibility)

In companies with a hierarchy culture (more in Chapter 12), employees expect communication to come from the top down. "If they expect me to do something," employees working in those cultures reason, "they'll tell me." Other company cultures expect and promote shared leadership.

Whether your team members expect face time with the corporate sponsor of your project or not, if they hear a senior leader lay out the benefits of your project team's work, they'll get excited and know the work they do matters.

Lack of a Shared Language

Companies develop their own language, slang, and jargon. Outsiders need a lexicon to break the jargon code. *API. DSN. Deep web. Sandboxing. MVP. A/B Testing. SaaS. Tech stack. Angry garden salad. Crapplet. Time porn.* If you work in tech, you get it. Those words represent a shortcut to communicating a bundle of information to those working in tech. But if you're in the finance, HR, or legal department on the same cross-functional team, most of that jargon means nothing.

Collaboration with a cross-functional team requires that each member becomes an insider. Using jargon and slang keeps them outside.

A great example of a cross-functional team is the partnerships that occur naturally between members of the C-suite in organizations. Executives speak the same language, possess deep understanding of the goals, and work together to get the right things done for their companies, communities, customers, and team members.

Lack of Dedicated Project Time

Many cross-functional teams rely on virtual teams (v-teams) from other areas in the company. As the team leader, you don't own that team member's time. Nothing creates more frustration for other leaders than when they're asked to offer up a team member for a project that lacks concrete time parameters and requirements spelled out in advance. And nothing creates team member resentment like being stuck between completing work on your team and work from their "day job."

Before the project begins, talk with the team member's

immediate supervisor about how much time the project will require and for how long.

Politics

"Silos," "the powers that be," and "turf wars" are concepts well-known in politically charged work cultures. It's possible you might end up with someone on your cross-functional team who was assigned to your project to maintain the *status quo* instead of to use their technical insights or skills.

Every office has some level of politics, where attitudes and behaviors serve to help a person or work area get or maintain power. Imagine being a software engineer on a team designed to promote the ease of cloud engineering. You might feel a bit threatened that the team's gain would come at your loss. Can you relate?

In Chapter 5, I shared that context is decisive. Leaders can shift team members away from politics to pragmatic optimism when they reinforce *why* the v-team exists and *how* the work of the team benefits the company, users, and individuals on the team. More on context shortly. But when you find yourself with a team member who seems more passionate about the politics of a project than the project itself, ask yourself, *What singular, compelling purpose offers enough meaning to each team member for them to put aside any potential political self-interest?* Once you can answer that question, your role is to unify your v-team around that purpose.

Most organizations use some version of a horizontal structure, meaning each person reports to a leader who reports to a leader, and so on. That horizontal reporting structure continues until it reaches the CEO of the company.

Tech companies, on the other hand, are often "flatter," meaning they don't have as many layers between the knowledge worker and the top of the organization. For example, Google doesn't put several layers of middle-management between the front line and the top. This fosters the sharing of ideas in real-time instead of using a long, formal chain-of-command to get answers. When tech companies get larger, their structures often consist of a hybrid between flat horizontal organizations and matrixed ones.

The v-team concept is an example of a vertical matrixed structure. With a matrixed team, decision-making takes place within the team outside of a formal, direct reporting relationship. Instead of relying on directives, the leader of a matrixed team empowers, aligns, and inspires team members to get the best output.

Even though matrixed teams have a leader, the leader acts less like a "boss" and more like a person championing collaboration and cooperation between equals.

Lack of Context, Vision, and Focus

Senior leaders spend enough time as a group to understand the *context* in which the company operates. They know the ins and outs of company and individual strengths, market share, profits and losses, customers, emerging markets, competition, as well as external market forces like regulations, supply-chain issues, etc.

Corporate success relies on them, knowing the context in which the business operates and sharing the same vision for the future.

Cross-functional team members haven't spent months and years working side-by-side. You need some glue to hold them together, and that glue is context. Each member must know what necessitated the project, if the project is in response to a problem or an opportunity, and if you're replacing or enhancing existing tech or are breaking new ground. And they need to know what market forces fuel the project.

In addition to providing sweeping context for your team, it's also crucial to share customized context to each team member. I've recruited multiple cross-functional team members by using context and vision that speak their "love language." I've recruited data scientists to a cross-functional team, while letting them know how much I needed their insight to help me understand the complex behaviors in a software product. I've done the same when asking user researchers to help me learn how users interact with our products and what users really want.

Finding the right selling point for team members isn't manipulation. Instead, it's offering them an opportunity to do something they love and increase their reputation while offering additional value to the organization.

Once you've created a clear context, it's time to communicate a compelling *vision*. A vision serves as an inspirational and often emotional picture of what the future holds.

Spotify and the Spotify product development team knows what it means to use a vision to get the right things done.

Product development happens in small, structured, cross-functional teams called *squads*. Each squad has a leader with a straightforward role: provide communication and context about the problem or opportunity that must be resolved. Put simply, *the leader establishes the vision* for the squad. But the real magic takes place within the squad when people collaborate to find the best solution. Team members enjoy endless autonomy to work toward their long-term mission, as directed by the vision. The team decides "what to build, how to build it, and how to work together while building it" (Fernandes 2021).

What vision can unite all members of your team? What does a brighter future look like, and how can you tap into your team to make that vision a reality? Take a lesson from the old marketing adage; remember that you're *selling the sizzle, not the steak.*

Context and vision help teams form. But they won't produce unless you provide focus.

If you pay someone to count the number of black cars that cross a particular intersection over the course of an hour, they could probably give you a rather precise accounting of black cars. But if you asked them at the end of the hour to tell you the number of red cars, they'd have no idea. Their focus on black cars made them oblivious to other cars that crossed the intersection.

Google cofounder Larry Page has been attributed with saying, "If you're changing the world, you're working on important things. You're excited to get up in the morning."

Focus on "changing the world" and accomplishing "important things" to foster intrinsic motivation within your v-team.

When you're leading in a cross-functional environment, the way you get things done is by helping team members stay focused on the right things. Work is full of distractions. In a cohesive v-team environment, people want to work on your project because it meets their needs, especially when their needs include desiring to be part of something transformational. The best leaders fulfill team members' unspoken desires for socialization, accomplishment, belonging, and achievement while focusing on intrinsic rewards.

Celebrating Results Only

Do you reward people for their efforts or for their results?

Your v-team environment must reinforce team member efforts. Effort is perpetual and ongoing, and you can see people exerting effort toward the right results. Catch people applying effort, and recognize them in the moment. Each time you recognize one team member, other team members learn quickly what you value and appreciate, causing them to offer similar effort.

Rewarding results instead of efforts can cause problems. First, results take place over time. When you were a child, did your parents wait until you graduated from high school or college before they celebrated your achievements? Or did they fill the front of your refrigerator with the pictures you drew and your A-papers?

Our bodies release dopamine as we get close to reaching a goal. Dopamine, one the "happy chemicals," gives us the added boost to keeping moving forward with increased energy as goal-completion nears (Livingston 2022).

Since approaching goal-completion releases this internally-produced boost of dopamine-fueled energy, consider creating smaller, more quickly-obtained goals so results are in sight as the project continues.

Second, celebrating results without celebrating effort can make team members shy away from tasks that won't create an immediate, positive result. That stifles experimentation and innovation as well as efforts that must be completed as part of day-to-day work.

DEVELOPING YOUR CROSS-FUNCTIONAL LEADERSHIP SKILLS

While leading cross-functional teams can be challenging, it's also rewarding. Following are some best practices for leading a cross-functional team.

Create and Use a Cross-Functional Team Mantra

As I shared earlier, cross-functional teams require collaboration. Most team members aren't your own, and joining your team means they're doing double-duty with an immediate supervisor, two teams, and you as a team lead. The right mantra can help you remember that these team members go above and beyond what others are asked to do.

Following are some examples to help you get started on your own collaboration mantra:

- *I lead the team, but the team drives the results.*

- *I can count on my team members' curiosity and ability to ask great questions.*
- *My team members offer limitless depth in their areas of expertise.*
- *Have I included all the necessary areas to ensure project success?*
- *We're one team in vision, efforts, and results.*

Maximize Your Kick-Off Meeting

The saying, "You only have one chance to make a first impression," holds true of your initial meetings. Regardless of what team members know, don't know, or think they know, the kick-off meeting sets the emotional tone for the team. If the first meeting leaves unanswered questions, skims over details, promises the world, or seems disorganized, team members may view their work as just another to-do instead of critical to the project's success.

Personally, I'm a strong believer in meeting face-to-face. Whenever possible, I pull team members together for dinner and drinks to build relationships before I ever ask them to start the hard work of getting things done. Seeing people in an informal, relaxed, and personal setting allows them to get to know one another as people and not just collection of corporate assets.

I suggest that your first meeting accomplish as many of the following as possible:

Answer the why, what, when, where, and how of the project. You may have developed, practiced, and refined your elevator speech a dozen times and shared it one-on-one with each team member prior to the kick-off, but this is your opportunity to connect every dot and answer any questions you didn't address.

Take the time to explain why this project requires a cross-functional effort. Don't assume that team members will intuitively understand why this team needs broader representation than just a singular team approach.

Invite the management/executive sponsor to speak at the kick-off. Most projects have a dedicated management or executive sponsor—a member of leadership responsible to get a project delivered on time, within budget, and meeting all requirements. Don't confuse the title of *project sponsor* with someone who knows the ins and outs of the project. Often, the sponsor has responsibility for many projects, and their sponsorship of the team is to remove barriers and report progress to senior leadership.

If possible, have the sponsor speak at your kick-off. If your sponsor doesn't know the project details, discuss some talking points with them before the meeting, asking them to highlight specific topics. Sponsors can speak to the big picture and vision of how a project benefits the enterprise, customers, shareholders, and other stakeholders.

Invest time in getting-to-know-you activities. If your cross-functional team hasn't worked together before, use an icebreaker to allow people to learn more about each other. Ask members to introduce themselves, mentioning where they work for their "day jobs," a bit about their areas of expertise, and anything else that could help the team form. Then, as I mentioned earlier, have each team member explain their roles and responsibility for the team.

Ask for team members' expectations up front. Some people asked to be part of your team; others were "voluntold." Whatever got them to the kick-off meeting, they all have an expectation about what they'll give and receive during your work together. Document what they say. Take special note of any expectations that your team may *not* be designed to meet. Circle back with people when necessary to explain why the team might not meet a certain expectation.

Create a team name. Don't skip this step. Collaborating on something as simple as brainstorming and choosing a team name sets the stage for future collaboration when the stakes are higher. Team unity thrives with owning a unique identity that sets it apart from all other corporate and team efforts (more on this later).

Create your team social code (See Chapter 8).

Clarify Your Expectations

Most members of your cross-functional project team have day jobs and other bosses. Keep that in mind when scheduling meetings, timeframes, due dates, etc.

Still, some expectations need to be spelled out early, including:

- What the team will accomplish
- How the team will interact with one another
- How all team members will contribute in their areas of expertise
- When you anticipate busy times on the project
- What you're responsible for, and what they're responsible for
- How you'll intervene when conflict arises.

It's better to share these expectations early than when you're in a crunch or stuck.

Ask Your Team Members Two Questions

In August of 2022, Google's CEO Sundar Pichai launched a program referred to as a Simplicity Sprint, a three-question all-Googler survey designed to boost productivity. The three questions were as follows:

1. What would help you work with greater clarity and efficiency to serve our users and customers?
2. Where should we remove speed bumps to get better results faster?
3. How do we eliminate waste and stay entrepreneurial and focused as we grow (Rella 2022)?

The first two questions are ones that every team leader should use regularly. Project clarity, like connecting the dots (See Chapter 5), comes from two channels: senior leaders and immediate supervisors. But when it comes to your project, no senior leader or project sponsor knows more than you. Ask your team members to tell you what they need in order to do their work effectively. Because while you know the work better than the project sponsor, your team members know the work better than you!

Then ask what obstacles prevent them from doing their best work. Their responses might uncover problems you never knew existed, allowing you to advocate for your team's needs.

Develop Your Team Identity

Unlike a functional, intact, or standing team, a cross-functional team is designed to remain permanent. The team joins talent around a specific shared interest. Once they've accomplished their goals, they return to their regular roles. But that doesn't mean cross-functional teams shouldn't have their own identity.

A cross-functional team, representing every department in a company with more than a hundred geographically remote sites, named themselves Double Helix. Since this company served the biotech industry, Double Helix referred to the structure formed by double-stranded molecules such as DNA.

One team member further explained, "The work of our team represents the DNA of the company. No matter what each team member does or what department they represent, we all share the same DNA—the core that matters most."

By creating a team identity connected to the values and "core" of the organization, Double Helix became a source of pride not just for the team members but for every person in the organization.

If possible, ask for a budget to promote team unity. Depending on the preferences of your team members, they might enjoy matching shirts with your team's logo/name along with the corporate logo. Some leaders schedule off-site retreats where spouses and significant others are invited, combining business with pleasure. Some cross-functional teams are given a dedicated workspace where the team can collaborate side-by-side for the duration of the project.

Leaders often think that the best way to value team members is with money. Research disagrees.

According to *Harvard Business Review,* a better thank-you than money is to offer experiences (Locklear et al. 2020).

Through the years, I've been given tons of tchotchkes, knickknacks, and gift cards for things like coffee, department stores, etc. They're a nice gesture of thanks. But one manager gifted me a zero-gravity adventure, something I'd never buy for myself but will never forget. The experience blew my mind! Each time I remember that experience, I remember that manager and the project I worked on that merited his gift.

Provide Regular Positive Reinforcement and Recognition

Since cross-functional team members are volunteers or "voluntolds" with other responsibilities, they'll miss out on getting any recognition they might receive were they in their functional teams full-time. Make it worth their while to work on your project.

Reinforce your team member with both tangible and social reinforcement.

Tangible reinforcements. If your budget allows, spend money caring for your cross-functional team members. Give them company and team branding clothes, travel mugs, or anything else of monetary value.

Social reinforcements. Social reinforcement is any social gesture that you can offer a team member

immediately. A smile, praise, or thumbs up can be a
social reinforcement. Use these liberally.

Blended reinforcements. Better than tangible and
social reinforcement is when you combine the two.
When you offer your team member something of any
monetary value while making a social event out of it,
you make your reinforcement even more memorable.

Maybe you can't pay them extra or offer them some sort of
Scooby Snacks for their efforts, but you can still value their
contributions.

A leader named Eric took one of his managers, Sue, to dinner
at a place in the Louisiana bayou where he ordered fried alligator. When the appetizer arrived, Eric offered some to Sue who
declined, saying, "Dinosaurs aren't on my diet." After Eric kept
saying how delicious it tasted, Sue finally tried a small piece.
And she loved it.

As they were leaving, Eric purchased a ceramic alligator sold
near the register. When they returned to the office, Eric gathered
up his team, told the story about trying fried alligator, and made
a presentation to Sue.

"Sue, you didn't want to try it, but once you did, you loved it.
Sometimes we find amazing surprises by pushing ourselves
outside of our comfort zones. So Sue, I present you with this
ceramic alligator with a challenge to make it a rotating award.
Whenever you see a team member working outside of their
comfort zone to get something done, please call us together to
present them with the alligator award!"

His one-time, $9 purchase rotated throughout the office and
even traveled to other sites within the company. Just like the
Stanley Cup in the National Hockey League, where the winning
team keeps the trophy until it passes to the winner of the next
playoff season, Eric used that alligator trophy to reward any team

member who pushed themself to accomplish a surprising, happy ending. That trophy offered bragging rights—something the team rotated until the alligator got lost in a move to a new office.

The late, great Maya Angelou famously said, "People will forget what you said, people will forget you did, but people will never forget how you made them feel."

Whenever you genuinely praise or thank someone for their efforts, you make them feel noticed, appreciated, and valued. Doing so costs you nothing, and your words might be the nicest, most-memorable event in that person's day.

If you're a small company with a limited budget, maybe you can only afford to bring in donuts or bagels to share with the team after hitting a milestone. Or maybe you can have a weekly lunch brought in to eat and bond together.

Some leaders create awards for team members for their unique contributions. A college president had a trophy made with ruby red slippers on top. Whenever she saw a team in the university do something above and beyond for a student or internal customer, she awarded them the ruby red slipper trophy at an all-staff meeting.

Create a Visual of Your Project Status

Yes, every project management tool comes with graphics that visually plot progress. You can print this and hand it out at a meeting, or you can just ask people to keep current on the project status through the intranet. But nothing beats a hand-drawn graphic showing your progress. In our highly technical word, it gets attention in the way a computer screen or printed handout doesn't. I've heard parents lament when their kids stopped making them cards for special days or imperfectly wrapping their inexpensive yet priceless presents—instead buying cards and presents. There's something special about a simple graphic drawn on a flip chart to show off at the beginning of a meeting.

You might be living in "project world" all day, every day. Cross-functional team members aren't. Give people: status updates in a fun way, reinforcement that they've made progress, and reasons to feel great about their contributions.

Set the Pace

Leaders set the pace on a team. Move slowly and cautiously, and your team will do likewise. Lead with passion and urgency, and your team will follow suit.

When you're facing a sprint, make the work as fun, reinforcing, and interactive as possible. Just like you get energy from them, they'll get energy from you. Even when you've finished the sprint and face a slower period, keep your enthusiasm and check-ins frequent.

We easily fall prey to the tyranny of the urgent. Between bosses, fellow team members, clients, and project work, the urgent can quickly take your cross-functional team members' eyes off the important work of the team. Checking-in, letting people know when to expect the next all-hands-on-deck, and staying connected will make it easier for your team members to reengage when they need to jump back into action.

Collaboration doesn't come naturally to every leader. Some must study collaboration techniques like a playbook, practicing each element slowly and deliberately to become fluent. But it's worth the effort.

There's one more piece of leading a cross-functional team to the highest level of performance. That's when a leader knows how to foster diversity, equity, and inclusion.

CHAPTER 10
FOSTER DIVERSITY, EQUITY, & INCLUSION (DEI)

"WHY DO I STRUGGLE TO HIRE FEMALE JOB CANDIDATES?"

Tech lead Juan's easygoing personality created loyal team members. Quick to joke, roll up his sleeves besides his colleagues, offer guidance, and even start an impromptu game of soccer with his teammates, Juan brought out the best in the people around him.

When he took a promotion to manager, he already had many of the skills necessary to be successful, but he didn't have much experience with hiring. Juan saw value in every job candidate he met, yet the ones he most wanted to hire turned down his offers, especially when trying to bring in diverse candidates.

"Can you give me a crash course on hiring for diversity?" Juan asked his HR partner, Jason. "I can't get females to accept a job offer from me to save my life."

After reviewing Juan's interviewing process—the questions, team interviews, and pre-hire assessments—Jason told Juan that everything looked solid.

"Would you like me to sit in on your next interview to observe your interviews firsthand?" Jason offered.

Jason sat in on Juan's next interview, taking notes throughout the process. Afterwards, he debriefed with Juan.

"Was this interview typical of the ones you have?" Jason asked.

"Yeah," Juan nodded in agreement.

Jason began. "First, overall, I think your comments and examples would work very well with male job candidates. However, I wrote down some words and phrases you used that are considered gender-coded language," Jason continued before pointing out this might not be as effective with female job candidates.

Here are a few potential inferences Jason shared with Juan, which could be interpreted based on things Juan asked or said in the interviews:

- *Does this place sound violent?* Juan made a reference to *The Art of War*, a book by Sun Tzu on military strategy. Such a statement could suggest that the work environment seems hostile, even dangerous.
- *Does this job require extra testosterone?* Juan's used words like "driven," "fearless," and "decisive." Those traits tend to appeal more to those with traditionally masculine traits, people favoring conquest and competition over the more traditionally female traits of cooperation and collaboration. The language used in an interview can send a subtle, unwelcoming message to female job applicants (Robinson 2021).
- *Wouldn't you rather hire Muhammad Ali for this job?* Juan included phrases like "crossing the goal line," "hitting a homerun" or "grand slam," "slam-dunk," "down for the count," "full-court press," and "bench strength." While reflecting Juan's passion for sports,

his words could easily lead someone to believe that a passion for sports was as important as being a solid contributor. And according to various researchers, many women find sports metaphors off-putting (Greeman 2021).

Diverse candidates include racial and ethnic minorities, women, people with disabilities, LGBTQ+ people, and members of other non-traditional groups.

Here are some stats on diversity and equity every leader should know:

• Men are twice as likely as women to be hired regardless of the gender of the hiring manager (Reiners 2021).

• White senior leaders hold 62.8 percent of senior leadership positions in the US (Zippia 2020).

• Minorities make up 36.3 percent of the US population (Jensen 2021) and hold about 22 percent of the jobs.

• Women make up 54.3 percent of the US workforce but hold only 28.8 percent of senior leadership positions (Zippia 2020).

• Women earn 82 percent of what men earn.

• People with disabilities are less likely to be employed than those without disabilities.

• The estimated global LGBTQ+ population is 9 percent. Yet only twenty-five of 5,670 (0.4 percent) board seats at Fortune 500 companies are occupied by openly LGBTQ+ people (Probasco 2022).

Looking at the CEO position in Fortune 500 companies, the numbers take on an even more telling depiction of an overall lack of diversity:

• Less than 13 percent of Fortune 500 CEOs are of racial or ethnic minorities (Black, Asian American, and Latin/Hispanic):
   • 4 CEOs are Black (0.8 percent) (Csiszar 2022).
   • 20 CEOs are Latin/Hispanic (4 percent) (Kurt 2022).
   • 40 CEOs are Asian (8 percent).

• Only 15 percent of Fortune 500 CEOs (8 percent) are women (Buchholz 2022).

• Only 4 (0.8 percent) of Fortune 500 CEOs are openly LGBTQ+.

Why should diversity, equity, and inclusion (DEI) matter to companies? Because the customers these companies serve are as diverse as the general population. When you look at companies on the top of the Fortune 500 list currently—Walmart, Amazon, Apple, CVS, and UnitedHealth Group—you would imagine they would benefit from having leadership teams that look more like the customers they serve.

Juan implemented Jason's feedback and developed examples, metaphors, and words that were outside of war, traditional masculinity, and sports. It paid off. The next female job candidate Juan interviewed accepted his offer.

THE BUSINESS CASE FOR DIVERSITY, EQUITY, AND INCLUSION (DEI)

Ageism. Sexism. Racism. Elitism. Nationalism. Nativism. Isolationism. These "isms" aren't new or unique to the US business culture. We as leaders must work intentionally to neutralize these "isms" so they don't destroy our companies and teams.

At Instagram, I led an area that was formed to expand equity by focusing on three areas:

- Helping every Instagram team member prioritize building equitable products and tools.
- Promoting fairness on the platform through our technology and automated systems.
- Using Instagram to create more opportunities for empowerment (Brooks et al. 2021).

Instagram isn't the only company that acts as champion for DEI for both team members and users. In 2020, Google and Alphabet CEO Sundar Pichai offered company-wide commitment to racial equality and reporting of their progress regularly. Similarly, Facebook has created multiple initiatives to build an equal workforce. In 2020, Apple reported that 50 percent of new hires came from typically underrepresented groups.

DEI are business practices that promote the representation and participation of individuals from minority groups. These groups include people of various ages, races, ethnicities, abilities, genders, religions, cultures, and sexual orientations.

Leaders must be intentional about applying DEI practices, because some industries tend to promote homogenous hiring. Here's a look at the current demographic working in the tech sector:

• 75 percent of tech jobs are held by men.

• 62 percent of tech workers are White.

• 83 percent of tech executives are White.

• Women in tech are offered salaries that are 3 percent lower than their male counterparts doing the same job.

• Black tech workers average 7 percent lower salaries that their White counterparts doing the same job.

• Compared with industries in general, the tech industry employs:
    • More White workers;
    • A smaller proportion of Black Americans (7.4 percent versus 14.4 percent), Latin Americans (8 percent versus 13.9 percent), and women (36 percent versus 48 percent).

Two final thoughts on the nature of the tech workforce. First, tech workers are predominately White and male; however, the *end users* of tech come from every demographic group. Second, females make up 25 percent of the tech workforce. At Google, females make up 33 percent (Ariella 2022). Google didn't reach 33 percent of female hires passively or accidentally. They created and followed a DEI plan to increase recruitment of diverse candidates.

How much better do you think your team would perform if every team member believed they—

- Belonged and *fit in* with other members of your team and the organization?
- Had the same opportunities to contribute, learn, grown, and work on high-visibility, high-impact projects?
- Were treated equally?
- Had a voice and felt safe using it?
- Could influence decision-making?

Let me make the question less hypothetical by sharing a thin slice of data for you to consider. Gen Y (aka, Millennials, meaning those born between 1981 and 1996) have become the largest cohort of employees in the US workforce. By 2025, Gen Y will make up 75 percent of all US employees. A Deloitte survey found that 83 percent of millennials reported that they would be more actively engaged at work if their company actively strove to create a diverse and inclusive culture (Jacimovic 2022). According to Gallup, actively engaged employees increase profitability of companies by 23 percent (Oak Digital Workplace). What could your team accomplish if they brought full engagement and discretionary effort to work each day?

Leaders must elevate DEI in the workplace. DEI is not "virtue signaling. It's vital to the success of your company and team.

Diversity means having a varied composition of people with different identities, backgrounds, thoughts, likes, dislikes, and experiences, to name a few. Traits such as race, gender identity, sexual orientation, religion, nationality, body shape or size, and age are also components of diversity. Beyond observable traits, top teams include a diversity in thinking. When a team has too many members who think A, you miss out on the perspective of those who think Z.

Equity is simply treating people fairly and giving them equal treatment, pay, training, access, opportunities, and career advancement.

Inclusion involves actively helping team members feel safe, seen, heard, and accepted at work. Inclusive work environments allow team members to share opinions and ideas without fear of being put down. Inclusive work environments foster respect for various styles of communication, leadership, and ways of getting things done (St. Bonaventure University 2022).

DEI Comes with a Huge ROI

DEI-savvy companies receive multiple returns-on-investment for their efforts: growing new markets, increasing revenues, and exceeding financial targets.

- *Harvard Business Review* found that companies with strong DEI practices are better positioned to grow in new markets.
- McKinsey & Company found that companies with diverse management teams see an increase in profits compared to their competitors.

- Companies employing an equitable split of male and female employees generate as much as 41 percent higher revenue.
- *Entrepreneur* reported that companies with strong gender equality practices are more profitable than those without such practices.
- Gartner found that 75 percent of companies with robust DEI practices exceed their financial goals (Carroll 2022).

Leadership practices that improve bottom-line financial results shouldn't be thought of as "soft" or "nice-to-haves." Instead, DEI practices are investments that grow financially-strong companies.

Additional benefits of DEI surface in the areas of product development, product testing, and design (Rainforest QA 2017). Companies with the highest levels of diversity reap fifteen times more product sales revenue than companies with the lowest levels of diversity. Teams comprised of diverse testers catch more bugs before products go into production. And diverse teams view design through the eyes of diverse users, allowing those teams to design products with the broadest end users in mind.

DEI Is Critical to Diversity of Thought

When Karen offered Yong-Sun a job, he had reservations. He wanted the job, but he didn't know if he could keep up with rest of the team. Most of those he'd met in the team interview were highly technical with a mixture of deep and wide skills in tech. Yong-Sun recently graduated college with a degree in digital marketing. He felt intimidated.

Instead of turning down the offer, he spoke again with Karen.

"Karen, I loved getting to know people on your team," Yong-Sun told Karen. "But if I'm honest, I'm not sure I can do what they do. Ava can code in her sleep. Tyler's an incredible programmer. You've got people who can write script. My studies and work in digital marketing are different. I don't want to let you or the team down."

"Let me stop you right there," Karen said. "You're right. I have brilliant people on my team. But I don't have a Yong-Sun. I need a creative thinker who sees, hears, and feels what users will see, hear, and feel. I need a Yong-Sun to help round out the creative side of my engineers."

Yong-Sun took the job and flourished.

The benefit of DEI comes when people with different skills, talents, and thinking join a project team. If you load your team with members who all think alike, you're likely to end up with groupthink instead of critical thinking that examines work from various perspectives.

DEI at Work Closes the Division in Our Nation

I'm not going to give undo attention to the rifts in the US. If you watch the news, you already know that much of the country is divided along political, social, economic, medical, gender, and racial lines. Fortunately, many organizations willingly step in to find and implement their own solutions around social issues.

According to the Edelman Trust Barometer, 86 percent of people surveyed said they expect CEOs to speak out on social issues, and 68 percent believe that CEOs must step in where the government has failed (Edelman 2021).

Businesses haven't shied away from bridging various social gaps that politicians aren't resolving. Consider these examples:

- When the government implemented immigration restrictions, Microsoft partnered with the International Rescue Committee to offer technology to teach digital skills to displaced people and refugees, especially women and girls.
- When the COVID-19 vaccine became available, IBM and Salesforce donated their own resources to promote vaccine distribution. Salesforce administered two billion vaccines to 190 countries.
- When various police officers were responsible for multiple racially-charged killings, Apple launched a $100 million Racial Equity and Justice Initiative (Kuryk 2021).

You don't have to own the company or sit in the C-suite to be a positive force for change as a leader. You can start by making your own team diverse, equitable, and inclusive.

Your Team Wants More DEI

Eighty percent of employees say that a company's DEI efforts are an important factor when considering a job. If you don't prioritize DEI and make your efforts transparent, you might not have an opportunity to interview and hire the top job candidates, because they won't even apply for your jobs.

DEI Brings the Diverse Experience and Thinking Shared by Your Diverse Customers

You need team members who are just as diverse as your customer base.

One survey found that 78 percent said that DEI gives companies a competitive advantage. We've all had to reach out to call centers with a customer service need. The automated intelligent voice response (IVR) call centers offer you the option to "for English press one, for Spanish press two." Given that Spanish is the second most spoken language in the US (by 13 percent of the population), it makes perfect sense that companies would want to connect in customers' native language (BBC 2018). Can you imagine trying to solve a problem over the phone if the person assisting you spoke a language other than your own? The only thing you'd get is frustrated. A person who doesn't speak your language, figuratively or literally, won't possess the same level of insight or ability to offer support.

When people launching programs and delivering services on your team similarly represent the same varied groups of customers you serve, you create a more personalized *user experience*. A diverse team can better answer the following questions around, for example, project design:

- How will this make the user feel?
- Are we using language our users are comfortable with?

- Does our visual design respect the beliefs, backgrounds, and sensitivities of our diverse customers (Berry 2021)?

MY INTRODUCTION TO DEI

When I worked at Google, we reached an interesting inflection point with Android. Whereas Android had become one of the most popular mobile OSs and OSs in the world, and we at Google had built many of the most popular apps on the platform, the developers inside Google found building the mobile experience to be complicated and cumbersome.

I led the team to streamline our work and make development faster and more reliable. As we proved our value, we eventually scaled from ten team members to 130, enabling the team to centralize mobile development across Google.

I loved the team. They already had a name when I started: the Mobile Ninjas. Yet our team was very male, and almost a little "bro-y." We all wanted more diversity on our team of engineers, but they had been struggling to do that since before I joined.

I did a little research about gender-coded language, and I learned that the name of a team impacts who applies for a job. Names like "ninja" and "rock star" tend to appeal to males while repelling female candidates.

I met with the team and told them what I'd learned about how our name might be working against us in attracting female candidates.

"Dang," one team member summarized the feelings of everyone in the room. "I love our name. It makes me feel good and special. But I get it. I've never seen a female ninja."

They agreed to changing, and they enjoyed the process of picking out a new name for our team, one that made everyone who joined us feel good and special. Within two months, I added two female senior engineers to the team. Both had heard of Mobile Ninjas, and neither applied simply because the name communicated that our team was for males only. Today, those two senior engineers have become a couple of the most important leaders in the group.

The NFL started using the Rooney Rule in 2003 to address the lack of diversity in the head coach, general manager, and executive roles. The Rooney Rule, named after the former owner of the Pittsburgh Steelers and chair of the NFL's diversity committee, recognized that nearly 70 percent of NFL players were Black, yet the league had no Black owners and only three Black head coaches.

In its application, the Rooney Rule mandates that interviews to fill top coaching and front-office jobs include multiple diverse candidates to choose from. That gives hiring authorities exposure to more qualified and diverse people.

Instagram uses the Rooney Rule for hiring, resulting in a much higher number of qualified minority candidates getting interviewed and hired for top jobs.

THE DEI-SAVVY LEADER

As I shared earlier, you don't need to own the company or serve in senior leadership to make positive DEI impact on your team. While you might not singlehandedly convince more females and minorities to pursue careers in tech, there are some things you can do, which we will explore next.

Create and Use a DEI Mantra

Today's leaders want the same things in the candidates they interview and ultimately hire and work with: a broad, diverse candidate pool, top talent, and a good fit for the needs of the team.

To meet those needs, start with a strong mantra to focus on your goals for DEI. Following are some examples to get you started on your own DEI mantra:

- *The greater the diversity of my team, the better we can meet the demands of our diverse customers.*
- *It's my job as a leader to make every member of my team feel like they belong.*
- *I'm a champion for equity in the workplace.*
- *The more diverse thinkers share their ideas, the more likely we are to create a brilliant solution.*
- *I'm glad you're here.*

Identify Opportunities for Improvement

If you find underrepresented groups such as women, minorities, those with disabilities, or older team members, you have a place to start. Comparing salaries between males and females might uncover pay inequity.

Senior leaders and HR in every progressive organization value leaders identifying and resolving DEI issues. Talk with HR to see if they will help you shrink any inequities in compensation between genders. Ask HR to help you recruit from a more diverse candidate pool.

Evaluate Your Current Team

You can't set a goal until you know how you're performing today. Get the data on your DEI. Many HR departments can share a report about the gender and racial diversity of your team, along with salaries. If your team is small enough, use your HR portal to collect the data yourself. As a final option, track down the data and enter it into your own spreadsheet.

Consider the information you discover as your baseline. You won't find it useful to compare yourself against other teams, organizations, or industries. When planning for tomorrow's improvements, what's most important is where you are today.

Communicate Your Intentions with Your Current Team

Since most team members want more DEI action from their organizations, your message will be welcomed news. Let your team know that you want input from the best and brightest, and then ask them where to find that talent when you have openings on your team. Be transparent that you need team "outsiders" to join you in an ad hoc, impromptu cross-functional team to get the broadest perspectives and ideas.

Let your team members know:

- Why DEI matters to you, the team, your organization, and your customers
- What steps you are taking to broaden diversity, create an equitable workplace, and foster inclusion for every team member
- That you welcome any team member referral of friends or former colleagues looking for work in the

tech industry who could help you achieve a more
balanced, diverse team

* That you want them to speak up if a project they're
  working on lacks inclusion from others or could
  benefit from broader diversity of thinking.

Use a Diverse Interviewing Group for Team Interviews

Telling your team that you value DEI is a great start, but to really
drive home the value of DEI, build a diverse, inclusive team to
conduct new hire interviews. Their different backgrounds and
skills will help you identify top talent.

Make Inclusion the Team Norm

No one who feels devalued or disrespected on a team can
perform at their peak performance. It's like trying to run as fast
as you can while looking over your shoulder. Fear shuts down
creative thinking and team member willingness to share opinions
in front of others.

As a leader, you likely can anticipate who will contribute the
most at your next team meeting. What about the person who
rarely contributes? Can you picture that person? Your goal is to
make speaking up and speaking out the norm. Call on people
who rarely contribute, and tell them that you're interested in
their thoughts.

Get Help

Group and societal norms change over time, as do words. It wasn't until 1986 that *The New York Times* wrote that they'd use Ms. when writing a woman's title. Prior to then, women were called Mrs. or Miss, revealing whether they were married or single (Varner 2018).

More recently, more people willingly share their gender identities and use nonbinary gender pronouns to describe themselves. Instagram was one of the first large platforms to promote this concept. Pronouns like *they/them* came into common use. Transgender and gender-queer team members may prefer pronouns like *zie/zim/zir/zis/zieself.* Don't assume that your team members —or even you personally—know everyone's preferred pronouns and are fluent in the most culturally-respectful way to address others.

You owe it to yourself and your team members to learn more about DEI. If your company offers training, attend. If you can attend an outside training session, go. Or take a class online. Learn as much as you can.

At the same time, encourage your team members to attend too. Usually when people hold contrary views about subjects like DEI programs and initiatives, the source of resistance comes from a lack of knowledge. To create a safe environment and maximize inclusiveness for all members of your team, make sure they are given time to learn more.

Take Advantage of the Blurred Lines Between Work and Home Life

Thanks to COVID-19 accelerating and expanding work from home (WFH) and the technology to keep teams connected, even those outside of tech have likely seen a naked child or two running in the background during a meeting. And it's now common for people to have a cat or dog make appearances during meetings. It's no longer easy to differentiate the walls of the office versus a living room.

Savvy leaders can benefit from the insights they have gained into the lives of others. As the boundary got smaller, you likely learned things about some team members that you would never ask at work, like, "Do you live alone?" Or "Do you have kids or pets?" You don't have to ask. You saw them on video!

More transformational than that, people have grown more comfortable sharing the stresses they face outside of work. Team members increasingly feel comfortable bringing up issues like daycare challenges, single parenting, and caring for elderly or sick family members. The more you and team members see and hear about common, shared issues, the more you build a sense that "we're in this together." By transcending the common, superficial work relationships and getting to know people on a more personal level, team members can better learn from and care for one another.

Scottish minister John Watson wrote under the pen name Ian Maclaren. While this famous quote has been attributed to Plato, Aristotle, and even Albert Einstein, most scholars believe that Maclaren was the first to write these words: "Be kind, for everyone you meet is fighting a hard battle."

As team members get to know one another personally, they can demonstrate empathy around common, shared struggles. This creates a team of supportive insiders who care for and protect one another.

As a leader, follow up on what you see and hear as a result of the thinner space between work and home. Ask team members about personal situations that the "new norm" illuminated. Show compassion for each person. This takes inclusion to a deeper level, when you find commonalities and connections you didn't know you shared.

Watch Your Words

Think about the common phrases you and others use at work that are either dated or no longer the most broadly accepted. This list isn't intended to be all-inclusive, but use it to start thinking about words or phrases you might say regularly that could make others feel less included:

Instead of saying...	Try saying...
guys	*people* or *team*
black and white	*at opposite extremes*
whitelist *blacklist* *blackballed* *black market*	*approved* *not approved* *rejected* *illegal*
handicapped	*a person with disabilities*
mental disability	*neurodiverse*
minority (yes, I've used this word throughout the section as a shortcut, and the word still appears in many recruitment ads)	*underrepresented people* or *underrepresented groups*

I've never known a leader personally who intentionally tried to offend people, but I've known several who misspoke without bad intentions. If you care about making your team members feel safe and communicating that they belong, educate yourself about common words and phrases that can come across as insensitive.

In Section IV, Strategic Leadership, I'll share some thoughts on strategies to exponentially increase your leadership effectiveness.

SECTION IV

STRATEGIC LEADERSHIP

Strategy outlines the long-range direction you wish to achieve and the plan you'll implement to get there. Strategies take time to develop. Tactics, on the other hand, are the smaller, more concrete and specific action steps needed to achieve a strategy.

Strategic planning in most organizations takes place at the C-suite level with the help of strategic planning departments—the analysts with access to both historical and trending data used to shape the direction.

When I discuss *strategic leadership*, I don't mean creating and driving the plans to direct the organization for years to come. Instead, I focus on what leaders can do strategically and immediately within their own teams to yield an exponential outcome.

Practicing these two strategic leadership concepts faithfully will give you and your team an edge when the organization needs a high-performing leader and team to assume projects with greater visibility and impact.

CHAPTER 11
TAKE OWNERSHIP, INITIATIVE, & ACCOUNTABILITY

IF THIS WERE YOUR COMPANY

Thinking back to my first job, I know I wasn't the ideal worker. I swept trash at Canada's Wonderland theme park. Let's just say that I didn't enjoy the work, and my attitude likely reflected in the outcome. I didn't take the job because of "perks"—like free daily admission to the park, a free trash-sweeping uniform, or first dibs at picking morsels out of the garbage. I took the job for a paycheck. I never saw Wonderland or sweeping as part of my future career. Like most first jobs, mine was a placeholder that I took because it was close to home, had somewhat flexible hours, and gave me a little spending money.

Since a common first job in the US resides in the fast-food industry, I'll use that as an example. If you worked in fast food—and remember, like my first job, you likely took it because it fit into the rest of your life—think about how you responded when you observed situations like the following:

- Trash blowing around the parking lot
- An empty soap dispenser

- A backed-up drain in the kitchen
- A freezer that got no colder than 40°F
- A long line at the cash register
- Ketchup stains on the tables
- No toilet paper in the bathroom
- Customers complaining about hot food served cold

If you were that teenager working in fast food, how did you respond to seeing these situations?

Even though fast food wasn't my first job, I'm pretty sure that my younger self would have looked the other way and pretended I didn't see anything that required my attention—unless, of course, my supervisor directed me to address it. Then I would do so. Reluctantly. Maybe you responded better than I imagine I would have.

I want to quickly point out that while my response may align with any fairly typical teenager in the same situation, that does *not* reflect my character and attitude today!

Now let's contrast you working in fast food as a teenager with you saving for several years to purchase your own fast-food business, a franchise that you hope to grow into a financial success. Having invested so much planning, time, money, and sweat equity into your new venture, how would you—as the business owner—respond to the same observations?

When you feel ownership, you take initiative and demonstrate accountability for every part of the business. After all, it's your money. You receive any profits, and you must absorb any losses. Just like Steve Jobs and Steve Wozniak pooling their resources to cofound Apple, you realize that success or failure rests 100 percent on your shoulders.

I can now say that I don't have to be the owner of a company to treat its resources and customers like they were my own. But I needed maturity and life experience to figure that out. Yes, some less mature team members may watch the clock, but *owners* watch and respond to each facet of the business, mindful that the organization represents their livelihoods and future while reflecting the nature of their characters.

Ownership encompasses taking initiative and being accountable. When you own something, you look for opportunities to preserve and grow it.

Human resources leader Dr. Jeanette Winters writes that employees have one of two mindsets: *renters* or *owners*.

About renters, she says that these employees "allow others to define them, detailing what and how they do their job. [They do] as instructed—completing transactions or tasks as directed. They operate within the 'lines' that management lays out for them."

In the example about the team member at the fast-food restaurant, a renter would fix problems…only once instructed to do so.

Winters contrasts renters with owners, saying that owners "take charge, fix what's broken, reap the benefits of their efforts by homing in on specific objectives…The critical difference between someone with an owner mentality and someone who shows up as a renter is that they invest in improving what irks them."

Leaders act like owners, take initiative, and hold themselves accountable. Companies with renters must point out opportunities and bugs, and then assign someone to address them before anything gets done (Winters 2020).

OWNERS LEAD FROM THE FRONT

Respected leadership speaker John Maxwell has been attributed with this statement: "A leader is the one who knows the way, goes the way, and shows the way." Knowing without acting is pointless. Acting without leading is like being a solo hamster on a wheel. The only way to lead is by going first—taking the right path while leading others through your example.

While the idea of leadership as a role model isn't new, there are four times that showing the way is most critical to leading others, which we'll explore next.

When Showing the Way Is More Effective than Pointing the Way

Tell people what to do, and they may resist. Leadership author Daniel Pink found a better way. He conducted an experiment that involved painting two lines on a sidewalk: one for people on their cell phones, and another for those who weren't. He outfitted his crew in orange vests and instructed them to line people up based on if they were on a cell phone or not. As you might imagine, people didn't comply. Many of them got angry!

Then he tried a different approach. Instead of instructing his team to tell people where to stand, he had them model the behavior of what actions were expected in each of the two lines. He had his team remove their vests, so they blended in with everyone else. In other words, these were no longer "leaders" identified by some sign of authority. They were just regular people.

Then he had members of his team who were on their cell phones line up in one line, while those who weren't lined up in the other queue. Guess what happened? The people on the street followed their examples (Barker 2014).

The same principle that gets people to line up based on their cell phone behavior works when it comes to taking initiative. If you wish your team members to take initiative, go first. Don't wait for a line to form. Start one. Lead from the front by your example.

When You're a New Leader

We tend to become like the people we spend the most time with. New leaders often shadow their bosses. Research shows that most leaders adopted their leadership styles from their immediate supervisors (Miller 2021). That's great news if you have a positive, strong leader to follow. But we don't just copy the strengths of our leaders. We also pick up their weaknesses.

Research in Motion's (RIM) Blackberry product took the business world by storm in 1999, and at its peak, Blackberry sales represented more than half of all smartphones used for business. By 2007, Blackberry had more than twelve million users and more than $42 billion in profits.

Co-CEOs Mike Lazaridis and Jim Balsillie decided to continue practicing business as usual instead of driving innovation, bringing new products to market, and behaving like owners in a company that would succeed for the long haul. But Apple's iPhone and Google's Android phone began cutting into Blackberry's market dominance. Leaders at RIM likely had followed their leader's cautious approach instead of taking initiative to push innovation. By 2017, the once venerated company and its ubiquitous Blackberry had no market share (CB Insights 2019).

Lazaridis and Balsillie set the tone at RIM, which spelled disaster. You can imagine that many other leaders at RIM embraced Lazaridis's and Balsillie's thoughts and behaviors, which further accelerated the company's decline.

Instead of blindly following the example of your immediate supervisor, look at their thinking processes and decisions objectively. Follow their positive examples, but guard against recklessly assuming a "monkey see, monkey do" approach.

When you're a new leader or leading a new team, your team members have little or no history with you. They can't "replay the tapes" of things that you've said, since they've never heard you say much. You'll have time to tell them about your values and expectations. But it's much easier to set the tone—showing them what you value and expect—by leading with your example.

When You Take Ownership

Many new leaders misunderstand the meaning of taking ownership. Following is a list of what taking ownership is not compared to what it is.

Ownership is NOT	Ownership IS
Being "the boss"	Empowering others to make decisions
Taking credit for successes	Giving credit to those who did the work
Blaming others for failure	Taking responsibility for team failure
Giving instructions	Showing others how to succeed
Taking charge	Leading the charge
Being hands-off	Being hands-on

Modeling ownership and accountability sets the tone for your team. They will adopt the same level of risk tolerance or risk avoidance that you show them. The same is true of how you deal with setbacks, screw-ups, and failures. Your response to those situations tells your team more than any series of workshops could.

When You Can Influence Others

When are leaders able to influence others? Whenever they're seen. "Leaders whose behavior is visible to followers are in a particularly powerful position to influence their followers' beliefs," researchers at *Journal of Economic Behavior & Organization* reported (Gächter & Renner 2018).

Acting like an owner, taking initiative, and accepting accountability are strategic—putting the best examples of leadership behavior on full display.

Think of a time when your team screwed something up. Maybe they followed a flawed process, left a job undone, or created a problem for someone else. Now imagine the impact if you claimed ownership and accountability for the problem and took initiative to fix it, saying something like, "I messed up, and we're going to take care of this."

This kind of strategic leadership builds trust with every team member, because it says, "I'll take the hit." It also demonstrates care for them and models your passion to make things right. That's what an owner would do, right? No fingers get pointed. No one is told to sit in the corner or don the proverbial dunce cap.

These strategic actions make your team feel safe, while encouraging them to demonstrate accountability without playing the blame game with peers or other departments. Finally, they tell people that mistakes aren't deadly. If you want your team members to hide the truth about problems, punish them for speaking up to identify bugs.

TAKING OWNERSHIP ON THE INTERNATIONALIZATION TEAM AT GOOGLE

When I worked at Google, I assumed accountability for the internationalization team. Much of our focus was on the way languages were represented on the web. If you speak and read only Mandarin, that's what you want to see when you conduct a search on your browser. My team helped create standards, build implementation across browsers and devices, create new fonts, and more.

At the time, we were EN-US-centric, and most of Google's revenue came from the United States, Great Britain, Australia, and other English-speaking countries. When I started leading this project called "The Forty Language Initiative," we wanted to ensure that Google products worked in forty languages and locales worldwide. We've far surpassed that scope today by having around one hundred languages and locales operational, but at the time, forty languages seemed like a Herculean task.

As various countries came online, I traveled there to gather firsthand information. I visited Myanmar to take part in the world's largest BarCamp, which is like an unconference where technologists get together to solve problems for a country.

It was there that I observed that nearly everyone I met from Myanmar had an Android device, but they were side-loading (the process of adding apps to a phone using USB cables, Bluetooth, or Wi-Fi or writing to a memory card from another smartphone or laptop) instead of downloading from the Google Play Store.

I got curious about why so many users had jumped through so many hoops instead of using the Google Play Store. After a little investigation, I learned that the Google Play Store didn't work in Myanmar. I filed a bug to have the problem resolved. That's when I learned that Myanmar had been blocked a few years prior, and even though restrictions should have been lifted, the bug still held. Several of my group filed bugs from Myanmar, and a team back home in the US "flipped the switch" to correct the problem.

Almost instantly, with the touch of a button instead of the cumbersome workarounds they'd been using, millions of people across the country had access to more apps on the Play Store. This simple fix served as an equalizer to making sure that information was democratically accessible to millions of additional people around the world.

No, I don't think my efforts in Myanmar should earn any special honor. All I did was observe a problem. But once I observed it, I owned the problem, reported it, and made myself accountable to the customers of Myanmar to ensure the bug got fixed. Then I shared in the excitement of my team back home and my new friends in Myanmar once Google resolved the problem.

Taking ownership, initiative, and accountability doesn't mean you'll need to rush into a burning building to save to your customers. Sometimes it's simply a matter of following up on what you know to ensure the right actions get followed through.

ELEVATING YOUR OWNERSHIP

Anyone can take ownership, initiative, and accountability. Following are some tips to elevate your game.

Create and Use an Ownership Mantra

We often get so busy that we forget to prime the pump that fuels our attitudes and guides our actions. Following are some examples of a mantra to help you lead as an owner, one who takes initiative and practices accountability:

- *How would my team perform if everyone followed my example?*
- *I will lead by example.*
- *I will take responsibility for any mistakes of my team while giving them credit for any success.*
- *When I see an opportunity, I will act on it. When I see a problem, I will fix it.*
- *I will treat my team as co-owners in the success of our company.*

Hone Your Observation Skills

Look around your office. If Warren Buffett walked down the halls while he considered investing in your company, would he see a place filled with "renters" or "owners"? Renters treat the property as a place to earn a paycheck. They take more than they give. They don't notice clutter, overflowing garbage bins, or trash on the floors. In tech, they write sloppy code, miss deadlines, work alone, and need to be asked before they work on the next logical, necessary task.

Look around your office as if you owned the place. Then ask yourself: *What does what I see say about our organization? What is my first impression of this operation based solely on what I see on the surface? What can I own to make this place look like a business that Buffett would want to invest in?*

Just as important as identifying opportunities to convert renters into owners is to tap into your team members who already act like owners. Think of those you would clone if it weren't for any ethical ramifications. How do they show that they are owners? How can you leverage them to create more owners? What opportunities would allow them to elevate their ownership, responsibility, and accountability across your team? You can't afford to lose these team members. What can you do to ensure that they stay engaged?

Make the Words "Accountable" and "Accountability" Part of Your Vocabulary

How often do you use the words *accountable* or *accountability*? And when you use them, how often is it in a positive context, such as, "Who was accountable for fixing this bug? You came up with a brilliant solution!"

The word accountable is misused, just like the word consequence. Both words seem to take on a negative connotation. But a consequence is neither positive nor negative. It's simply what happens after a behavior occurs. The consequence for missing deadlines might be a reprimand; the consequence for continual, outstanding performance might be a promotion or reward.

When you need something done on your team, ask, "Who will be accountable to get this done?" When a task is done well, ask, "Who had accountability for this success?" Using those words demonstrates to your team that accountability is an opportunity to own a task and perform it in a memorable way.

After a company conducted an employee engagement survey, the CIO was shocked to see low scores and negative comments from his employees about the lack of feedback they received. He shared the results with his direct reports, who were equally surprised.

On a hunch, the CIO wondered if employees considered feedback only as formal, scheduled, one-on-one sessions with their immediate supervisors. He suggested that each time a leader offered feedback, they start the conversation by saying, "Hey, I'd like to offer you some feedback."

In the next survey twelve months later, the employees wrote positive comments about the amount and quality of feedback they'd received. The only behavior change the leaders made was to say the word *feedback* while offering feedback! That simple addition connected the dots for employees, showing that feedback didn't happen exclusively in formal meetings.

Volunteer for Meaningful Work and Encourage Team Members to Do the Same

What "non-work" task or project interests you—meaning one outside of the role you were hired for? It doesn't need to be one that you have experience in. The only requirement is that the organization has identified it as important to the business, like enhancing corporate visibility in your community. Maybe you want to explore new opportunities outside of your current expertise, or you want to get involved in a project with social impact like heading up United Way initiatives or volunteering in the community.

How about your team members? How can you get them involved? Ask them to invest their energies in an area of their passions. By giving them ownership, initiative, and accountability for an outcome on work time, you foster their personal development. When team members feel fulfilled, that energy shows up in the work they do for your team.

Become a Champion

As I shared, renters wait to be told what to do; owners, on the other hand, look for opportunities. Perhaps you don't know of any existing projects or teams to join that could benefit from your leadership. To get started, ask yourself:

- *What am I passionate about?*
- *How could my passion benefit the company?*

Take ownership of fixing an existing problem or improving a current situation. Become a champion of what matters most to you.

One growing leader became passionate about helping his local community when he read that children in his city were more likely than those in other cities within his state to grow up in single-parent homes, live below the poverty line, and drop out of high school. He wanted to improve the lives of those families while also creating a potential pipeline for future hires in his organization.

With support from his senior leadership team, the mayor's office, and the chamber of commerce, he created an army of volunteers. At first, these volunteers beautified the local schools by cleaning, painting, and updating old classroom furniture and technology. After the first year, his group extended into the community—refurbishing playgrounds, parks, and even some homes of the poorest residents. By the third year, his team started providing mentorship, tutoring, and job training for at-risk kids. What started with one person became a corporatewide initiative where team members were given paid time off to volunteer locally.

This leader found a need and sought to address it. He rallied likeminded people to join his cause, and financial support poured in from his own company and the city.

Here's the question: how do you think his passion and efforts to take ownership of that initiative impacted the reputation of his company in that community?

Practice Followership

The US Army leadership model uses the word *followership* to mean "the capacity or willingness to follow within a team or organization." Those who would lead must also know how to follow corporate guidelines, cultural norms, and others within the team (Duran-Standon and Masson 2021).

Are you modeling how to be a strong follower? I'll ask the same question again that I asked as a potential mantra: *how would my team perform if everyone followed my example?* Think about that in terms of how you demonstrate ownership. Consider how you take initiative when you identify a problem and opportunity. Finally, imagine overhearing your team members talk between themselves about how you take accountability. What would they say?

Look for Ways to Empower Your Team

Toyota created a tool known as the Andon Cord. The cord was nothing but a rope in the manufacturing plant. Pulling on the Andon Cord immediately shut down the entire manufacturing plant. That cord didn't exist for the managers or floor leaders who may have been in their offices instead of on the assembly line. No, that cord could be pulled by any team member who spotted a problem within the assembly process. Once the cord got pulled, everyone would assemble to discover why it was pulled and what the team must do to resolve the problem (Six-SigmaDaily 2018).

That's empowerment. You can tell your team that they're empowered a dozen times each day, but unless you encourage them to put the brakes on the component of a project when they detect a problem, empowerment is just a trendy word.

Do you empower and trust your team enough to give them access to the "kill switch"? Are you willing let your team conduct ad hoc sprints to create workarounds and fixes as needs arise? Are you able to accept accountability for your team's actions, even when they might "make you look bad" to others?

Remain Vigilant

Thomas Jefferson, the writer of the US Constitution, admonished his compatriot to guard against any attacks on the new law of the land by saying, "Let the eye of vigilance never be closed."

Business leaders should follow that same advice. Whether you run a dry cleaner or a product team, it's imperative that your eyes remain open for both threats and opportunities to grow your business. Research emerging trends inside and outside your own industry. Look for successes you can apply to your own industry while identifying potential threats that could weaken your market share. Be discontent with the status quo, remembering that customers forever ask, "What have you done for me lately?"

From its beginning in 1921, RadioShack, the retail chain that once had more than four thousand stores across the US, was a haven for electronics buffs and hobbyists for generations. But by the time RadioShack entered the mobile phone distribution race in the1990s, the company was already too far behind to catch up to businesses that had anticipated consumer trends and demands. After declaring bankruptcy, RadioShack never recovered (Day and Schoemaker 2019).

Had RadioShack monitored emerging trends in consumer electronics, they would have responded to changing consumer demands more quickly. Additionally, they would have identified market shifts ahead of their competition.

Master Curious Inquiry

Owners not only practice active vigilance, but they also use *curious inquiry* to determine what the research and trends mean for their own business.

When I've asked project managers (and PjMs) who've been in their roles for decades to reflect over their entire careers and identify the biggest threat or opportunity they've encountered in their roles, the answer surprised me: Microsoft Excel. Some believed Microsoft Excel would make the project management discipline obsolete overnight; others saw the same technology as a tool that would free up their time so they could focus on the purpose behind their jobs: keeping projects on time and within budget.

The difference between PMs that viewed MS Excel as a job-killer or a game-changer came down to their perspectives and the questions they asked themselves when faced with a new tool. Those with a fixed mindset asked themselves questions like these:

- *Is this going to cost me my job?*
- *Is using MS Excel mandatory?*
- *What might I do to stall implementation?*

However, those PMs with a growth mindset and a spirit of inquiry became even stronger project managers, and they asked themselves questions like these:

- *How might I apply this to my work?*
- *How can this benefit my work, team, and organization?*
- *What must I do to realize the benefits and seize the opportunity?*
- *How can I get others to get excited about the possibilities?*

Curious inquiry is a leadership mindset, and it allows leaders to own the outcomes of their decisions and work.

Warren Buffett, the chair and CEO of Berkshire Hathaway known as the "Oracle of Omaha" because of his business insight, asks several questions before he invests in a business. Here are two of those questions:

1. Does this business successfully violate industry norms?

2. Does this business have efficient systems and teams?

The first question seeks to learn if a company is a disrupter in its space. As Dr. Jesse Green said, "Business as usual is not exciting for Buffett. It needs to violate industry norms."

The second question is to determine the assets of the business that are wired into its success: process and people. When Buffett buys into a business, he's not solely interested in its products. Processes and people will be around long after products evolve or become obsolete (Green 2020).

Imagine that you "own" a department that Buffett is

considering investing in, knowing that an investment from Buffett will lead other investors to follow suit. Personalize those questions to your leadership of your team:

1. Do you ask questions that disrupt status quo thoughts and actions?

2. Do you ask questions that inspire your team members to hardwire ownership into how they work?

Ownership, initiative, and accountability have nothing to do with "being the boss." They're traits of servant leadership, leading by example, and being accountable to get the right things done.

In the next chapter, I'll lay out how a leader serves as the cultural steward for the organization and their team.

CHAPTER 12
BECOMING A CULTURAL STEWARD

THE GREAT RESIGNATION

Researchers studying employment trends started using the term "The Great Resignation" or "The Big Quit" in late 2020, although some experts believe this trend began more than a decade ago.

Regardless of when it started, the Great Resignation picked up momentum during COVID-19. Some businesses closed their doors, displacing "non-essential" workers; other companies instituted sweeping work from home (WFH) initiatives to maintain business without risking team members' health to exposure in an office setting.

According to the Pew Research Center, low pay fueled volunteer attrition in some industries. But that's not the only reason employees quit. Pew reported the top three reasons that employees left jobs as "low pay (63 percent), no opportunities for advancement (63 percent), and feeling disrespected at work (57 percent)" (TheStreet 2020).

Advancement opportunities and respect directly relate to company culture.

An employee at a tech start-up pinpointed the moment when he knew his company was going to fail: "For me it was getting into a screaming match with the CEO over him eating canned tuna in the office" (Heald 2022).

I'm thinking, *Tuna as the straw that broke the camel's back?* Perhaps it wasn't the tuna as much as it felt like disrespect that the CEO would eat something so pungent in an open work environment. Or maybe the cheap lunch signaled that the company had no money. Either way, the only screaming at work should be sounds of delight and excitement at achieving a breakthrough, not shouts from prolonged periods of relentless stress.

Revelio Labs studies public employment records to help them understand workforce trends, and CultureX compiles data to create insights about improving employee engagement and business results. Those two research organizations joined forces in using AI to analyze more than 1.4 million Glassdoor reviews written by current and former employees, as well as other various data points, to better understand the impact of culture on employee retention (Sull et al. 2022).

Here's a summary of what they learned:

- While the media singled out employee dissatisfaction with pay as the largest driver of turnover in the Great Resignation, pay ranked sixteenth as a predictor of employee turnover.
- An employee's perception about their corporate culture proved a more reliable predictor of industry-adjusted attrition than compensation.

According to the research, the top four drivers of employee turnover are as follows:

1. *Toxic corporate culture.* When employees feel disrespected at work and believe their organization doesn't value diversity and inclusion, employees feel like they can't get ahead unless they embrace the company's dysfunction. A toxic corporate culture showed itself as 10.4 times more powerful in driving turnover than pay.

2. *Job insecurity/reorganizations.* Layoffs and reorgs cause teams to lose faith that their organization has a bright future. Such insecurity drives team members to take control of their careers, even if it means starting over at a new company and job.

3. *High levels of innovation.* Jobs that require ongoing, high levels of innovation force team members to work longer hours under higher stress just to conform to their peer norm. When teams must work both creatively and under continuous stress, some would rather take a pay cut for a job that requires less from them.

4. *Failure to recognize team-member performance.* When an organization doesn't treat, recognize, and reward high performers differently than average (or poor performers), morale plummets. This practice tells high performers that their ability to get ahead isn't linked to their efforts or results.

Bottom line: corporate culture determines team-member retention.

As challenging as it is for organizations to minimize the negative impact of "the great resignation," an even more insidious problem lurks in some companies: "quiet quitting." While quiet quitting is a new term for employees who keep their jobs but stop going above and beyond in their work efforts, the concept has been around forever. Gallup would call these employees disengaged. A consultant friend of mine called these R.O.A.D. warriors: employees who were *Retired On Active Duty.*

Team members who take 100 percent of their paycheck without giving 100 percent of their best efforts can be called quiet quitters, disengaged, or R.O.A.D. warriors. Whatever you call them, they cost organizations money, and they often hide in the open.

I'd love to see research on the correlation of quiet quitting and toxic work cultures. I'd expect to see that team members working in toxic cultures account for most of the quiet quitting across the country.

WHAT IS CULTURE?

Think of corporate culture as the personality of a company that shapes how teams think and feel about their workplace. Culture includes the written and unwritten rules about how things get done within the organization—ultimately impacting how teams approach their work. And while every company has a culture, no two cultures are identical.

Leaders serve as stewards for their organization's culture. If a leader doesn't believe in, support, and serve as a cultural ambassador, they should work elsewhere.

Being a cultural steward means two things. First, it means

exemplifying and elevating the best parts of the company's culture to your team. Second, it means developing a *team* culture that brings out the best in each member.

Kim Cameron and Robert Quinn from the University of Michigan popularized the idea of four distinct corporate cultures. According to their research, companies operate in a *clan, adhocracy, market, or hierarchy culture* (Sharkey 2022).

- *Clan culture.* Clan cultures are friendly, collaborative, participatory, consensus-driven, and team-centric. Instead of traditional bosses, leaders serve as mentors. Instead of rulebooks, clan cultures teach through their history and legacies, while adhering to a company's long-standing traditions. Clan cultures care greatly about the people, and these organizations prioritize developing the next generation. This makes sense, since these cultures feel like one big, extended family.
- *Adhocracy culture.* This culture works well for creative teams operating in fluid, ever-changing environments. These cultures require innovation, risk-taking, learning agility, and change-readiness to meet the dynamic demands of the business and customers. Creative team members who thrive on developing new products and services do well in adhocracies. These companies move quickly, disrupt the status quo, and learn from their mistakes. Tech companies are often adhocracies, since their businesses require team members to work autonomously as well as collaboratively to quickly identify problems and jump on new opportunities.
- *Market culture.* If you're in a business that demands constant results, you would enjoy working in a market culture. These companies are "all business,"

and operate with a "what have you done for me lately?" philosophy. Getting things done and achieving goals comes ahead of everything else. Their environments feel competitive, the leaders seem demanding, and the employees understand that they exist to get results. Market cultures focus on goals and results, not feelings and hugs. The metrics that drive a market culture include capturing market share, beating the competition, and driving up stockholder value.

- *Hierarchy culture*. This culture asks employees to "do it our way." In hierarchy cultures, "our way" means the way things have always been done as outlined in the formal policies, procedures, and processes and mandated in the structured work environment. Leaders in these organizations value "tried and true" practices that reduce costs, risks, and uncertainty. Hierarchy cultures adhere to a strict command-and-control leadership model (detailed in Chapter 8). Employees who succeed in hierarchy cultures learn quickly to fall in line and do as they're told.

When Jerry took a job with an internationally-known social services organization, he felt excited to work for them.

During his interview, Jerry's boss, Lynn, let him know that while other organizations were moving to business-casual attire every day of the week, their company didn't follow the trend. "People visit head-quarters from around the world each day. We want to look professional in everything we do, so we require workers in headquarters to wear a coat and tie to work. Of course," Lynn said with a laugh, "you can take off your coat in the office. Just put it on when you walk around."

Jerry didn't care about the dress code. He only cared about the company's mission. He enthusiastically moved into his new office, thrilled to be part of a company with deep pockets, an outstanding reputation, and global outreach.

A couple of days into his new job, Lynn stopped by to check on Jerry.

"Are you finding everything OK?" Lynn asked.

"Yes," Jerry said with a smile. "This place is amazing, and people have been helpful in pointing me in the right direction. I really love the work."

"I'm so glad to hear that," Lynn said. "Just wanted to make sure that we're treating you well. Hey, before I forget," Lynn added, "I saw you heading to the bathroom the other day. You forgot to put on your sports coat."

"Right," Jerry said, "You're right. I forgot, and I remembered that I forgot as soon as I went to hang my coat on the door hook of my stall. But I couldn't because I left it in my office," Jerry laughed.

"I understand," Lynn nodded. "It takes time to develop new habits. Speaking of which, I noticed that you have your sleeves rolled up."

"I'm a lefty, so I tend to drag my entire arm through fresh ink when I write," Jerry answered. "I've lost a few shirts that way. Is it a problem to roll up my sleeves?" Jerry asked, feeling confused.

"No, that's fine," Lynn said with understanding. "Especially on hot days like today. But could I ask you to roll your sleeve inside your shirt instead of on the outside? It looks tidier and more professional."

And at least once a week, Jerry learned a new

"rule" that everyone else seemed to know and follow. After six months, Jerry quit, citing health reasons. Jerry's "health reason" was stress. He loved the nature of the job, the campus, the cafeteria, and his coworkers. But he experienced intense anxiety about all the rules that came along with the job. He believed he would either blow up at work or end up in the hospital for stress.

Sound unbelievable? I wish it were, but this is the norm in hierarchy cultures. Another company insists that team members cover tattoos and remove piercings when meeting with clients. Companies with reams of unwritten rules that people must learn and follow before they learn how to "get things done" have become rare in recent years, but they live on in legacy, family-run companies.

SIGNS OF A TOXIC CULTURE

More important that knowing precisely what kind of culture your company has is understanding the traits of *toxic* and *healthy* cultures. Researchers have pinpointed the top five toxic descriptors of a corporate culture, which we will explore in this subsection.

Disrespectful

Toxic cultures ignore the feelings and opinions of their team members. Leaders often lack common courtesy and fail to treat others with dignity. When you pass a leader in the hallway of a company full of disrespect, don't expect a friendly "hello," wave, nod, or eye contact.

Non-inclusive

Toxic cultures often practice cronyism and nepotism—using inequitable practices in how they treat people based on sexual orientation, disability, race, age, and gender issues. When team members resemble photocopies of one another and leaders practically mandate "groupthink," you know that inclusivity isn't valued.

Facebook (Meta) uses an exercise to avoid groupthink. When working with a problem or opportunity, they brainstorm in three phases: individual reflection, paired reflection, and group reflection. This ensures that individual team members' thoughts don't get buried in groupthink (Meta 2022).

Unethical

Toxic cultures breed dishonesty and have a lack of rigor, even on regulatory compliance. When a company makes headlines with words like "fined" and "penalized," it's a good bet that they got caught for illegal and/or unethical practices.

Since 2000, just five companies—Bank of America, JP Morgan Chase, BP, Volkswagen, and Citigroup—have paid out more than $205 billion due to illegal business practices. Bank of America alone accounted for more than $82 billion of the total (Good Jobs First 2022).

Besides outright illegal business practices, companies can see their reputations and revenues drained by unethical practices such as making false product claims, unethical accounting practices, poor working conditions, pay imbalances, unfair competition, defamation, selling customer data, and more.

Cutthroat

Toxic cultures foster an environment of unhealthy competition as well as backstabbing behaviors between team members. You see this in cultures where promotions are based on how much you discredit other candidates instead of showing your own merit.

Abusive

Toxic cultures often breed bullies along with harassment allegations and lawsuits.

Cofounders of CultureX, Donald and Charlie Sull, summarized what they learned about cultures this way: "A vibrant culture can not only keep employees happy — it can also be the difference between financial success and failure" (Sull and Sull 2022).

More than 75 percent of Fortune 500 companies share their corporate culture statements publicly (Sull et al. 2019). However,

I've never seen such a statement that asks their leaders and team members to be disrespectful, non-inclusive, unethical, cutthroat, or abusive. Yet these toxic behaviors exist.

Enron touted itself a "global corporate citizen" with four core values: respect, integrity, communication, and excellence (Kunen 2002). They even had these words etched in twelve-inch letters on the marble façade in their lobby.

Help me remember...Why did Enron go bankrupt? Oh yeah, their leaders perpetuated one of the biggest accounting frauds in history.

Words on a page or even etched in marble for all the world to see don't always translate into leaders internalizing them and using them as a moral compass. Words are cheap. Actions tell the whole story.

Obviously, no company publicly promotes unethical and illegal behaviors. Yet some companies allow toxins to leach into the business, costing them in fines, customer loss, diminished market share, and reputation. Consider the following two situations that captured the headlines:

- In 2016, Gretchen Carson sued and won a $20 million settlement against Twenty-First Century Fox for the sexual harassment by Fox news chief, Roger Ailes; a year later, Twenty-First Century Fox agreed to a $90 million settlement of shareholder claims arising from the sexual harassment scandals by Roger Ailes and anchor Bill O'Reilly (Stempel 2017).

- In 2021, the Equal Employment Opportunity
  Commission sued Ford for Pregnancy Discrimination
  (EEOC 2021).

Enough on toxic corporate cultures. Plenty of organizations build and maintain healthy corporate cultures. Following are some companies that typically make the top-ten list for best corporate cultures (Patel 2017).

1. Zappos	6. Squarespace
2. Warby Parker	7. Google
3. Southwest Airlines	8. REI
4. Twitter	9. Facebook
5. Chevron	10. Adobe

I spent more than fifteen years at Google, have worked in the Meta (formally known as Facebook) umbrella of companies for nearly two years, and Tony Hsieh invited me to speak at an all-team-member meeting at Zappos. I know firsthand why these three company cultures are frequently on the top of the best companies list. Once you've worked in a healthy culture, you know how critical culture is to your mental health and professional success.

Are you thinking that these top-ten organizations offer catered meals served on a rooftop lounge, late morning massages, lunchtime swims at the company's health spa, beer-and-pizza Fridays, unlimited vacation days...all free to team members? As a matter of fact, some of them do. But while generous compensation, deep benefits, and rich perks can play a role in culture, they aren't necessary for a healthy culture. Remember that a company culture is akin to its personality—

what a company *feels like* as well as *how things get done* inside an organization. Even if you eat for three hours each day at work, that doesn't compare to the hours you spend breathing in your organization's culture. Pay, benefits, and perks can't compensate for toxic office air!

HR and organizational culture experts know that a healthy culture is based on how leaders demonstrate care for their teams. Whereas turnover reflects disengaged people and a toxic company culture, retention reflects engaged team members and a healthy company culture.

Here are seven things that organizational leaders do to build and maintain healthy cultures (Damian 2021):

1. Care for others, which includes their wellness and mental health (Chapter 4).
2. Provide coaching and timely, constructive feedback (Chapters 7 and 15).
3. Promote diversity and inclusion in the workplace (Chapter 10).
4. Communicate with transparency (Chapter 5).
5. Foster learning agility (Chapters 2 and 11).
6. Recognize contributions and provide positive reinforcement (Chapters 9 and 15).
7. Connect the work to the company's core values (Section III: Collaborative Leadership and Chapter 11).

Up until this point in the chapter, I've defined company culture, given you examples of toxic and healthy ones, and listed how healthy cultures are differentiated them from toxic or average cultures. *What does this have to do with me?* you might be wondering. Or more specifically, you might think, *I'm just a team lead. My team makes up 0.03 percent of the total team member population. I have almost no influence over the culture!*

True, one team leader in an organization of thousands can't turn a toxic culture into a healthy one. But one team leader can create a healthy culture *within their team,* despite the organization's culture.

REINFORCING YOUR COMPANY CULTURE AND ENRICHING YOUR TEAM CULTURE

You can love your job, leaders, team, and company but not *be in love* with every part of the culture. Think of the parts you don't care for as *quirks* in someone's personality. You might not love each quirk, but you can still love the overall person and their personality. Quirks aren't deal-breakers. But I do consider any of the five toxic cultural traits I shared earlier as deal-breakers.

Another deal-breaker for me would be to work for an organization with products, services, values, or a mission that is diametrically in opposition to my own values. For example, if I were a member of People for the Ethical Treatment of Animals (PETA), I wouldn't find working in a slaughterhouse or as a furrier a good fit based on my values.

When you choose to work for an organization, you chose to live by their cultural values. If you love your culture, it's much easier to support your culture. If you don't, you should consider moving to a job that aligns to your needs instead of staying and trying to promote what you don't believe in.

When you were a child, you probably played Follow-the-Leader or Simon Says. But you probably never volunteered to play a game of Obey-the-Boss or Simon Commands…unless you could play the part of the boss or Simon!

As a leader, you want team members to follow you willingly, not because you strong-arm them. You can't instruct people to "love our culture." Instead, you show them the cultural aspects that you love while leading the charge to create a best-in-class culture inside your own team.

Sub-cultures exist inside every culture. Some of them work against and subvert the prevailing, healthy corporate culture (like a counterculture); other sub-cultures serve as higher or customized versions of the prevailing company culture.

Following are ways to be an ambassador for your culture while creating your special subculture within your team.

Create and Use a Cultural Mantra

A cultural mantra serves to remind you of the best parts of your company's values and culture. Use these as a starting point to creating your own:

- *My company cares about me and earns my loyalty.*
- *The culture of my company makes me feel valued and respected.*
- *I love working for a company that values ____, ____, and ____.*
- *My team deserves a team culture that makes them feel safe, cared for, and appreciated.*
- *I want my team members to choose my team because of the culture we created.*

Connect Perks to the Company Culture and Values

It's easy to think of benefits and perks as a company's cost of doing business. Job candidates consider perks and benefits as part of the overall compensation package. But perks and benefits also indicate the company's culture and the value placed on people.

As a leader, connect the dots for people that the perks and benefits of your organization demonstrate its care for team members. Note the following examples.

Benefits/Perks	The Cultural Value Demonstrated
Generous or unlimited time off	Cares about work-life balance and team member well-being
Rich compensation/401k	Cares about people and their futures
On-site cafeteria/free meals	Handles the little things, so team members can focus on the big things
On-site or discounted workout facility	Invests in team-member health and wellness
Seminars, workshops, and learning opportunities	Cares about and invests in team member development

Google offers something called the "20 Percent Rule" or "20 Percent Project" which encourages Googlers to invest up to 20 percent of their work time exploring projects that interest them, which could potentially offer the company opportunities in the future (Xu 2020). Here are three different ways a manager *could* interpret the 20 percent rule for their team members:

Cynical translation. "The company makes so much money that they're willing to throw it away."

"Boss" translation. "It's just one of the benefits Google offers. Take advantage of it if you want, but I still expect you to get 100 percent of your work done."

Leader translation. "We trust you, and we want you to use your unique skills, talents, and passions to the fullest, even if we don't see an immediate ROI."

Leaders find ways to translate company benefits and perks to deepen team members' relationships and connections to the company's culture and values.

By the way, if you've ever used Gmail, Google's email platform, you've benefited from a Googler's innovation and use of the 20 percent rule. Googler Paul Buchheit used the 20 percent rule to develop search capacity for his email. When Google launched Gmail on April 1, 2004, the product had so much storage and speed that many users thought it was an April Fool's Day hoax! (Smith 2021).

Renew Your Own Appreciation of Your Company Culture

When I work from home or the office, I see my son each day. He doesn't change or grow quickly while I'm watching him. But my perspective changes when I leave on business for a week. Seeing him after I've been traveling, I notice and appreciate things about him that I can't see change daily. When I hug him close, his head seems to come up higher on me, as if he's grown. When I listen to him talk, I hear new words in his vocabulary.

Once we've worked in an organization for a while, we tend to take things like a healthy culture for granted. Were we to take a job somewhere else with a less healthy culture, we'd recognize the difference immediately.

Ask yourself these questions:

- *What do I enjoy most about my organization's culture and values?*
- *What sets my organization's culture and values apart from other companies I've worked for?*
- *When things get challenging, why is my company still the best place to work?*

If you struggle to come up with a long list of things you appreciate about your culture, keep thinking until you can list at least ten factors. By dwelling on what makes your company great, you shift from spotting grievances to experiencing gratitude. Hold onto that gratitude. Return to your list when you feel triggered by a quirk you don't like. Be known for pointing out to your team members the parts of the company culture that you love. Doing that will encourage them to challenge their own negative thoughts over an aspect of the culture that they don't enjoy.

Define the Culture You Want to Create

Let's put aside company culture and focus on your team culture. As I stated earlier, one team leader can't turn a toxic organizational culture into a healthy one. But one team leader is all that's required to create a healthy team culture.

What words do you want your team members to use when they describe the sub-culture you've created in your team? The following list contains thirty words that team members might use to describe their ideal culture. I left four boxes blank, so you can add your own words if you don't see the ones you want. Look at the list and put a checkmark by the ten words you'd most like to hear your team use when talking about your team culture.

Rewarding	Nurturing	Supportive	Flexible
Exciting	Engaging	Challenging	Collaborative
Progressive	Connected	Transparent	Inclusive
Fun	Welcoming	Innovative	Positive
Hard-working	Passionate	Empathetic	Dedicated
Autonomous	Respectful	Healthy	Empowered
Motivating	Inspiring	Rewarding	Loyal
Open-minded	Results-oriented	Customer-centric	Diverse

Review the ten words you've marked, and circle the top five words you'd like team members to say about your culture.

You're almost done. Now go back and put a star by the top three words.

Southwest Airlines frequently tops the lists of the most loved airlines by customers, highest employee engagement in the industry, and best work culture. One of the reasons Southwest builds such loyal customers is the culture they've created.

Southwest Airlines has clarity of purpose, which is to "connect people to what's important in their lives through friendly, reliable, and low-cost air travel." Their vision is "to be the world's most loved, most efficient, and most profitable airline."

And their employees live the company's purpose and vision. It started with founder Herb Kelleher and the culture he created. Here are some of Kelleher's behaviors, which built his culture:

He served as a mentor. When he worked as a lawyer, Kelleher hired and developed his administrative assistant, Colleen Barrett, a woman without a degree or legal training. Kelleher mentored Barrett, brought her over to Southwest Airlines when he started the company, and developed her. In 2001, after serving in multiple leadership roles, Barrett assumed the role of president of Southwest Airlines.

He made himself accessible. The *Dallas Morning News* wrote, "Mr. Kelleher is not happy unless he's talking with employees." Even as the airline grew, Kelleher loaded baggage, worked flights, gave in-flight announcements, handed out peanuts, drove out to the airplane hangars, and went to great lengths to meet employees wherever they happened to be (Maxon 2019).

He put employees first. Kelleher believed that at Southwest Airlines, "people made the difference," and he treated them like they were the number-one priority. During a financial crunch, Kelleher sold an airplane to avoid laying off employees (Kerstein 2019).

He insisted on having fun and built a company around fun. Can you imagine working as a flight attendant and having the CEO pop out of an overhead compartment on your plane? If you worked with Kelleher, you expected it, just like you expected that some days he'd dress like Elvis and ride his Harley-Davidson motorcycle to an employee party. Kelleher said, "It's much better to have fun in life than not have fun. I really don't believe that you have to be boring to be successful" (Schwartz 1996).

I've not found any record from Kelleher about what

kind of culture he envisioned creating or what he wanted those around him to say about his leadership. But based on his legacy, I think his goals included creating a fun, employees-first company that prioritized mentorship and customer service.

In 2022, J.D. Power awarded Southwest Airlines as the best airline in the country for economy and basic economy flights. Southwest Airlines proves that culture is a business differentiator (Chen 2022).

Convert Cultural Ideals into Actions

Review the exercise you completed wherein you prioritized three words you wish team members would say about your culture. Now write your distinct *culture word* on each of the three lines of the list below. Next, from the point of view of your team, how do you believe they'd currently rate each culture word on a four-point scale (1=Low, 4=High)? Write that number into the *current rating*.

Culture Word	Current Rating	Stop	Start

Now comes the work to make those themes come alive in your culture. The goal for this next exercise is for team members to rate your team culture a 4 in all the areas that mean the most to them. The purpose of this activity is to foster collaboration, elevate trust, get team member buy-in and input about the culture they want, and develop new norms.

Step One. Be transparent with your team about the exercise you completed. Explain that you came up with your top three words and rated how you think your team currently performs on those traits using a four-point scale. Explain that you wish to build a culture within the team that makes it the best place to work within the company.

Step Two. Ask for their help by completing the same exercise, so you can capture the opinions of each person as well as get a sense of the team's priorities. Send them the list of thirty words, and ask each person to narrow down the list to the top three words they'd like to see come alive in the team culture. They will share their three words in Step Four. *Note: In low-trust cultures, consider using an anonymous survey tool so individuals aren't identified. In high-trust environments, you can have team members complete this exercise in a room using Post-it notes.* Finally, ask them to rate (1 to 4 scale) how the team lives up to the three culture words they chose.

Step Three. Have each team member debrief the three culture words they chose with a partner, sharing why they chose those words and how they believe the team currently performs.

Step Four. Have each person write their three culture words on a Post-it note (one word per note) and stick them on a whiteboard. As a participant, put your own three words on the whiteboard along with the others.

Step Five. Ask a volunteer to cluster the words into common responses and report how many "votes" each word received.

Step Six. Ask the volunteer to facilitate an open discussion with the team to decide the top three to five words that best capture the ideal culture for the team.

Step Seven. Once they decide on three to five words, have your facilitator lead a discussion to rate each word based on your current team culture.

Step Eight. Break your team into smaller groups. Assign one group to brainstorm and record the behaviors that must STOP for the team to reach a 4 rating on each of the three to five culture words. Assign the other group to do the same with which behaviors the team must START in order to reach a 4 rating on each of the words.

Step Nine. Debrief the STOP group's results, asking the START group to make any additions to STOP behaviors. After the START group shares, ask the STOP group to add anything that's missing.

Step Ten. Remind the group that reaching a 4 rating isn't the goal, nor is it to master three to five words while ignoring the rest. Instead, the goal is to identify the culture the team wants, remove behaviors that weaken the culture, and add behaviors that strengthen the culture—while holding each other accountable in the process.

Compile the final lists and circulate them to all team members. Challenge each person to catch others engaging in affirming START behaviors that reinforce best cultural traits, or engaging in STOP behaviors.

Step Eleven: Add the topic of culture to weekly team meetings. Start each meeting asking a few people to share the best-in-class behaviors they saw in others during the previous week.

Resurvey your team every twelve months to evaluate the progress you've made in enhancing team-member perception around the three to five words you team wishes to elevate.

While this activity can start repairing an unhealthy culture and creating a healthy one, it does more than that, including the following:

- It shows your team members that leadership is about taking care of people and responding to their needs and desires.

- It practices collaboration in real-time around a "soft" issue. While teams sprint and huddle around bugs, collaboration is just as helpful around people issues.
- It increases engagement and spotlights the importance of DEI work. Every team member is given a voice and encouraged to use it.
- It empowers your team members to take ownership for the culture they want.
- It shares the accountability between you and each team member instead of making you responsible for all the effort.
- It provides countless opportunities for positive reinforcement within the team.
- It creates a common cultural team goal as a blueprint for a positive sub-culture within the corporate culture.

Kasey served as a tech manager for a large corporation with a healthy culture. Unlike her peers who managed "heavy tech" projects like infrastructure, architecture, network engineering, and system administration, her department did non-technical administrative support for the division. Since her team didn't require "hot skills," their salaries were smaller, and most of her jobs were considered entry-level. Even with robust recruitment inside and outside the company, Kasey struggled to find qualified workers who would take these jobs.

Kasey understood that the work and function of her team were different from other departments, so she set out to create a sub-culture that worked best for her team. She undertook a similar exercise as the one shared in this chapter. Her team distilled the culture they wanted into three words: *fun, engaging, and customer-centric.*

At their STOP and START meeting, Kasey learned from her employees that her team's culture didn't quite follow the *adhocracy culture* of the larger division. Much of their STOP/START discussion revolved around building a subset within the team so they could function as a *clan culture*, more like a small family.

Did it work? The proof was in the result. Before she defined and created the kind of culture that her team needed, it took her an average of 117 days to fill open positions in her team. Eighteen months after she and her team codesigned their team culture, Kasey filled openings within thirty days, with many of the applicants coming word-of-mouth through current team members.

Your company and team already have a culture. The kind of culture you reinforce and build—whether it's toxic or healthy—is up to you as the leader.

In the final section, Executional Leadership, I'll share ideas on how to use goals, planning, and feedback to influence your team's success.

SECTION V

EXECUTIONAL LEADERSHIP

Adopt the best mindset. Prioritize your people. Foster a collaborative team environment. Develop strategies and visions that others believe in and wish to follow. A leader following these best practices will win over the hearts and minds of their team.

But without execution—including the knowledge and skill required to get results—a leader won't see the rewards for their effort. Strategies don't implement themselves. They must be executed through intentional, focused leadership.

Companies struggle with too many, too few, or too confusing priorities to execute. Consider these survey results from executive leaders across the globe in various industries:

- 64 percent believe that their organization has too many *competing priorities*. Organizations with consistent above-average profitability and revenue growth credit their success to having three or fewer strategic priorities.
- 66 percent believe that their capabilities fail to support their corporate strategies (Sommerfield Communications 2011).

Leaders must create clear top goals for their teams. Then they must develop and execute plans to align their team's capabilities to the desired results. Finally, leaders must provide ongoing feedback throughout execution to reinforce the best efforts, offer course correction when needed, and reward outcomes.

CHAPTER 13
FOCUS ON TOP GOALS

GOAL-SETTING: THE FIRST STEP OF EXECUTION

Saving for retirement. Improving physical health. Enjoying marital harmony. Living in peace. Eating a balanced diet. Sleeping seven hours each night. Taking a dream vacation. Achieving work-life balance. Rearing independent children. Losing/gaining weight. Running a marathon. Becoming debt-free.

We set goals around a variety of things throughout our lives. We can achieve some goals in a relatively short time; other goals require constant focus, effort, and years to accomplish. It doesn't matter if you're trying to grow a 200-pound pumpkin, launch a new operating system, or move from a knowledge worker to a leader, the first step is the same: you must set a goal.

BENEFITS OF GOAL-SETTING

I don't think I need to belabor the point on why setting goals in our lives and work is critical to success. But let me share a handful of benefits that goal-setting helps you achieve.

Ted Turner, serial entrepreneur and founder of Cable Network News (CNN), summed up the intrinsic value of setting goals by this statement attributed to him, "You should set goals beyond your reach, so you always have something to live for."

Clarity

Setting a goal requires you to develop a clear picture of your desired achievement. When you build goals collaboratively with your team, they also get clear on what must be accomplished.

Focus

Where should you and your team expend effort? Goal-setting allows you to focus on what's most important instead of getting caught up in non-critical tasks and distractions.

Communication

In Chapter 5, I gave four reasons why leaders don't communicate. One is that they didn't always know *what* to communicate. Goals and goal updates give you something relevant to communicate with your team, peers, and immediate supervisor.

Commitment and Accountability

In Section III: Collaborative Leadership, I spelled out the benefits of collaborating with your team around joint projects. Imagine what happens to team member commitment when instead of informing them about your goals, you invite them to work with you to develop them. In my experience, creating goals with my teams secures both their commitment and accountability to those goals. After all, they aren't my goals. They're *ours*.

Feedback

I'll elaborate on this in Chapter 15. For now, I'll say that goals serve as the foundation for feedback with your team members, whether you're redirecting their efforts or acknowledging their successes.

Tracking

Goals give you a reason to measure successes as well as insight to any adjustments you need to make mid-course. Tracking or monitoring can sound like "big brother." But when tracking is linked to goals that team members understand, commit to, and make progress towards, tracking tells them how far they've come while giving them an earned sense of accomplishment.

GOAL-SETTING SYSTEMS

You know the benefits of goal-setting, and even if you work for a small company, you have goals that you're paid to achieve. The question is, what kind of goal-setting should you use with your *team*? For years, businesses followed "Management by Objectives" as outlined by in Peter Drucker's 1954 book, *The Practice of Management* (Drucker 1954). Hewlitt-Packard favored this goal-setting practice. But it's obsolete today.

Before telling you my favorite goal-setting process, I'll give you a short tour of models, tools, and strategy-management frameworks that remain popular in executional leadership today.

S.M.A.R.T. Goals

In 1981, George Duran, a consultant and former director of corporate planning for Washington Water Power company, wrote a paper called, "There's a S.M.A.R.T. Way to Write Management's Goals and Objectives." Doran created the *S*.M.A.R.T. model, which stands for *specific, measurable, attainable, realistic,* and *timely* goals. For many years, business schools and organizations followed this practice (Doran 1981, 35–36).

S.M.A.R.T. objectives and goals are concrete, which lets you know when you've successfully met a goal. But that strength also underscores its weakness. S.M.A.R.T. goals tell you about the result, but they don't offer a true road map of what's necessary to *achieve* those results.

Key Performance Indicators (KPIs)

Key performance indicators (KPIs) aren't goals; rather, they're part of a goal management system used to measure performance linked to goals. Many companies that use KPIs combine them with *balanced score cards* (BSCs) to create dashboards with easy-to-interpret graphics, letting you how you're performing against a goal. KPIs allow you track the progress of specific objectives or goals over time. The insights generated by KPIs can inform necessary redirection and decisions that must be made along the route (Qlik 2022).

A business consultant provided a great example of the weakness of KPIs by evaluating two employees against the KPIs and her personal observations. The consultant spent time studying Leah and James, two call-center employees. Leah answered one hundred calls per hour and was up for an award because of her impressive call volume. James handled only fifty calls per hour, and he was slated to receive performance coaching to get his numbers up.

But the numbers didn't tell the story about *how* each employee performed their jobs. Leah's customers complained about her abrupt tone, some even claiming she hung up on them. Many of the callers Leah "helped" needed to call back again, because Leah didn't resolve their problems. James, on the other hand, managed outstanding first contact closure with each caller, all while his customers called him courteous and respectful (King 2015).

If you looked just at the metric for calls the two employees handled, you would believe the company should clone Leah and coach James out the door, which would have proven a mistake. Quantity metrics can be readily quantified; qualitative data, though, needs a different tool for measurement.

I believe a weakness of KPIs is that they're often linked to compensation bonuses. This can encourage team members to put off tasks that aren't measured by the KPIs, so they can focus on only tasks linked to pay bonuses. And in the case of the two call center employees, Leah would receive a large bonus, while James would be looking for another job.

Balanced Score Cards (BSCs)

Balanced score cards (BSCs) are a part of the goal-setting process. BCSs are a strategy management framework that examines a corporate strategy from four perspectives: *financial, customer, internal process*, and *learning and growth*. BCAs are further broken down into *objectives, measures, initiatives,* and *action items* (Lucco 2022).

As stated earlier, many companies use BSCs as part of their KPIs. As a strategy map, BSCs clarify the metrics that define results and show the connection between multiple objectives.

But BSCs have their drawbacks. First, in my experience, leaders don't reevaluate them often enough. In most organizations, BSCs are written once a year and essentially forgotten. BSCs are as useful for the day-to-day execution as driving your car forward by using your rearview mirror.

Second, executives develop the BSC with little input from the departments doing the work. Since these goals are top-down, they lack the collaboration and accountability of goals created from the bottom up or sideways.

Third, like KPIs, most BSCs are linked to compensation bonuses. The challenge with linking goal obtainment with compensation is that humans set the goals. What human doesn't want to set an obtainable goal and reap a reward for reaching it? When I see a company achieving every goal they set, I assume that they set their goals too low (Marr 2021).

Finally, while BSCs provide an at-a-glance view of how the organization is performing on corporate strategic goals, they are too high-level to be of much use to a front-line leader.

Objectives and Key Results (OKRs)

Under Andy Grove's leadership at Intel, he moved the company from memory chips to microprocessors—thereby adding power to PCs while driving down their cost and increasing Intel's revenues from $1.9 billion to $26 billion. How did he manage a project of this scale? He created a strategy and then implemented it with something he called *objectives and key results* (OKRs) (Pines 2018).

One of Grove's disciples, John Doerr, worked with Grove at Intel where he first learned about OKRs. When he left Intel, he joined Kleiner Perkins Caufield & Byers, which became a major investor at a new company named Google. That's where he taught the concept of OKRs to Google cofounders Larry Page and Sergey Brin (Perdoo 2022). Later, Doerr wrote *Measure What Matters: How Google, Bono, and the Gates Foundation Rock the World with OKRs* (Doerr 2018).

Okay, enough about OKR history. But I wanted to be sure you know the pedigree of OKRs. Companies like Google, Adobe, Amazon, Dell, LinkedIn, Microsoft, Salesforce.com, Netflix, Oracle, Dropbox, Mozilla, Twitter, Nerd Wallet, Facebook, Spotify, and Yahoo all use OKRs to set their goals and achieve outstanding results.

WHAT ARE OKRS?

Unlike other goal-setting methods where goals are meant to be easy to obtain, OKRs involve setting high, ambitious goals—almost unrealistically high by intention. The "goal" of OKRs is less on goal-obtainment than giving the team a lofty target. Even if the team doesn't meet the OKR, teams accomplish more than if they were given a goal they could reach in their sleep. OKRs force team members to keep a clear focus on what they strive to achieve. Forget comfort zones and status quo thinking. Great successes require equally great leaps into new thinking.

Martial arts legend Bruce Lee could have been talking about OKRs in this statement commonly attributed to him, "A goal is not always meant to be reached; it often serves simply as something to aim at."

THE SIX CHARACTERISTICS OF OKRS

What makes OKRs such an effective goal-setting tool is their unique characteristics:

1. They are *specific,* removing any ambiguity of what you wish to achieve.
2. They are *concentrated,* allowing for a focus on top priorities.
3. They are *measurable,* giving you the ability to know your performance in real-time.

4. They are *flexible,* affording you the opportunity to change as needed, such as by adjusting cycle times.
5. They are *simple,* eliminating complicated processes and systems.
6. They are *transparent,* meaning they are public to everyone in the organization, letting other areas know what you're working on so they can see how they can help and understand where you share accountabilities (Tú 2021).

When US President John Kennedy told the audience at Rice University about his intention to reach the moon, he communicated a clear, specific objective about what he wished to see accomplished.

"We shall send to the moon 240,000 miles away, a giant rocket, more than 300 feet tall on an untried mission to an unknown celestial body, and then return it safely to Earth," Kennedy told the crowd (Taylor 2021).

Not only did Kennedy state his vision with specificity and crispness, but his objective also seemed impossible, since what he hoped to achieve fell into the category of challenges that had never been attempted.

Similarly, OKR goals aren't meant to be easily obtained.

While not a specific characteristic of OKRs, I want to add one more distinction: *OKRs aren't linked with compensation or bonuses.* Unlike other goal-setting and reporting systems that rely on "pay-for-performance" as a large part of the motivation to get them done, OKRs rely on collaborative teamwork, team members doing what they do best, and intrinsic motivation.

OKRs start with lofty *objectives*, a statement describing an ideal future, development, or accomplishment. Here are some OKR objectives for tech:

- Accelerate product revenue growth.
- Improve product reputation (Google 2022).
- Delight our customers (Castro 2021).

Remember, objectives shouldn't be obtained easily. Hence the word *lofty*. Instead of "improve such-and-such by 3 percent," OKR objectives require a big stretch and an all-team effort.

The NFL evaluates leg power of potential draftees by putting athletes through the Standing long jump at the National Scouting Combine. In 2015, Byron Jones set a world record by jumping 12'3". Contrast that with an NFL draftee rated as "excellent" in the long jump if they can leap 8' and 2 ½". We non athletes would need three jumps to clear 12 feet! (Wood 2008).

Think of an OKR as a goal set to beat the standing long jump world record, an accomplishment that beats *excellent* by 4 feet and 150 percent!

Objectives detail the *what*, not the *how*. How to accomplish an objective is detailed with three to five *key results*, which serve as mini-goals to be accomplished on the journey toward the *objective*. Under each key result follows several action items outlining the specific work needed to support the key results and, ultimately, the objective.

Key results themselves are written to describe outcomes, not activities and tasks. Tasks come later. A key result spells out *what will be accomplished* and *by when*, like, "Create a new data center in the Midwest region by September 30, 20XX," or, "Increase the number of data recovery sites from three to five by July 1, 20XX."

Key results are further broken into *tasks* (and *action plans*) that support the work required to fulfill each key result. As the name states, tasks outline the specific actions that will be taken.

Here are some examples of OKRs:

Example Number One
Objective: Improve release quality
Key Results:

- Reduce post-release bugs from twenty-five to six average
- Increase code unit test cover from 25 percent to 50 percent
- Increase pre-release team member testing from one to three average

Example Number Two
Objective: Improve stability of product releases
Key Results:

- Reduce monthly average unscheduled downtime from eighty-two minutes to ten
- Reduce emergency production batches average from eight to two average
- Increase on-time releases from 40 percent to 75 percent

MAXIMIZING YOUR OKRS

If you've ever made New Year's resolutions, you know how unlikely you are to keep them. Let's say on December 31 of any given year, you resolve to drop twenty pounds and run a marathon the next year. Most people are more likely to order pizza delivery and pass out on the couch by 1:30 a.m. on January 1 than to drop the weight and start running. Research says that about 25 percent of people stick with their "resolutions" throughout January; only 8 percent stick with their goals throughout the entire year (Prossack 2018).

When you set a personal goal and make a conscious decision to achieve it, your chances of success range from 10 to 25 percent. But certain behaviors increase your success rate. For example:

- Creating a specific plan for how you will achieve that goal increases your success to 50 percent.
- Sharing your goal and plan with another person to demonstrate your commitment to achieving success and make you accountable to your goal increases your success rate to 65 percent.
- Scheduling and conducting follow-ups with that person to report on your progress improves your chances for success to 95 percent (Wissman 2018).

Those success rates hold true for goals where you have direct control over the outcomes, since they involve personal willpower and behavioral change. OKRs, on the other hand, involve complex, moving parts that require the alignment and action of a team to achieve objectives, since they are set at high levels.

Personal goals and OKRs aren't exactly an apples-to-apples comparison, but they both share a secret to improving results: *collaboration* and *accountability*.

Following are some tips to get started with your OKRs.

Create and Use an OKR-centric Mantra

Setting goals might not seem like the type of work that could benefit from a mantra, but I think the traits of OKRs made them mantra-friendly. Look at this list to kickstart your thoughts on creating and using your own OKR-centric mantra:

- *Our success is based on our focus.*
- *If we can envision it, we can achieve it.*
- *My job is to ensure that all team members know our priorities.*
- *If our work were easy, anyone could do it.*
- *High goals give me something to shoot for.*

Involve Your Team in the Process

Top-level, high-impact OKRs are normally set at the corporate level by the executive team by engaging with teams in the process. Then each leadership level creates their own OKRs in support of the higher-level OKRs.

Some leaders create OKRs for their teams. But then those become *your* OKRs and *your* responsibility to accomplish. Instead, I collaborate with my team in the process. My role is to provide clarity, communicate, demonstrate commitment, and show accountability for achieving great things within our team. I use the Eisenhower Matrix to help my teams prioritize our work.

The Eisenhower Matrix comes from a 1954 speech former US President Dwight Eisenhower delivered at Northwestern University: "I have two kinds of problems, the urgent and the important. The urgent are not important, and the important are never urgent."

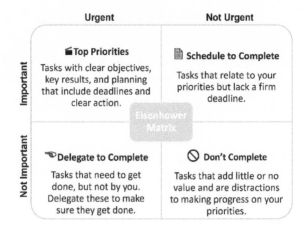

Also known as the Eisenhower Decision Principle, the Eisenhower Matrix helps leaders think through tasks to differentiate *urgent* from *not urgent* as well as *important* from *not important*. Tasks that are both urgent and important serve as your top priorities. We label things that are *urgent and important* as P0; *not urgent but important* as P1; *urgent but not important* as p3; and *not urgent and not important* as p4. Obviously, we prioritize our work and time starting with 0 followed by 1, 2, etc.

I'll explain where the Eisenhower Matrix works well with your team shortly, but first, I suggest taking the following steps in creating your OKRs.

Step One: Do prework. If possible, schedule an in-person meeting with your team, ideally in a room with a large whiteboard. Pre-write each objective high up on the board, leaving room underneath and next to them for later work. Have pens and stacks of Post-it notes on hand.

Step Two: Review objectives. Start the meeting by reviewing each objective. Ask the team for their ideas on refining the objectives until it is written clearly and concisely enough so that nearly anyone in the organization could read and comprehend it. That means leave out in-team or subject-matter expert jargon.

Andy Grove, the former CEO of Intel and creator of the OKR process, asked two questions of his team when they met to develop OKRs:

1. "Where do I want to go?" which uncovered the *objective*.

2. "How will I pace myself to see if I am getting there?" which outlined the *key results* (Grove 1983).

Step Three: Develop key results. You'll spend most of your time adding key *results* and *tasks* to your *objectives*. As a leader, you should already know the skills and abilities of each team member, but each team member is the subject-matter expert of what they personally "bring to the table." Remember, this isn't about assigning a to-do list to people; this is tapping into their strengths, thoughts, and passions while securing their commitment to progressing on your OKR.

As an example, let's say my team's objective is to: "Improve page performance on the landing pages." Then I prime the pump by saying, "I think one of the key results would include KR1: reduce page full loading time from four seconds to one second."

Then I ask them to write one possible key result per Post-it note for several minutes, until they each have written several key results. Once they've run out of ideas, I'll ask them to post their key results on the whiteboard under "Objective Number One." I'll ask for a volunteer to read off each key result from the Post-it notes on the whiteboard and work with the team to cluster like ideas together.

Once all key results are clustered, I'll ask the team to discuss what they believe are the top three to five key results that will give us the best start towards *objective number one*.

Step Four. Evaluate key results using the Eisenhower Matrix. I've used the Eisenhower Matrix frequently enough within my teams that they quickly identify the results that are *urgent* and *important*. Once we've narrowed down our top three to five key results through the lens of the Eisenhower Matrix, we'll work as a team to write out each key result in the most clear, measurable language.

Using the example of "Improve page performance on the landing pages," my team might add the following key results:

[P0] KR1: Reduce page full loading time from 4 seconds to 1 second.

[P1] KR2: Increase page security rating from 60 to 80.

[P2] KR3: Increase page structure score from 50 to 80 percent.

Notice that each key result is prioritized using the P0–P4 system. At times, we end up with P5 or more. Those key results are bigger stretches but also lower priorities, so we rarely get to them. But this process allows us to document thinking that may be valuable for future projects and OKRs.

Step Five: Develop tasks. Following the same process used to develop key results for *objective number one*, I have my team brainstorm on Post-it notes the tasks required to complete key results, starting with *key result number one*.

> Tasks are nothing more than drilling down the steps we
> plan to take at a granular, actionable level.

Again, I'll ask a volunteer to cluster like-tasks under the key result and facilitate a team discussion on which tasks seem most relevant to reaching the key result.

Step Six. Evaluate key results through the Eisenhower Matrix. Once again, I'll use the lens of the Eisenhower Matrix to identify the tasks that are both *urgent* and *important* to accomplish.

When you finalize *objective number one*, develop three to five key results supporting the objective, and add multiple tasks that support each key result, you've completed your first OKR. Follow the same process for each of your OKRs.

Now That You Have Direction...

I believe OKRs are the best goal-setting process used today. Even in organizations that use KPIs, doing OKRs with your team provides you a crisp roadmap as you set a vision, identify top priorities, and nail down actionable results. Simultaneously, the OKR process reinforces multiple leadership themes already shared in this book. For example, the process does the following:

- Encourages personal and professional growth (Chapter 1)
- Equips you to embrace and lead change (Chapter 2)
- Stretches the team to "stay hungry, stay foolish" (Chapter 3)

- Demonstrates your care for team members as you value their opinions, skills, and contributions (Chapter 4)
- Connects the dots about *why* and *how* you will move forward (Chapter 5)
- Fosters team member engagement (Chapter 6)
- Provides focus to your coaching efforts (Chapter 7)
- Fosters collaboration (Chapter 8–10)
- Empowers others to take ownership, initiative, and accountability (Chapter 11)
- Fuels a positive, healthy team culture (Chapter 12)

Developing and working OKRs with your team makes reaching milestones a collaborative team effort. The process reinforces that no single person can achieve results on their own. OKRs give you ready-made agenda topics, and each meeting focuses on updates to progress and barriers that must be removed for success.

I consider OKRs as the best execution tool at my disposal as a leader. Another tool I like is one developed at Facebook called a *postmortem*, a process we use to troubleshoot project roadblocks and failures before they happen (Meta 2022). Without going into detail about the exercise, the leader asks team members to envision that the project is over, and it failed. The exercise asks team members to think through what caused the project to fail. This process allows teams to avoid following down those paths of failure before the project even begins.

Armed with your OKRs, it's time to build capacity to drive your results forward.

CHAPTER 14
BUILD CAPABILITIES TO DRIVE RESULTS

STRATEGIES CAN'T REMAIN STATIC

Research, business intelligence, data analytics, market research, trend analysis, and key metrics all play a part in developing corporate strategies. Data is so important that former Netscape CEO Jim Barksdale has been attributed as saying, "If we have data, let's look at data. If all we have are opinions, let's go with mine."

Let's simplify the objective of most organizations: make money. How a company chooses to accomplish that comes from a host of strategies. The following list is incomplete, but it gives you an idea of strategies that organizations use to generate revenue.

Any of these strategies can work, depending on your internal capabilities and willingness to change course when needed.

Increasing cross-sales	Promoting sustainability
Capturing a growing market	Increasing customer retention
Reducing customer acquisition costs	Pricing strategies
Enhancing customer service	Improving product innovation
Selling new products	Improving quality of existing products
Improving the ease of doing business	Developing new technology

What industrialist Andrew Carnegie has been quoted as saying about investments is just as true about strategies: "Put all your eggs in one basket, and then watch that basket." His sage wisdom wasn't advocating just watching your resources as they "go to hell in a handbasket." Instead, his words served as a warning to carefully monitor your "basket," so you can do an about-face when external or internal drivers require a new direction.

Not every organization follows this wisdom. German-Hong Kong shipbuilding firm MV Werften spent years and $1.6 billion constructing the world's largest cruise ship, Global Dream II. Built to carry nine thousand passengers, the ship boasts an indoor waterpark and a full-size movie theater (Newman 2022).

The strategy to build the world's largest cruise ship was put in motion at the peak popularity of cruising. All data and business intelligence indicated that the world could use a bigger, more luxurious cruise ship.

Then in 2019, nearly a dozen cruise ships made the news for being, as CNN called them, "incubators for measles and other diseases," such the chicken pox, influenza, norovirus, campylobacter, rotavirus, and even E. coli (Chavez 2019). Cruise lines suffered from the bad press. Then another nail got pounded in the cruise-line coffin: COVID-19. Cruise lines, having no other revenue streams besides booking people to travel in floating disease incubators, were hit hard.

Left with a $1.6 billion dollar investment with $200 million needed to complete Global Dreams II in the declining cruising industry, MV Werften went bankrupt. Their unwatched and unaltered strategy is scheduled to be sold for scrap in 2023 (Buitendijk 2022).

TWO WAYS STRATEGIES DEVELOP

Strategies develop in a planning phase but get refined throughout execution. This happens via two methods, which we'll explore in this subsection.

Deliberative

When most people think of developing a strategy, they think of a small room of business leaders poring over business intelligence. In such a process, executive teams at the planning table follow a deliberate process to negotiate the best strategy based on everything they know. By the time they're finished, they sit back, look over their strategy document, and say something like, "Here's our best thinking. Now we need to act. We'll do some additional planning, and then we can implement this."

This process seems obvious, logical, and foolproof. Starting with a blank piece of paper, executives develop data and research-based strategies that grow into implementation plans—like the strategic thinking and implementation planning to build the world's largest $1.6 billion cruise ship as the industry continued to grow. MV Werften and their investors likely followed an equally linear, logical, and foolproof strategy. And they failed.

No one can fault a company for building a strategy around business intelligence. The error doesn't lie with the strategy. The problem lies with believing a deliberative strategy is like an arrow leaving a bow string, which once launched, has an immutable trajectory. Strategies must evolve and change based on business and economic conditions as well as business insights learned from those implementing the strategy.

When the "rubber" of the deliberative process of strategy development hits the "road" of execution, the people closest to implementation must tap into their own insights to change direction midcourse.

Trial and Error

While less prescriptive than the work of developing a strategy, trial and error relies on continuous learning, experimentation, and adjustments during execution. Execution requires implementation leaders to think differently: "We planned to execute X, but X seems unreachable at this time. Have we learned enough to try X again? Is it time to rethink X and execute Y?"

The "best" strategy developed today may fail to show a return on investment, unless those implementing the strategy apply trial and error, learning to tweak their approach. In the case of MV Werften, COVID-19 should have been a final warning for the company to stop work and cut their losses unless a buyer could be found.

Scottish poet Robert Burns got it right when he wrote, "The best laid plans of mice and men often go awry."

Even when corporate executives develop world-class strategies, those strategies must grow, evolve, morph, and change throughout implementation. That happens when "people on the ground" start creating, acting, testing, rethinking, and reimagining throughout the execution phase.

REVISITING MOUNT FUJI

Let me revisit bringing the Google Street View project to the mountaintop. Our strategy was simple: travel to each mountain, climb it, and photograph panoramic views from the seven tallest mountains in the world.

Climbing Mount Fuji happened in a serendipitous way. A colleague and I were already in Tokyo on business. We'd scheduled our climb to Mt. Everest Base Camp a few months down the road. But then we started thinking, *Heck, since we're already so close to Mount Fuji, why not check this one off our list?*

"It's not that big," my friend added excitedly. "We can be in and out in a day!"

We had a strategy, photography equipment, and proximity to Mount Fuji. What more did we need?

Well, it turns out we were grossly underprepared for our first attempt. We hoped to make our "short climb" up Mount Fuji before daylight, so we could catch the sunrise from the peak. The night before our climb, instead of resting and conducting rigorous preplanning for the climb, we watched a sumo wrestling competition late into the night while drinking too many beers. Our lack of study meant we didn't know we'd planned to scale Mount Fuji at the worst time of year.

"Whatever," we shrugged. "We're just going to do it anyway."

"Doing it anyway" included having neither the proper permits nor clothing for the climb. We also hadn't thought about transportation from Tokyo to Mount Fuji, so we took a taxi to the base of the mountain. We had no idea that Mount Fuji was sixty-plus miles from Tokyo or that our cab ride would cost $700!

But we had a strategy to implement, right? *We're just going to do it anyway* started to ring hollow in my head.

After five hours of arduous hiking, we were only halfway to the top. This "little hike" took ten hours in freezing temperatures, leaving the two of us huddling together in our inadequate clothing while our bones quaked from the cold. Everyone else on the mountain wore GORE-TEX jackets and hiking boots with crampons and used walking sticks to support their weight. Not us. In tennis shoes and fleece jackets, we might as well have been wearing flipflops and Speedos while carrying bottles of beer.

But we didn't quit. We knew if we made it to the top, we'd have stories to tell and lessons to take with us. Finally, we reached the summit and felt the adrenaline of achievement soothe our tired bodies.

We learned many things on this first climb. First, we needed to conduct our own due diligence to know the environment we climbed in. Our strategy looked great on paper (and in our heads), but when that strategy met the mountain, we were utterly ill-prepared. Second, we had to get the right equipment. The sweat from our efforts turned to ice, and our bodies trembled. While we expected cold weather, we hadn't anticipated the extreme butt-freezing temperatures we'd hit at 14,000 feet. Finally, we learned that it's much easier to craft a broad strategy than to execute that same strategy. That strategy we crafted in some distant, safe, climate-controlled office didn't look at all like what we experienced the second we stepped out of the taxi at the base of Mount Fuji. With a little more planning based on real-world conditions, we would have chosen a route that would have cut off half the distance to the summit.

Our strategy wasn't flawed, but we needed to apply onsite intelligence and planning to be successful. Trial-and error learning turned our static strategy into a dynamic one. Each lesson we learned, even the most grueling ones, seeded our next successes. In fact, we took those lessons with us the during our next attempt to reach the Everest Base Camp, as well as Mount Kilimanjaro where what we learned yielded success.

ALIGNING THE ORGANIZATION AROUND YOUR STRATEGY

At the beginning of the skyscraper age, architect Louis Sullivan gained renown for his steel-framed buildings that reached ever-higher. "Form follows function" served as his mantra, indicating Sullivan's belief that the shape of each building he constructed should be based on how the building would be used.

His protégé, Frank Lloyd Wright, took Sullivan's mantra one step further: "Form follows function—that has been misunderstood. Form and function should be one, joined in a spiritual union." In other words, everything between drafting a blueprint to the end use were inseparable (Guggenheim 2022).

What's true for architecture is also true for how your team should be organized to achieve a strategy. Your team and business strategy must be entwined in that "spiritual union" that Wright spoke about.

So what if you hired people to do X, but the new strategy calls for Y? Is it time to replace your team members?

Instead of replacing your entire team each time a new strategic direction emerges, it's possible to merge form and function into an almost spiritual union. In this subsection are three tips to help you maximize your existing talents to reach new heights.

Tap into Organization-Wide Capabilities

After you work with a team for a short time, you develop a good sense of what each individual and the team collective bring to the table around project execution. I shared earlier that I regularly meet with people outside of my own organization to learn what other leaders are working on. Instead of waiting for dots to connect themselves in front of me, I went looking for the dots so I could make some of my own connections (Chapter 5). I didn't only connect with leaders around projects but also around their people and capabilities. Why would I rush out to hire someone with a Y skillset, if I could tap into someone with immediate capabilities to support my strategic imperative?

Leaders must look beyond their own team capabilities to scan organizational capabilities. If you find internal capabilities, you've saved your organization money while shortening the learning curve for new hires getting up to speed on your project and culture.

Separate "Everyday" Tasks from Strategic Work

Cofounder and managing partner at Navalent, Ron Carucci, believes that when the lines blur between required "everyday work" and strategic work, the effort and outcomes on projects linked to your differentiation strategy suffer. Everyday tasks include "necessary evils" and tasks that could be handled by nearly any team member. Strategic work is what drives progress on core priorities (Carucci and Shappell 2022).

Ted served as a tech manager in a non-tech business where he oversaw a team working on change control for a large rollout within the company. As the launch date approached, he wanted to travel to the location where most of his team members worked so he could support them. But when he called to book travel, his corporate credit card didn't work. Confused, he called someone in finance for help.

"We had your card suspended," the finance office told him. "While your payment with your company card is up-to-date, our records indicate that you haven't submitted any corporate reimbursement forms for the last three months."

"That's because as we get ready to launch," Ted responded, giving the name of the project he'd been spearheading, "I've been traveling every week. I plan to complete those forms once the launch is done."

"Once you do, I'll have your card reinstated," the person on the other end told him.

Bureaucratic "everyday" tasks linked to policies and procedures interfered with Ted's ability to oversee strategic work. Ted immediately assigned a team member to go into the corporate portal and catch him up on entering receipts. That's when he found another barrier: he'd need to share his login information with his employee, a compliance no-no.

Long story short, Ted took the time to complete his expense reports. After his project launched, he worked with HR, finance, and legal to change their policy. He and his team created a separate reimbursement page where employees could exchange passwords. After that, he forever delegated that "everyday" task to someone who could do it instead of him.

Sometimes policies and "busywork" get in the way of the most meaningful work. Once again, using the Eisenhower Matrix (differentiating between urgent,

important, non-urgent, and non-important) can help
you spot and "outsource" tasks that aren't strategic.
And when you find ones that don't add value, work to
eliminate them.

If you feel like you have limited resources, ask yourself if
your team members with the greatest competence are drowning
in everyday work instead of focusing on strategic work. Hire
entry-level team members to do the required busywork, so your
top resources can free up time to tackle work of strategic importance. This practice brings new people into your pipeline who
can grow and develop their skills to assume work of greater
significance over time.

Move Decision-Making Next to Execution

If you work in a large corporation, you know the three plagues
that choke team members: *death by PowerPoint*, *death by
committee*, and *death by executive decision-making*.

Nothing disrupts progress on high-impact projects like
needing to be granted permission from an executive to make
day-to-day decisions. Imagine working on a project where the
sole decision-maker is an executive. This executive not only
works in a different office, but they also work across the globe in
a different time zone. Each time your project reaches a cross-
road, you must wait to receive the go-ahead from headquarters.
That's like trying to thread a needle when you hold the thread
and someone else holds the needle…miles away.

I don't enjoy being micromanaged, and I can't imagine
micromanaging other professionals. Projects require differing
levels of approvals in organizations. Unless there's a specific

reason to do otherwise, I push decision-making down as close as possible to where the work takes place. By doing this, projects benefit from the trial-and-error insights team members learn while testing new ideas. This practice also rewards earned autonomy. Once team members show me that they can handle decision-making responsibly, I empower them to call the shots with matters that match their expertise and experience.

Learn to Read the Signs

While climbing to the Everest Basecamp, we used local guides. Fortunately, our guide spoke decent English, so we could ask questions and learn from him during our ascent.

"I noticed that you never consult a map or a compass," I said to him while we trekked. The mountain looked like a white sheet dotted with rocks. At times, we reached forks with footprints in the snow going in both directions. "How do you know where to go or if we're on the right path?"

"Well," he said, "I grew up here, so I know the mountain well."

"But how do you remember every trail?" I persisted. "We must have come to a dozen forks in the trail, and you seem so sure that we're on the right one."

"That's true," he laughed. "I can't possibly remember every trail. But you see, there are markers along the way. If you know what to look for, the rock cairns point the way."

He pointed to a cairn near the trail. "See that? Those stones mark the path."

After he told me what to look for, I spotted cairns everywhere we trekked. *How have I climbed so many peaks and never noticed these?* I wondered.

Later in the trek, I heard members of our group asking each

other, "How do we know we're on the right route?" Armed with new knowledge, I told them about the cairns.

But our sherpa held even more secrets. At times he would stop, scan the horizon, sniff the air, and lead us to a different path.

"Why are we switching trails?" I asked.

"It's going to rain on that side," he said confidently. "It will be too dangerous to pass. There's a river over there. Once it floods, the trail will become impassable."

While I'll never be a "native" to a mountainous environment, I've learned to spot warning signs at work. Once I learned what to look for, I could sense impending doom or success on the projects I worked on.

Early in my career at Google, I got put on a project team for Google Plus to work the privacy side of the team. As a newbie, I was like a sub-sub team lead. The project was deemed a failure, and the failure had nothing to do with technological limitations or lack of innovation. Some would say it failed because of pride and not watching the signs. With quite a bit of skepticism and internal debate about this project, some would say the project lead made poor decisions. Tired of hearing tough questions from within the project team, one of the leaders asked that they lock down the dashboards so we couldn't watch how the product was performing. Instead of practicing transparency, welcoming tough questions, and empowering team members to fix bugs that they found, this decision kept any of us from knowing just how buggy the platform had become.

Since that time, I've known how to read the cairns and warning signs. I also learned through that leader's bad example that top tech leaders are open, vulnerable, and instill trust in their teams. I've also conditioned my mindset not to dwell on flaws but rather any positive lessons I can glean from each experience. And I've structured the contents of this book with positive exam-ples to help evolving tech leaders avoid these pitfalls of poor leadership. By learning to read the positive signs in the environment and project team, you can maximize project success and minimize the risk of encountering "bad weather" on your journey.

BALANCING SPEED AND FLAWS

"Move fast and break things" has long been the mantra in Silicon Valley, a phrase that taps into the hacker roots of many early tech team members. Breaking things isn't actually the goal; instead, breaking things is often a necessary byproduct when innovating quickly. If you're creating bug-free solutions, you aren't moving quickly enough.

Another phrase that captures the need for speed in tech is "innovate now, optimize later." Pushing an imperfect solution forward will create some *technical debt*— which pushes to a later date the errors produced when prioritizing speed over perfection —and that's to be expected.

When a software engineer for OKCupid pushed a small change to their website, the system crashed. One small enhancement "broke things," and the server went down for hours.

Did the engineer get fired? Did he, at the very least, get reprimanded or demoted to making coffee for the other engineers?

No. In fact, OKCupid CEO Mike Maxim had a saying: "We can't sacrifice forward momentum for technical debt."

Technical debt, and the rework required to fix imperfect innovations, gets addressed later. Maxim wisely understood that technical debt grew at the same pace of the speed of innovation, and he didn't expect the absence of technical debt if it meant slowing innovation.

The engineer concluded that, "Even if you spend a whole bunch of time trying to make something that's perfect, you won't necessarily succeed" (V.C. 2018).

Flawless execution sacrifices speed. And in tech, speed is everything.

On the other hand, technical debt, like monetary debt, must be paid off. Otherwise, it accumulates more debt in the form of interest. In tech, unpaid debt is like building a house on an off-kilter foundation. While the foundation might look square as it sets on the ground, as soon as you add walls and height, the structure becomes less stable. Unless you fix the unstable foundation before continuing work, the system will eventually come crashing down.

Adherent of the "move fast and break things" mantra for years, Mark Zuckerberg rethought his position as Meta grew and evolved. Knowing that unpaid technical debt would eventually bring development to a halt, Zuckerberg revised his mantra to "move fast with sustainable infrastructure." He explained, "[W]hen you build something that you don't have to fix ten times, you can move forward on top of what you've built" (Statt 2014).

While the risk tolerance of senior executives sets the balance between speed and imperfection at the corporate level, the immediate leader strikes the right balance during day-to-day execution.

KNOW YOUR DEVELOPMENT VELOCITY

In tech, velocity is "an indicator or an estimate of how much work a development team can complete, based on previous timeframes of similar work." Calculating your average team velocity allows you to better forecast the amount of time your team requires to reach milestones and goals (Dumitrescu 2021).

Velocity is a measurement of speed, not quality. The measurement can't differentiate between simple work and critical work, or rework and new work. It's rather a measurement of work completed. If your team spends days developing a feature with marginal value that no one cares about, that adds into your *developmental velocity*.

You can see how important developmental velocity is as a leader. Knowing what your team can deliver *and* when to shepherd your team's efforts into high-value efforts increases the value your team adds to the organization.

You can measure developmental velocity by units of work (engineering hours, user stories, story points, and so on), or you can measure by units of time (iterations, sprints, and weeks). However you choose to measure velocity, the results give you a snapshot of your team's current capabilities. If your velocity needs to be increased, you may need to add capabilities through hiring or adding hours to your current team. Or you may need to identify non-value-added work that can be eliminated or delayed.

UNDERSTAND YOUR KEY METRICS

Knowing your developmental velocity allows you to adjust staffing levels by utilizing expertise from outside your team. You can also reprioritize where your team spends their time. Metrics, though, give you the big picture of the impact your team and organization are making towards higher-level goals.

Let's say you have an OKR of "[P0] O1: Increase the quality of our mobile app." What corporate metric does it connect to? If your OKR links to a strategic priority, the proof should be reflected on a metric.

This book isn't about developing business strategies and

metrics, but you should be familiar with some of the most common metrics that organizations track. Not only will the metric provide you with insight on how your work impacts the organization's success, but it also gives you data to show your team the results of their efforts. Remember, when people believe their work ties into something that could change the world, they don't hold back.

Following are some of the most common business metrics.

Customer Acquisition Cost (CAC)
CAC measures the total cost to your organization to close a new customer.

Customer Lifetime Value (CLTV)
This metric estimates how much a customer will spend on your business over their lifetime.

Monthly Recurring Revenue (MRR)
This metric estimates how much revenue you generate each month.

Churn
This metric tells you how many customers you're losing.

It costs a company five to twenty-five times more money to keep an existing customer than to secure a new one. That's why churn serves as a critical metric. The best sales team in the world will struggle to find new customers if the rate of exiting customers grows too high (Gallo 2014).

Some metrics see common use in tech development. Following is a short list of tech metrics.

NPS and CSAT Scores

Net promoter scores (NPS) and *customer satisfaction scores* (CSAT) tell you what your users think of your work. The NPS score can show if your customers love your product and will likely tell others, or if they hate it and may tell others about their negative experiences.

Referrals

While your NPS tells you about the customers' loyalty to your product, referrals measure their behavior after they have become loyal. If they bring other customers with them through referrals, they are considered brand ambassadors and a powerful piece of your informal salesforce.

Activation

Activation measures how many people started using your product. It records when a customer first starts using your product or if they use your free trial and find enough value to become a paid subscriber. *Time to value* is often measured as part of activation, and it tells you how long a customer must use your product before they realize the value of what you offer.

DAU/MAU Ratio

The *daily active users* (DAU) to *monthly active users* (MAU) ratio measures how often people engage with your product. DAU tracks unique users who engage with your product in in a twenty-four-hour period. MAU reports the number of unique users who engage with your product over a thirty-day window (Geckoboard 2022).

Retention

Just like team-member retention rates can give leaders insight about tenure and engagement, retention at the product level tells you about repeat customer use and interaction with your product.

Engagement
Twitter, LinkedIn, Facebook, Instagram, Snapchat, and other social media platforms want more than a user to sign up for a free account. They measure user *engagement* to evaluate how a customer uses the service, how often they check their feeds, who they interact with, and what features add the most value (Ajiboye 2021).

HOW TECH LEADERS MAXIMIZE TEAM CAPABILITIES

Maximizing team capabilities isn't a one-and-done endeavor. Each new project and any churn in your team, refinement of corporate strategy, or OKR requires a leader to maintain their ability to deliver results.

Earlier I shared about the study we did while I worked at Google called Project Aristotle, which explored what makes a team great. The project name was taken from an Aristotle quote: "The whole is greater than the sum of its parts." That's what top leaders do. They maximize *the team's* ability to execute.

While it might sound like a matter of semantics, the first thing Project Aristotle did was differentiate between a *work group* and a *team*. Google found that teams are highly interdependent in how they make decisions, plan work, solve problems, and review progress. Team members need one another to get work done.

Google determined that the top performing teams had more to do with *how the team functioned together* than with *which individuals were on the team*. Google identified five critical features of great teams (Rozovsky 2015):

1. *Psychological safety* (shared in Chapters 4 and 7)
2. *Dependability.* Team members consistently complete quality work on time.
3. *Structure and clarity.* Team members know what's expected of them, the roadmap for meeting those expectations, and the critical nature of individual performance on the team.
4. *Meaning.* Team members find purpose in their work.
5. *Impact.* Team members believe their work makes a difference.

Look at those five items. How do you maximize the performance of your team? Create a team environment where each member is afforded psychological safety, rewarded for dependability, offered structure and clarity, given meaningful work, and knows how they make a positive impact.

Create and Use Capability-Building Mantra

If you've ever run a marathon, you know the thrill, sweet pain, adrenaline, and utter joy of crossing the finish line. Running a marathon is awesome. Training for a marathon is, well, a bit less awesome. Tech offers many "sexy" roles in engineering and development where creativity and innovation rule the day. Tech leaders, though, know that *building capability* within their teams can be just as sexy.

A mantra will help you treat building capability as a priority. After all, OKRs and strategies don't implement themselves. Only by building capability can you put any main plan into action.

See if any of these mantras can help you develop and use your own capability-building mantra:

- *I will build a team where the whole is greater than the sum of its parts.*
- *I will guide my team using data as well as ground intelligence we gather along the journey.*
- *If I can borrow talent from within the organization, I don't need to hire additional people for my own team.*
- *We will move fast on top of stable architecture.*
- *I am on the lookout for signs that we need to change directions.*

Launch and Iterate

Both Google and Facebook practice a "launch and iterate" philosophy where teams move quickly to get an experiment out the door, while learning and iterating as it progresses. Be willing to execute your best plan based on the intelligence you have at the time, and look to learn and make changes along the way.

Carefully consider various approaches to your challenge. Don't shy away from a viable solution just because you lack the skill set within your team. Shop within your organization for those who can partner with your team. Keeping your mind and options open to nonlinear solutions often reveals optimum solutions. And learn as you grow!

Accelerate Your Development Velocity

Terminal velocity is a physics term referring to the constant speed a freely-falling object reaches when the friction of the medium through which it falls (like air or water) prevents further acceleration. A skydiver in a belly-to-earth freefall position reaches the speed of about 120 miles per hour (mph); however, by tightening your form, focusing on what you're trying to achieve, not allowing distractions, and making sure you have the right training and skills before you jump, you can accelerate your velocity, increasing your speed to about 200 mph.

Tech leaders can shape development velocity in much the same way as a skydiver can increase their velocity through the air. Making sure your team has the

$$V_t = \sqrt{\frac{2mg}{\rho A C_d}}$$

right internal tools and processes, you can shave precious developer time required to build and ship to market.

At Google, I did quite a bit of work on data-driven approaches to measuring and improving engineering productivity. We created a *goals/signals/metrics* (GSM) framework to inform our metrics (Jaspen 2021).

Goals are a statement of our desired end result, remaining mindful of five key factors called QUANTS:

- *Quality* of the code
- *Attention* from engineers
- *Intellectual* complexity
- *Tempo* and velocity
- *Satisfaction* of engineers

Signals are things we want to measure, but they might not be measurable. When we couldn't measure a signal, we'd create a metric that closely reflected the measure of the key signal.

Maximizing team capabilities requires a blend of art and science. If expanding the capabilities within a team had a "secret sauce," that sauce would be called a leader—one who balances team member care with data.

In the final chapter, I will tie all the principles of this book together around the magical elixir called *feedback*.

CHAPTER 15
OFFER (AND RECEIVE) ONGOING FEEDBACK

PUTTING THE PIECES TOGETHER

In Section I, Personal Leadership, I focused on the mindset that leaders must have before they can lead others. Mindset is a prerequisite to leadership. No one will follow if you try to take charge with a fixed mindset—determined to resist change and act incurious and risk-averse. Team members will go as far as you take them. You can't equip them with the right skills if you attempt to lead with glaring deficits.

Section II on People Leadership described the proper motivation for leading others. Don't expect team members to help you become a successful leader if your primary motivation is to gain title, prestige, or a few more dollars in your paycheck. The top leaders have a passion to care for, communicate with, engage, and coach their teams.

Collaborative Leadership came next, in Section III. From the moment you accept the role of team lead, your success is no longer about what you personally achieve. Rather, it's about what you lead others to accomplish, and that requires collaboration.

Section IV, Strategic Leadership, equipped you to model accountability, ownership, and initiative for your team while serving as a cultural steward for your organization.

Finally, Section V on Executional Leadership has so far delved into how to maximize your resources through focusing on top goals and building capacity to deliver on results.

So you've fostered a leading mindset, demonstrated continual care to your team members, built a high functioning and collaborative team, exemplified the behaviors you wish to see in others while serving as a cultural evangelist, and created OKRs with the help of your team. The skills you've exhibited as a leader are almost complete. But the glue that holds them together is the *feedback* you provide your team.

There's a reason why the last chapter is about the power of feedback. Once you've applied the other concepts, feedback anchors all the other skills in your tech leadership.

THE FEEDBACK DEFICIT

A whopping 86 percent of team members surveyed reported they believe a diverse workforce would help their companies yield better results (see Chapter 10). Seventy-six percent of people surveyed reported that they want jobs that bring an opportunity to balance work and their personal lives (Minahan 2021). But did you know that 65 percent of US workers say they want more feedback at work? More than two-thirds of US workers report that they're hungry for more feedback, an activity that costs leaders nothing except time (Mazur 2022).

How important is feedback to team members?

- 85 percent *take on additional initiative* when they get feedback at work.
- 75 percent believe that feedback is valuable to *improving their productivity, performance, and skills.*

- 72 percent of millennials who receive accurate and consistent feedback *feel fulfilled* in their jobs.
- 69 percent believe they would *work harder* if they received some acknowledgment through feedback.
- Those who receive feedback at least once per week are four times more likely to be *highly engaged* (McLain and Nelson 2022).

Despite the multiple benefits on team member performance from receiving regular, ongoing feedback, only 28 percent of team members say they receive at least weekly feedback.

If you're a leader who fears delivering feedback the "wrong" way, you might be interested to know that 22 percent of team members who receive negative feedback disengage at work. That's not great, right? But it's not bad compared to the 40 percent of workers who report that the reason they disengage at work is because of receiving no feedback!

What does this research mean? It means that leaders who provide regular feedback increase engagement, improve morale, create a positive work culture, demonstrate care, increase team-member initiative, and generate more productivity. These are leaders who don't miss out or create disengagement (quiet quitting, etc.).

WHY DON'T LEADERS PROVIDE FEEDBACK AS OFTEN AS TEAMS NEED?

If you were to ask leaders why they don't provide regular, meaningful feedback to their team, you'd hear one answer over and over: "I don't have time."

Not to sound contrarian, but when I hear a leader say, "I don't have time," my brain translates that to, "I'm not willing to make time." We all have twenty-four hours in a day and get to choose where we invest those hours. See if you've ever heard or made similar excuses about how you prioritize one activity over another:

- "I don't have time to cook a nutritious, balanced dinner," but then you spend an hour in your car to visit a drive-through on your way home from work.
- "I don't have time to exercise each day," while you never lack time to binge-watch a favorite show on Netflix.
- "I don't have time to make coffee at home," but you have plenty of time to stop at Starbucks on your way to work.
- "I don't have time to give my team feedback each week," yet you make time for twenty to twenty-five hours in weekly meetings.

All of these are actions which experts say come with a huge cost of lost opportunity compared to investing that time with teams (Murphy 2021).

It's not so much that we lack *time* to provide feedback as that we prioritize other activities, many of which are time *wastes* that accomplish little, instead of time *investments* that come with an ROI.

As a tech leader with twenty years of trial-and-error to build my leadership skills and help my team deliver consistently outstanding results, I can say without fear of contradiction that the time I spend giving feedback to my team members creates an exponential return on quality, productivity, creativity, risk-taking, initiative, team cohesiveness, morale, and overall performance.

Top leaders spend their time differently than average leaders. Most CEOs spend an average of forty-five minutes each day working out and another forty-five minutes on self-development (Patel 2016). They *make* time, and so should you.

Vice president of product at Microsoft, Adam Harmetz,

spends 22 percent of time coaching and offering feedback (Harmetz 2021). Harmetz *makes* time, and so should you.

ALIGNING YOUR FEEDBACK TO THE SITUATION

When doing a multiple-day mountain trek with friends, I had to give and take feedback every step of the way. Once while hiking with some advanced climbers, I let them set the pace the first day. That night, I felt like I'd run two marathons.

Before starting out the next morning, I gave them some feedback. "Dudes, your pace is killing me," I admitted. "If we keep up that speed, I'll fall behind. Can we slow down a bit today?" In about twenty-five words, I'd offered feedback from my perspective. We were friends. I didn't find it hard to say those words or request that we make a change. No one ridiculed me or ostracized me. They took my feedback as I intended it: how to make the climb work for all of us.

Other times on the climb, I had an easier time scaling a steep climb than the taller members of the team. They asked me if I would slow down!

At work, I use various types of feedback with my team. Following are the ones I use most often.

Steering Feedback

Steering feedback comes before work commences or as soon as the team reaches a decision point, as a form of proactive context-setting.

Early on, I let the team know of any known constraints that shouldn't be tackled in our development process. I also use steering feedback to keep the team on track as work begins. Let's say team members are pursuing different approaches to fixing a problem or developing a new product. Or our team might be duplicating the efforts worked in another team. In those cases, I use steering feedback to align my team around one approach, so we can maximize development velocity.

If you've ever seen "kiddie bumpers" at the bowling alley, you understand that when the bumpers engage, they prevent the ball from entering the gutter. Similarly, steering feedback keeps the project from entering the gutter or stalling.

Technical Feedback

I provide technical feedback early in the design review process. As a tech leader, I stay current on the technology that goes into design. While I might not have all the answers, I make it my business to connect expert resources when necessary to provide feedback and suggestions as the tech enters development.

Consider writing a design document (design docs) for your project. While design docs vary, most contain the facts (content and scope), requirements (goals and non-goals), and best solutions (actual design). Google engineers include varying degrees of information in their design docs, such as the following:

- System-context-diagrams
- APIs
- Data storage
- Code and pseudo-code
- Degree of constraint (Ubl 2020)

Protocol Feedback

Every tech organization follows set protocols for issues like reporting bugs and conducting *postmortems* after a project is complete. Facebook and other large tech companies use something called an SEV review for big production issues (Wolff and Dellamaggiore 2019). The only difference between a postmortem and SEV is the scale and scope. In most tech organizations, the leader is responsible to ensure that protocols are adhered to and documents are kept, so the lessons learned can serve as a historical repository to inform future work.

A postmortem implies something like, "This project died, and now we need to find out who killed it!" But it's not a finger-pointing session. Instead, it's a discovery and debrief session. I love conducting these feedback sessions, because the team gives me a wealth of information, and I get another opportunity to reinforce individual contributors for their parts in the effort.

Kudos Feedback

My favorite type of feedback—and, not surprisingly, the easiest for me to give and team members to receive—is positive feedback. "Nice job on ____," takes almost no time to deliver. Unfortunately, inexperienced leaders might miscalculate its simplicity as unimportant. Nothing could be more wrong.

A study in the US asked participants to write as many emotive words as they could think of in two minutes. Half the words people used expressed negative emotions, 30 percent shared positive emotions, and 20 percent described neutral emotions. When they replicated the study in nearly forty different languages, they found that most cultures use these seven words most frequently when describing emotions: joy, fear, anger, sadness, disgust, shame, and guilt. Of those seven, only one is positive (Dye 2005).

Beyond just the words we absorb and use, our entire brains seem hardwired with a *negativity bias,* a phenomenon of which psychologist Rick Hanson said this: "The brain is like Velcro for negative experiences and Teflon for positives ones" (Hanson 2016). We tend to remember negative experiences and forget positive ones. Researchers Frederickson and Losada have suggested that every negative experience we encounter requires five positive ones to counterbalance the negative load (Brown 2021).

Here's my point: we as leaders must not only counter the negativity from others and the negativity bias in our brains, but we also must help counter any feedback that a team member perceives as negative. How do you accomplish that? Simply by pointing out when someone has done something well.

Corrective Feedback

This is feedback of last resort, and I don't find myself using it frequently. However, some situations must be corrected, because the consequences of continued errors are severe. Here are some examples:

- A team member writing sloppy code
- Building errors into the system
- Compliance, privacy, or legal violations
- Pushing code without tests or monitoring
- Communication issues between team members
- Bypassing normal operating processes

THE F.A.S.T. FEEDBACK MODEL

While you must align the feedback you use to each situation, the F.A.S.T. Feedback model provides an excellent general guide to delivering meaningful feedback (Pokorny 2015). Although written more than two decades ago, Bruce Tulgan's book *Fast Feedback* is just as relevant today as it was then. F.A.S.T. not only describes how speedy it is to deliver effective feedback, but it's also an easy-to-remember acronym—which we will explore next.

Frequent

Just as the situational leadership model suggests that you coach others based on their current level of proficiency, Tulgan doesn't suggest a one-size-fits-all approach to the meaning of the word *frequent*. Depending on where each team member falls on their learning curve and experiences, and even the complexity of a particular task, leaders should be prepared to offer feedback at a frequency level the situation calls for.

Accurate

Tulgan describes *accurate* as feedback that is correct, balanced, and appropriate. Saying to a team member, "Your code is a hot mess," might make you feel temporarily better if you're frustrated. But that description isn't accurate; it's subjective. While parts of the code might be awful, that kind of feedback isn't balanced, nor is it appropriate. Any leader using vague or inappropriate criticism should expect their them to push back and resist additional feedback.

Specific

Whether your feedback is positive or pointing out room for improvement, it needs to focus on specifics. Imagine your boss calling their direct reports into a conference room and saying, "I just wanted to tell you that you're all doing great work." It's better than nothing, right? But would that kind of feedback make you wonder if your boss even knows what anyone is working on? Wouldn't it come across as a very general statement, one that doesn't seem based on firsthand knowledge or supporting examples?

Or what if that same boss called your group of leaders to say, "I'm disappointed with all of your teams' performance." *Really? All of our teams are failing? There isn't one team that is doing OK?* And if that's where the meeting ended, would you have any idea how to "fail less" or perhaps become successful?

What makes feedback meaningful is its specificity, like focusing on what's working well, what could be improved, and what to do next.

Timely

The final part of the acronym involves *when* it should occur. Feedback is most likely to be well-received and meaningful to your team when it comes as close to the action as possible. Timeliness applies both to praise and correction. Telling a team member, "That project you headed up last April didn't go well.

I'd like to talk to you about it," would have been helpful last April. Bringing it up now seems like you're going out of your way to be critical instead of helpful.

FEEDBACK IS A GIFT

Up to this point, I've focused on the feedback you provide others. But what about the feedback you request and receive from others? Do you get enough?

Whenever someone offers me feedback, I embrace it like a gift. We can learn tons through trial and error, but that process often takes time. On the other hand, feedback gives me a learning shortcut or even teaches me things I likely wouldn't have learned on my own.

If you've put into practice the principles I've shared up to this point, you should feel secure in asking your peers and team members for a gift: feedback. By building up trust with your peers and team members, most will gladly give you feedback about your performance or behavior. Doing so would be a big risk for them. They wouldn't know how you might respond, and they may fear you'll dismiss their thoughts or even use their gift against them! Build their trust first.

Your aim as a leader is to create an environment where feedback is an ongoing, two-way street. You offer feedback to others, and they accept it in the spirit in which it's given. You request and receive feedback, and you take it as a gift and proof that you've established a trusting relationship.

HOW TO EXPERIENCE THE REWARDS OF FEEDBACK

In its purist application, feedback is holding a mirror up for others to see themselves, their actions, and their performance. The leader's job is to reflect what they see back to team members. But a leader must see things as they are with accuracy (as in the A in F.A.S.T. feedback), not a funhouse mirror full of distortion based on their own biases or frustrations. The mirror helps others see what you see, while allowing them to adjust accordingly.

Next, we will explore how to make the practice of giving regular feedback a worthy, rewarding investment.

Create and Use a Feedback Mantra

If you're not in the habit of giving regular feedback, or if you save up your feedback for formal sit-down sessions, start with a mantra that puts feedback in the right context. Feel free to use any of these, or come up with your own:

- *Planning on its own won't provide feedback to my team on how they are performing against the plan.*
- *The drive behind my feedback is to let my team members know how they are performing.*
- *When I see someone doing something I want to see again, I will stop and say something. When I see someone doing something I don't want to see again, I will stop and say something.*
- *My feedback will reinforce solid performance and redirect problem performance.*
- *I will inform my team members about what I see in their blind spots, so they can learn and improve.*

Don the Right Attitude

Would you let someone you care about walk around all day with spinach in their teeth? Probably not. And you certainly wouldn't let a friend walk around with a toilet paper streamer trailing the sole of their shoe.

Your attitude before providing feedback, just like your mantra, should project your desire to provide value to your team. When your attitude comes from care and a desire to offer support, few people will resist.

Make Feedback Spontaneous and Immediate

As I've shared, many leaders say they don't have time to give feedback (aka, they don't make time), because they see feedback as an annual, formal, sit-down affair with in-depth documentation. That's a performance review, not feedback. Feedback is often spontaneous and based on specific situations. Just like the Transportation Security Administration's (TSA) slogan of, "If you see something, say something," feedback can happen on the spot.

Make Feedback a Habit

Habits form by repetition. James Clear, *New York Times* bestselling author of *Atomic Habits* explains that new habits are formed using four steps: *cues, cravings, response,* and *reward* (Clear 2022).

Let's explore this model through the example of the leader who doesn't provide enough positive feedback.

Cues. A cue for a leader to deliver regular feedback might be as simple as looking for feedback-worthy behaviors at work. Start by looking for positive behaviors, ones you wish to see again, which are a cue to offer feedback. In this case, seeing good performance serves as a cue to offer praise or thanks.

Cravings. Does that mean you crave giving feedback? Probably not. But you do crave your team performing to the best of their collective and individual abilities— operating at top creativity, efficiency, and performance. How does that benefit you? As a leader, the only accolades you'll receive are based on what your team achieves. There's nothing wrong with a leader craving kudos for creating a high-producing team.

Response. This is where you form the habit: giving feedback. Your cue is when you see a behavior you wish to see again. That fuels your craving to see every member perform at the highest level of their abilities. Your response? Stop and say something. Acknowledge what you saw. Tell your team members why you liked it. Thank them for the specific, desirable trait you saw, such as taking initiative, perseverance, resilience, creativity, etc.

Reward. The reward comes after you see a cue, respond to your craving to create a team of optimal team, and respond by stopping and saying something immediately. Some rewards are immediate, like someone smiling or telling you, "Thanks for noticing." Other results come later, like when that same person works even harder to earn your attention and appreciation.

Be on the Lookout for Positive Behaviors to Reinforce

I used positive feedback in the previous example for a reason. Remember that our human brains already work with a negativity bias, recalling negative events more clearly than positive ones.

As a result, leaders must provide team members with multiple positive experiences to counter just one negative experience.

If you were to develop one habit only as a tech leader, providing positive feedback is the one you should prioritize. Positive feedback demonstrates team care and fosters a collaborative culture. When positive feedback is linked to the tasks and behaviors needed to execute on your OKRs, the positive words from a leader propel others to work harder and focus on top goals.

I've heard this technique referred to as "bathroom feedback." Each time you get up to use the restroom, refill your coffee, take a stretch break, etc., make it a point to provide positivity to one person when you leave, and another person when you return. You can stop by their workstations, or if you work virtually, you can send messages.

If you get up ten times each day, you could positively impact twenty team members. It won't take you much extra time, and it conditions your team to look forward to seeing (or hearing from) you.

Share Customer Feedback with Your Team

CEO of Apple Tim Cook gets up each morning at 3:45 a.m. and reads his emails. As a CEO, you'd imagine that he'd have an assistant culling through the hundreds of emails he receives each day. But he does it himself. He also reads emails from customers, some of them praising Apple, some critiquing Apple's products, and some offering product suggestions (Dormehl 2019).

What have customers said about the products your team helped develop? Tech leaders can take a page from Tim Cook's habit of reading customer emails. Thanks to social media and bold customers, there are likely multiple other methods to learn about your customers' experiences with your products and services. You can then share examples of what your customers said about your work with your team.

A friend of mine served as an executive in a multibillion-dollar healthcare organization. In his role, he received customer feedback and even handwritten notes about the company and specific services. He would personally respond to most of the customers' notes. He also shared some of those notes with his team and his leaders who managed claims, customer service, tech, strategy, and product innovations. Eventually, he started reading customer stories at every annual senior and executive leadership retreat, so other leaders could hear the customers' perspectives.

In addition to telling the customers' stories, he expressed appreciation to the multiple departments and divisions which had a hand in allowing customer service to provide such stellar results. Before long, other departments asked for these customer experiences to show teams how their work had such a positive impact.

Voice of the customer feedback is gold, regardless of if they love your product or hate it. Positive feedback reinforces your team for their parts in creating those results, while negative feedback often surfaces opportunities to explore in the future.

Request and Receive Regular Feedback

Feedback is the key to accelerated learning. As I've stated, if you've created safety for others to share feedback with you, be willing to ask them for more. Say, "I really value your opinion, and I think we have a great working relationship. Would you do me a favor and give me your honest feedback about _____?"

Many people say, "I want feedback," but by the way they receive feedback, it's clear that they want praise, not honesty. Ask people whose opinions you trust, and be prepared to listen. What they're offering you is a gift, if you receive it.

Never forget the effort you've put into becoming a leader. Execution can be the most difficult strategy to achieve. But feedback anchors your work. Your results will grow as strong as your feedback. By heading off problems before they arise, providing technical guidance, taking advantage of lessons learned as teaching moments, praising, and correcting people when needed, your team can grow to be unstoppable.

AFTERWORD

At the beginning of *Tech Leadership: The Blueprint for Evolving from Individual Contributor to Tech Leader*, I shared my belief that you could become a tech leader if…

- You are a high performer in your current role.
- You are willing to develop a leader's mindset.
- You have an insatiable desire to learn new things.
- Your colleagues come to you for help because they see you as both knowledgeable and eager to share what you know.
- You believe you can create a deeper positive impact by leading others rather than being a sole knowledge worker.

Every lesson I've outlined here can be learned, which means I believe anyone can become a tech leader *if they feel called to lead* and are willing to put in the effort. In this book, we covered how:

- Personal Leadership fuels your mindset.
- People Leadership shows your care for others.
- Collaborative Leadership builds your team.
- Strategic Leadership develops your plan.
- Executional Leadership gets your results.

As CEO of Apple Tim Cook has been credited with stating, "Work takes on new meaning when you feel you are pointed in the right direction. Otherwise, it's just a job, and life is too short for that."

I've pointed you in the right direction to lead in tech. Don't make leadership your job. Make it your passion.

Now get out there and lead!

ACKNOWLEDGMENTS

I thought that writing a book would be a solitary endeavor, but I have found is it to be a wonderfully social experience where I was able to connect and reconnect with wonderful people along the way. I am so lucky to have the support, guidance, and assistance of many individuals who have made this book possible.

First and foremost, I want to express my heartfelt gratitude to my mother for all of her support over the years, my wife Sara, and my son Artan. Their encouragement, support, and patience created the space for me to invest time in writing and editing this book. Without their love and support, this book would not have been possible.

I would also like to extend my sincere thanks to my friends and colleagues who have taught me so much over the years. I've had the honor of working with amazing teams that helped shaped the internet product landscape for almost 20 years. Working with these amazing people has provided me with wonderful insights and has been invaluable in shaping my ideas and refining my philosophy. I am fortunate to have had such a talented and generous group of people in my life.

I also want to acknowledge the contributions of Alana Karen, Kathy Polizzi, Bill Coughran, Jonathan Rosenberg, Alistair Croll, Yan Budman, Alan Eustace, Caitlin Pantos, Mike Curtis, Gabriel Mecklenburg, Lee Maliniak, Nestor Hernandez, Matthew Stepka, Rachel Potvin, who generously volunteered their time to review the manuscript and provide valuable feedback. Their attention to detail and thoughtful critiques were instrumental in improving the final product.

Finally, I would like to thank all the readers who have taken the time to read this book. I hope that the insights and knowledge shared here will be of value to you and that you will find it informative and useful on your journey through leadership in Tech. This book is a reflection of the wisdom, generosity, and kindness of those around me, and I am grateful for the role each of you has played in its creation.

REFERENCES

"10+ OKR Examples for Information Technology." 2022. OKRexamples.co. 2022. https://okrexamples.co/technology-engineering-rnd-okr-examples.

"2021 Edelman Trust Barometer." 2021. Edelman. 2021. https://www.edelman.com/trust/2021-trust-barometer.

"25 Employee Engagement Statistics You Wouldn't Believe." 2022. Oak Digital Workplace. Oak Engage. September 13, 2022. https://www.oak.com/blog/employee-engagement-statistics/.

"4 Ways Effective Leadership Inspires Employee Engagement." 2019. Slack. February 27, 2019. https://slack.com/blog/collaboration/effective-leadership-inspires-employee-engagement.

"5 Whys: Getting to the Root of a Problem Quickly." 2021. MindTools.com. Emerald Works. 2021. https://www.mindtools.com/pages/article/newTMC_5W.htm.

"7 Ways to Build a Healthy Company Culture." 2021. Human Resources Director. KM Business Information US. June 10, 2021. https://www.hcamag.com/us/specialization/mental-health/7-ways-to-build-a-healthy-company-culture/257612.

"About Ikea." 2022. About IKEA. IKEA. August 25, 2022. https://about.ikea.com/en/about-us.

"The Achiever Pre Employment Assessment." 2020. Saterfiel & Associates. 2020. https://www.employment-testing.com/Achiever.htm.

Ajiboye, Damilola. 2021. "Metrics That Matter." Bootcamp. Medium. March 29, 2021. https://bootcamp.uxdesign.cc/metrics-that-matter-2e1df4f8a14.

"Amazon's Global Career Site." 2022. Amazon.jobs. Amazon. 2022. https://www.amazon.jobs/en/principles.

"The Andon Cord: A Way to Stop Work While Boosting Productivity." 2018. Six Sigma Daily. Bisk. January 8, 2018. https://www.sixsigmadaily.com/what-is-an-andon-cord/.

Ariella, Sky. 2022. "Diversity in High Tech Statistics [2022]." Zippia. April 14, 2022. https://www.zippia.com/advice/diversity-in-high-tech-statistics/.

"Bank-of-America: Violation Tracker." 2022. Violation Tracker. Good Jobs First. 2022. https://violationtracker.goodjobsfirst.org/parent/bank-of-america.

Barker, Eric. 2014. "5 Non-Evil Ways to Get People to Do What You Want, from Dan Pink." Barking Up The Wrong Tree. November 2014. https://bakadesuyo.com/2014/11/how-to-deal-with-difficult-people/.

Bass, Dina. 2022. "Microsoft Cuts Jobs, but Plans Increased Headcount This Year." Bloomberg.com. Bloomberg. July 12, 2022. https://www.bloomberg.com/news/articles/2022-07-12/microsoft-cuts-jobs-but-plans-increased-headcount-this-year.

Berkovic, Paul. 2017. "Google's Unwritten Rule for Team Collaboration." Edited by Charlotte Dillon. I Done This Blog. July 6, 2017. http://blog.i-donethis.com/google-team-collaboration/.

Berry, Ray Slater. 2021. "Why Tech Teams Need to Be More Diverse & Inclusive than Ever Before." Codility. March 29, 2021. https://www.codility.com/blog/why-tech-teams-need-to-be-more-diverse-inclusive-than-ever-before/.

Boyd, Anthony. 2022. "7 Emotionally Intelligent Ways Leaders Show They Care about Their Team." Medium. Leadership By Anthony Boyd. July 31, 2022. https://byanthonyboyd.com/7-emotionally-intelligent-ways-leaders-show-they-care-about-their-team-591937ed2318.

Brooks, Rachel, Stacy Houston, and Chrisina Wadsworth. 2021. "Equity Updates – What We've Been up to and What Comes Next." Instagram Blog. Instagram. April 26, 2021. https://about.instagram.com/blog/announcements/equity-updates-what-weve-been-up-to-and-what-comes-next.

Brown, Nick. 2021. "The Curious (and Completely Flawed) Case of the Positivity Ratio." Talent Quarterly. September 21, 2021. https://www.talent-quarterly.com/the-curious-and-completely-flawed-case-of-the-positivity-ratio/.

Brownlee, John. 2011. "Before/Apple/After: How Apple Has Led the Tech Industry Every Step of the Way." Cult of Mac. September 14, 2011. https://www.cultofmac.com/113454/before-apple-after-how-apple-has-led-the-tech-industry-every-step-of-the-way-gallery/.

Buchholz, Katharina. 2022. "How Has the Number of Female CEOS in Fortune 500 Companies Changed over the Last 20 Years?" World Economic Forum. March 10, 2022. https://www.weforum.org/agenda/2022/03/ceos-fortune-500-companies-female/.

Buitendijk, Mariska. 2022. "Cruise Shipbuilder MV Werften Files for Bankruptcy." SWZ Maritime. SWZ. January 10, 2022. https://swzmaritime.nl/news/2022/01/10/cruise-shipbuilder-mv-werften-files-for-bankruptcy/.

Burke, Adrienne. 2013. "Why Zappos CEO Hsieh Wants to Enable More Collisions in Vegas." Forbes. Forbes Magazine. November 15, 2013. https://www.forbes.com/sites/techonomy/2013/11/15/why-zappos-ceo-hsieh-wants-to-enable-more-collisions-in-vegas/?sh=5d04405f1100.

Burns, Robert. n.d. "To a Mouse." Poetry Foundation. Accessed October 19, 2022. https://www.poetryfoundation.org/poems/43816/to-a-mouse-56d222ab36e33.

C., V. 2018. "Move Fast and Break Things Is Not Dead." The Startup. Medium. September 14, 2018. https://medium.com/swlh/move-fast-and-break-things-is-not-dead-8260b0718d90.

Carbonara, Scott. 2013. "Communication: The Art of Asking Others to the Dance." Essay. In *Manager's Guide to Employee Engagement*, 191. Madison, WI: McGraw-Hill.

Carbonara, Scott. Zoom interview with author, May 20, 2022.

Carroll, Emily. 2022. "How to Conduct a Diversity and Inclusion Survey." Drive Research. June 2, 2022. https://www.driveresearch.com/market-research-company-blog/diversity-and-inclusion-survey/#.

Carucci, Ron, and Jarrod Shappell. 2022. "Design Your Organization to Match Your Strategy." Harvard Business Review. Harvard University. June 6, 2022. https://hbr.org/2022/06/design-your-organization-to-match-your-strategy.

Castro, Felipe. 2021. "OKR: Learn Google's Goal System with Examples and Templates." FelipeCastro.com. August 30, 2021. https://felipecastro.com/en/okr/what-is-okr/.

Chapman, Gary D. 1992. *The Five Love Languages*. Chicago, IL: Northfield Pub.

"Charles Babbage." 2022. Encyclopædia Britannica. August 22, 2022. https://www.britannica.com/biography/Charles-Babbage.

Chavez, Nicole. 2019. "Here's Why Cruise Ships Are the Ideal Incubators for Measles and Other Diseases." CNN. Cable News Network. May 3, 2019. https://www.cnn.com/2019/05/03/health/measles-diseases-cruise-ships.

Chen, Eve. 2022. "Which Is the Best Airline in the US? Depends on the Class. See JD Power's 2022 Rankings." USA Today. Gannett Satellite Information Network. May 11, 2022. https://www.usatoday.com/story/travel/airline-news/2022/05/11/southwest-jetblue-best-airlines-2022/9718400002/.

Chen, James. 2022. "Analysis Paralysis." Edited by Gordon Scott and Vikki Velasquez. Investopedia. August 9, 2022. https://www.investopedia.com/terms/a/analysisparalysis.asp.

Cherry, Kendra. 2022. "How Does Self-Determination Theory Explain Motivation?" Edited by David Sussman. Verywell Mind. September 22, 2022. https://www.verywellmind.com/what-is-self-determination-theory-2795387.

Chism, Marlene. 2018. "Don't Let Politics Ruin Thanksgiving." LinkedIn. March 7, 2018. https://www.linkedin.com/pulse/dont-let-politics-ruin-thanksgiving-marlene-chism/?articleId=6205439354400186368.

Chrislip, David D. 2002. *The Collaborative Leadership Fieldbook: A Guide for Citizens and Civic Leaders*. San Francisco, CA: Jossey-Bass.

Chui, Michael, James Manyika, Jacques Bughin, Richard Dobbs, Charles Roxburgh, Hugo Sarrazin, Geoffrey Sands, and Magdalena Westergren. 2019. "The Social Economy: Unlocking Value and Productivity through Social Technologies." McKinsey & Company. McKinsey & Company. February 13, 2019. https://www.mckinsey.com/industries/technology-media-and-telecommunications/our-insights/the-social-economy.

Clear, James. 2022. "How to Start New Habits That Actually Stick." JamesClear.com. August 31, 2022. https://jamesclear.com/three-steps-habit-change.

"Coaching by Leaders and Managers – Why It Can Fail and How You Can Make It Work (Part 1 of 5)." 2014. Metattude. June 3, 2014. https://metattude.com/coaching-leaders-managers-can-fail-can-make-work-part-1-5/.

"College Enrollment Rates." 2022. National Center for Education Statistics. U.S. Department of Education. 2022. https://nces.ed.gov/programs/coe/indicator/cpb/college-enrollment-rate.

"Complete History of the MITS Altair 8800." 2021. History-Computer.com. October 19, 2021. https://history-computer.com/altair-8800-complete-history-of-the-mits-altair-8800/.

Cooks-Campbell, Allaya. 2021. "Are You Languishing? Here's How to Regain Your Sense of Purpose." BetterUp. October 27, 2021. https://www.betterup.com/blog/what-is-languish-how-to-flourish.

Cortland, Pat. 2022. "Which Way Is the Bus Going? Kids Do Better on This One than Adults." Hella Life. August 2, 2022. https://www.considerable.com/life/education/bus-brain-teaser-solution/.

"Council Post: 15 Tech Leaders Share the Top Challenges They're Facing in 2022." 2022. Forbes. Forbes Magazine. March 24, 2022. https://www.forbes.com/sites/forbestechcouncil/2022/03/24/15-tech-leaders-share-the-top-challenges-theyre-facing-in-2022/.

Crandall, Mike. 2021. "'Gentlemen, This Is a Football!'." Edmond Business. February 23, 2021. https://edmondbusiness.com/2021/02/gentlemen-this-is-a-football/.

Creasey, Tim. 2022. "Why Some Communications Work and Others Don't." Prosci. October 3, 2022. https://www.prosci.com/blog/understanding-why-some-communications-work-and-others-dont.

Cross, Rob, Reb Rebele, and Adam Grant. 2021. "Collaborative Overload." Harvard Business Review. Harvard University. August 30, 2021. https://hbr.org/2016/01/collaborative-overload.

Croucher, Lauren. 2022. "Change Management in Times of Crisis." RevGen. September 1, 2022. https://www.revgenpartners.com/insight-posts/change-management-in-times-of-crisis/.

"Cruise Ship Outbreak Updates." 2022. U.S. Centers for Disease Control and Prevention. June 7, 2022. https://www.cdc.gov/nceh/vsp/surv/GIlist.htm.

Csiszar, John. 2022. "There Are Only 4 Black Fortune 500 CEOS." GOBankingRates. June 2, 2022. https://www.gobankingrates.com/money/business/fortune-500-includes-only-4-black-ceos/.

"Dau/Mau Ratio: KPI Example." 2022. Geckoboard. 2022. https://www.geckoboard.com/best-practice/kpi-examples/dau-mau-ratio/.

Dawson, Victoria. 2015. "The Epic Failure of Thomas Edison's Talking Doll." Smithsonian.com. Smithsonian Institution. June 1, 2015. https://www.smithsonianmag.com/smithsonian-institution/epic-failure-thomas-edisons-talking-doll-180955442/.

Day, George S., and J. H. Schoemaker. 2019. "How Vigilant Companies Gain an Edge in Turbulent Times." MIT Sloan Management Review. Massachusetts Institute of Technology. November 18, 2019. https://sloanreview.mit.edu/article/how-vigilant-companies-gain-an-edge-in-turbulent-times/.

de Maine, Bridget. 2017. "How Many Good Experiences Finally Outweigh a Bad One?" Collective Hub. May 15, 2017. https://collectivehub.com/2017/05/how-many-good-experiences-finally-outweigh-a-bad-one/.

Deutschman, Alan. 2007. *Change or Die: The Three Keys to Change at Work and in Life*. New York, NY: HarperBusiness.

"Digital Around the World." 2022. DataReportal. Kepios. July 2022. https://datareportal.com/global-digital-overview.

"Diversity, Equity, and Inclusion: Why It Matters." 2022. St. Bonaventure University Online. St. Bonaventure University. February 16, 2022. https://online.sbu.edu/news/why-dei-matters.

Dixon, Mike. 2022. "Do You Spend 80% Of Your Time Communicating?" Center for Management & Organization Effectiveness. 2022. https://cmoe.com/blog/do-you-spend-80-of-your-time-communicating/#.

Doerr, John. 2018. *Measure What Matters How Google, Bono, and the Gates Foundation Rock the World with Okrs*. New York, NY: Portfolio/Penguin.

Dolan, G. T. 1981. "There's a S.M.A.R.T. Way to Write Management's Goals and Objectives." *Management Review* 70 (11): 35–36.

Dormehl, Luke. 2019. "Yes, Tim Cook Does Read Your 'Dear Tim' Emails." Cult of Mac. February 25, 2019. https://www.cultofmac.com/608606/yes-tim-cook-does-read-your-dear-tim-emails/.

Drucker, Peter F. 1954. *The Practice of Management*. New York, NY: Collins.

Duffin, Erin. 2022. "Educational Attainment in the U.S. 1960-2021." Statista. June 10, 2022. https://www.statista.com/statistics/184260/educational-attainment-in-the-us/.

Duignan, Brian. 2019. "Dunning-Kruger Effect." Encyclopædia Britannica.

July 26, 2019. https://www.britannica.com/science/Dunning-Kruger-effect.

Dumitrescu, Sorin. 2021. "What Is Development Velocity and How Do You Measure It?" Bunnyshell. August 13, 2021. https://www.bunnyshell.com/blog/what-development-velocity.

Duran-Stanton, Amelia, and Alicia Masson. 2021. "Lessons in Followership: Good Leaders Aren't Always out Front." Association of the United States Army. May 18, 2021. https://www.ausa.org/articles/lessons-followership-good-leaders-arent-always-out-front.

Dweck, Carol S. 2016. *Mindset: The New Psychology of Success*. New York, NY: Ballantine Books.

Dye, Lee. 2005. ABC News. ABC News Network. February 2, 2005. https://abcnews.go.com/Technology/DyeHard/story?id=460987&page=1.

"EEOC Sues Ford for Pregnancy Discrimination." 2021. U.S. Equal Employment Opportunity Commission. September 28, 2021. https://www.eeoc.gov/newsroom/eeoc-sues-ford-pregnancy-discrimination.

"Empathy Definition: What Is Empathy?" n.d. Greater Good. University of California, Berkeley. Accessed October 17, 2022. https://greatergood.berkeley.edu/topic/empathy/definition.

"Executives Say They're Pulled in Too Many Directions and That Their Company's Capabilities Don't Support Their Strategy, According to Booz & Company Survey." 2011. GlobeNewswire News Room. Sommerfield Communications, Inc. January 18, 2011. https://www.globenewswire.com/en/news-release/2011/01/18/1209299/0/en/Executives-Say-They-re-Pulled-in-Too-Many-Directions-and-That-Their-Company-s-Capabilities-Don-t-Support-Their-Strategy-According-to-Booz-amp-Company-Survey.html.

Faulk, Kathryn E., Christian T. Gloria, and Mary A. Steinhardt. 2013. "Coping Profiles Characterize Individual Flourishing, Languishing, and Depression." *Anxiety, Stress & Coping* 26 (4): 378–90. https://doi.org/10.1080/10615806.2012.708736.

Feloni, Richard. 2016. "Facebook Engineering Director Describes What It's like to Go through the Company's 6-Week Engineer Bootcamp." Business Insider. March 2, 2016. https://www.businessinsider.com/inside-facebook-engineer-bootcamp-2016-3.

Fernandes, Thaisa. 2021. "Learn More about the Spotify Squad Framework-Part I." PM101. Medium. February 24, 2021. https://medium.com/pm101/spotify-squad-framework-part-i-8f74bcfcd761.

Ferrazzi, Keith. 2019. "How to Lead without Authority." KeithFerrazzi.com. 2019. https://www.keithferrazzi.com/talks/how-to-lead-without-authority.

"Flourishing." 2022. APA Dictionary of Psychology. American Psychological Association. 2022. https://dictionary.apa.org/flourishing.

Flynn, Jack. 2022. "25 Trending Tech Industry Statistics [2022]: The State of the U.S. Tech Industry." Zippia. September 22, 2022. https://www.zippia.com/advice/tech-industry-statistics/.

"Form Follows Function." 2022. The Guggenheim Museums and Foundation. 2022. https://www.guggenheim.org/teaching-materials/the-architecture-of-the-solomon-r-guggenheim-museum/form-follows-function.

Fredrickson, Barbara L. 2009. *Positivity: Top-Notch Research Reveals the 3-to-1 Ratio That Will Change Your Life.* New York, NY: Three Rivers Press/Crown Publishers.

Fredrickson, Barbara L. 2013. "Updated Thinking on Positivity Ratios." *American Psychologist* 68 (9): 814–22. https://doi.org/10.1037/a0033584.

Freeman, Bruce. 2021. "Name It to Tame It: Labelling Emotions to Reduce Stress & Anxiety." Oral Health Group. NewCom. May 3, 2021. https://www.oralhealthgroup.com/features/name-it-to-tame-it-labelling-emotions-to-reduce-stress-anxiety/.

Frei, Frances X., and Anne Morriss. 2021. "Everything Starts with Trust." Harvard Business Review. August 31, 2021. https://hbr.org/2020/05/begin-with-trust.

Frick, Don M. 2021. "Robert K. Greenleaf Biography." Greenleaf Center for Servant Leadership. 2021. https://www.greenleaf.org/about-us-3/robert-k-greenleaf-biography/.

Gallo, Amy. 2014. "The Value of Keeping the Right Customers." Harvard Business Review. Harvard University. October 29, 2014. https://hbr.org/2014/10/the-value-of-keeping-the-right-customers.

Glowasz, Marcus. 2022. "Information Overload Is a Choice." DataDrivenInvestor. Medium. July 23, 2022. https://medium.datadriveninvestor.com/information-overload-is-a-choice-970165fe846a.

Goldberg, Rick, and Jim Ruehlin. n.d. IBM. Accessed October 12, 2022. https://www.ibm.com/garage/method/practices/culture/failing-fast.

Grant, Adam. 2022. "'That's My Opinion and I'm Sticking to It' Is a Self-Limiting Way to Live. People Who Never Let Go of Their Views Never Evolve. Growth Is Not Just about Embracing New Ideas. It's Also about Rethinking Old Ones. Refusing to Change Your Mind Is a Decision to Stop Learning." Twitter. September 2, 2022. https://twitter.com/AdamMGrant/status/1565730168261443587?cxt=HHwWhoCw1dvSy7orAAAA.

Greeman, Hanna. 2021. "Can Sports Jargon Exclude Women in the Workplace? ." 3 Plus International. February 23, 2021. https://3plusinternational.com/2021/02/can-sports-jargon-exclude-women-in-the-workplace/.

Green, Jesse. 2020. "Questions Warren Buffet Asks before Investing in a Business." Savvy Dentist. June 12, 2020. https://savvydentist.com/questions-warren-buffet-asks-before-investing-in-a-business/.

Grove, Andrew S. 1983. *High Output Management*. New York, NY: Souvenir Press.

Gächter, Simon, and Elke Renner. 2018. "Leaders as Role Models and 'Belief Managers' in Social Dilemmas." *Journal of Economic Behavior & Organization* 154: 321–34. https://doi.org/10.1016/j.jebo.2018.08.001.

Hankel, Isaiah. 2021. "How a PhD Gives You an Edge over Other Job Candidates." Cheeky Scientist. October 9, 2021. https://cheekyscientist.com/phd-gives-you-an-edge-at-a-job-interview.

Hanson, Rick. 2016. "Overcoming the Negativity Bias." Dr. Rick Hanson. November 30, 2016. https://www.rickhanson.net/overcoming-negativity-bias/.

Harmetz, Adam. 2021. "Where Does a Tech Product Leader Spend Their Time?" LinkedIn. March 21, 2021. https://www.linkedin.com/pulse/where-does-tech-product-leader-spend-time-adam-harmetz/.

Harter, James K., Frank L. Schmidt, Sangeeta Agrawal, Stephanie K. Plowman, and Anthony Blue. 2016. "The Relationship between Engagement at Work and Organizational Outcomes." Gallup.com. Gallup. May 25, 2016. https://www.gallup.com/services/191558/q12-meta-analysis-ninth-edition-2016.aspx.

Harter, Jim. 2022. "Percent Who Feel Employer Cares about Their Wellbeing Plummets." Gallup.com. Gallup. August 11, 2022. https://www.gallup.com/workplace/390776/percent-feel-employer-cares-wellbeing-plummets.aspx.

Harter, Jim. 2022. "U.S. Employee Engagement Slump Continues." Gallup.com. Gallup. September 28, 2022. https://www.gallup.com/workplace/391922/employee-engagement-slump-continues.aspx.

Headlee, Celeste, and Andrew Swerdlow. 2013. Exploring The World's Highest Peaks From Your Couch. Other. *NPR.com*. Washington, DC: NPR.

Heald, Melody. 2022. "'For Me It Was Getting into a Screaming Match with the CEO over Him Eating Canned Tuna in the Office': Tech Worker Pinpoints the 2 Moments He Knew His Company Was about to Go Under." The Daily Dot. July 28, 2022. https://www.dailydot.com/irl/tech-worker-start-up-fail/.

Hersey, Paul, and Kenneth H. Blanchard. 1969. *Management of Organizational Behavior: Utilizing Human Resources*. Englewood Cliffs, NJ: Prentice-Hall.

"The History of Ikea." 1999. About IKEA. IKEA. 1999. https://about.ikea.com/en/about-us/history-of-ikea.

"How to Improve Employee Engagement in the Workplace." 2022. Gallup.com. Gallup. August 23, 2022. https://www.gallup.com/workplace/285674/improve-employee-engagement-workplace.aspx.

Jacimovic, Darko. 2022. "The Importance of Diversity in the Workplace - 20 Key Statistics." What To Become. August 3, 2022. https://whattobecome.-com/blog/diversity-in-the-workplace-statistics/.

Jacimovic, Darko. 2022. "The Importance of Diversity in the Workplace - 20 Key Statistics." What To Become. August 3, 2022. https://whattobecome.-com/blog/diversity-in-the-workplace-statistics/.

Jaspen, Ciera. 2021. "Measuring Engineering Productivity." O'Reilly Media. Medium. January 5, 2021. https://medium.com/oreillymedia/measuring-engineering-productivity-a6da8605ffae.

Jeans, David. 2022. "Better.com CEO Who Fired 900 Workers on Zoom Call Reinstalled." Forbes.com. Forbes Magazine. January 20, 2022. https://www.forbes.com/sites/davidjeans/2022/01/18/better-ceo-vishal-garg-returns-softbank/?sh=597a80a43595.

Jensen, Eric. 2021. "Measuring Racial and Ethnic Diversity for the 2020 Census." The United States Census Bureau. August 4, 2021. https://www.-census.gov/newsroom/blogs/random-samplings/2021/08/measuring-racial-ethnic-diversity-2020-census.html.

Jobs, Steve. 2005. "You've Got to Find What You Love." Stanford News. Stanford University. June 12, 2005. https://news.stanford.edu/2005/06/14/jobs-061505/.

Kahn, W. A. 1990. "Psychological Conditions of Personal Engagement and Disengagement at Work." *Academy of Management Journal* 33 (4): 701. https://doi.org/10.2307/256287.

Kanter, Rosabeth Moss. 1997. *On the Frontiers of Management.* Boston, MA: Harvard Business School Press.

Kenny, Conor. 2020. "'The Single Biggest Problem in Communication Is the Illusion That It Has Taken Place'." The Irish Times. November 9, 2020. https://www.irishtimes.com/culture/books/the-single-biggest-problem-in-communication-is-the-illusion-that-it-has-taken-place-1.4404586.

Kerstein, David. 2019. "What Southwest Airlines' Co-Founder Taught Me about Retail Banking." BAI. Bank Administration Institute. February 1, 2019. https://www.bai.org/banking-strategies/article-detail/clear-for-takeoff-what-herb-kelleher-taught-me-about-retail-banking/.

Kiger, Patrick J. 2020. "6 Inventions by Thomas Edison That Took the World by Storm." History.com. A&E Television Networks. March 6, 2020. https://www.history.com/news/thomas-edison-inventions.

King, Sonia. 2015. "Key Performance Indicators Are a Waste of Time." LinkedIn. February 20, 2015. https://www.linkedin.com/pulse/key-perfor-mance-indicators-waste-time-sonia-king.

Klemmer, E. T., and F. W. Snyder. 1972. "Measurement of Time Spent

Communicating." *Journal of Communication* 22 (2): 142–58. https://doi.org/10.1111/j.1460-2466.1972.tb00141.x.

Kunen, James S. 2002. "Enron's Vision (and Values) Thing." The New York Times. January 19, 2002. https://www.nytimes.com/2002/01/19/opinion/enron-s-vision-and-values-thing.html.

Kurt, Daniel. 2022. "Corporate Leadership by Race." Investopedia. February 28, 2022. https://www.investopedia.com/corporate-leadership-by-race-5114494.

Kuryk, Hildy. 2021. "Fast Company | Business News, Innovation, Technology, Work Life and Design." Fast Company. Mansueto Ventures LLC. January 19, 2021. https://www.fastcompany.com/.

"Languishing." 2022. APA Dictionary of Psychology. American Psychological Association. 2022. https://dictionary.apa.org/languishing.

"Learn More about the History of Remote Work and Where It's Going!" 2022. We Work Remotely. 2022. https://weworkremotely.com/history-of-remote-work.

Lev-Ram, Michal. 2017. "Microsoft CEO Satya Nadella Says Empathy Makes You a Better Innovator." Fortune. October 3, 2017. https://fortune.com/2017/10/03/microsoft-ceo-satya-nadella-says-empathy-makes-you-a-better-innovator/.

Lieberman, Matthew D., Naomi I. Eisenberger, Molly J. Crockett, Sabrina M. Tom, Jennifer H. Pfeifer, and Baldwin M. Way. 2007. "Putting Feelings into Words." *Psychological Science* 18 (5): 421–28. https://doi.org/10.1111/j.1467-9280.2007.01916.x.

Livingston, Mercey. 2022. "Naturally Produce More Dopamine, Serotonin, Endorphin and Oxytocin for a Happier Brain." CNET. September 20, 2022. https://www.cnet.com/health/mental/you-can-actually-hack-your-brain-to-produce-more-happy-chemicals/.

Llopis, Glenn. 2015. "6 Things Wise Leaders Do to Engage Their Employees." Forbes. Forbes Magazine. February 2, 2015. https://www.forbes.com/sites/glennllopis/2015/02/02/6-things-wise-leaders-do-to-engage-their-employees/?sh=753a8daf7f5d.

Locklear, Lauren R., Shannon G. Taylor, and Maureen L. Ambrose. 2021. "Building a Better Workplace Starts with Saying 'Thanks.'" Harvard Business Review. April 5, 2021. https://hbr.org/2020/11/building-a-better-workplace-starts-with-saying-thanks.

Loewenstein, George. 1994. "The Psychology of Curiosity: A Review and Reinterpretation." *Psychological Bulletin* 116 (1): 75–98. https://doi.org/10.1037/0033-2909.116.1.75.

Lucco, Joseph. 2022. "Balanced Scorecard: The Comprehensive Guide." Clear-

Point Strategy. April 12, 2022. https://www.clearpointstrategy.com/full-exhaustive-balanced-scorecard-example/.

Majors, Melissa. 2022. "Empathy: The Gateway to Trust & Psychological Safety." Melissa Majors Consulting. February 21, 2022. https://www.melissamajors.com/blog/updbldg3wo8v4uc3avals3ka3y6ct9.

Maraniss, David. 1999. Essay. In *When Pride Still Mattered: A Life of Vince Lombardi*, 265. Thorndike, ME: Thorndike Press.

Marr, Bernard. 2021. "OKRs vs BSC: What Is the Difference?" BernardMarr.com. July 13, 2021. https://bernardmarr.com/okrs-vs-bsc-what-is-the-difference/.

Maxon, Tery. 2019. "Why Covering Airlines around the Genuinely Friendly Southwest CEO Herb Kelleher Could Be 'Dangerous'." The Dallas Morning News. January 5, 2019. https://www.dallasnews.com/business/local-companies/2019/01/05/why-covering-airlines-around-the-genuinely-friendly-southwest-ceo-herb-kelleher-could-be-dangerous/.

Maxwell, John C. 2008. *Leadership Gold: Lessons Learned from a Lifetime of Leading*. Nashville, TN: Thomas Nelson.

Mazur, Caitlin. 2022. "20 Essential Employee Feedback Statistics [2022]." Zippia. June 29, 2022. https://www.zippia.com/advice/employee-feedback-statistics/.

McLain, Denise, and Bailey Nelson. 2022. "How Fast Feedback Fuels Performance." Gallup.com. Gallup. January 1, 2022. https://www.gallup.com/workplace/357764/fast-feedback-fuels-performance.aspx.

"Meta Think Kit: Pre-Mortem." 2022. Meta for Business. Meta. 2022. https://www.facebook.com/business/m/thinkkit/exercises/strong-starts/pre-mortem.

"Meta Think Kit: Think, Pair, Share." 2022. Meta for Business. Meta. 2022. https://www.facebook.com/business/m/thinkkit/exercises/move-forward/think-pair-share.

Miller, Jennifer V. 2021. "Monkey See Monkey Do: New Leaders Emulate Their Bosses." People Equation. October 12, 2021. https://people-equation.com/monkey-see-monkey-do-new-leaders-emulate-their-bosses/.

Minahan, Tim. 2021. "What Your Future Employees Want Most." Harvard Business Review. Harvard University. March 31, 2021. https://hbr.org/2021/05/what-your-future-employees-want-most.

Moore, Martin G. 2022. "5 Things That Change When You Become a Leader." Harvard Business Review. January 20, 2022. https://hbr.org/2022/01/5-things-that-change-when-you-become-a-leader.

Morin, Amy. 2019. "The Top 10 Fears That Hold People Back in Life, According to a Psychotherapist." Inc.com. November 4, 2019.

https://www.inc.com/amy-morin/the-top-10-fears-that-hold-people-back-in-life-according-to-a-psychotherapist.html.

Murphy, Bill. 2022. "How People with High Emotional Intelligence Use the 'Chick-Fil-A Rule ...'" Inc.com. August 27, 2022. https://www.inc.com/bill-murphy-jr/how-people-with-high-emotional-intelligence-use-the-chick-fil-a-rule-to-make-much-better-decisions.html.

Murphy, Mark. 2021. "Your Leaders Are Spending Their Time in the Wrong Areas." TLNT. Ere Media. August 11, 2021. https://www.tlnt.com/your-leaders-are-spending-their-time-in-the-wrong-areas/.

Muñoz, Simón. 2019. "Disagree and Commit: The Importance of Disagreement in Decision Making." HackerNoon. January 17, 2019. https://hackernoon.-com/disagree-and-commit-the-importance-of-disagreement-in-decision-making-b31d1b5f1bdc.

Nassira. 2021. "Book Summary: 'On Becoming a Leader' by Warren Bennis." Oeconomia Finance. WordPress. April 20, 2021. https://oeconomiafinance.-wordpress.com/2021/04/20/book-summary-on-becoming-a-leader-by-warren-bennis/.

Newman, Jack. 2022. "World's Biggest Cruise Ship Costing £1.2billion to Be Sold for Scrap before It Has Set Sail." Daily Mail Online. Associated Newspapers. September 1, 2022. https://www.dailymail.co.uk/news/article-11167999/Worlds-biggest-cruise-ship-costing-1-2BILLION-sold-scrap-set-sail.html.

Nusca, Andrew. 2014. "IBM's Rometty: 'Growth and Comfort Don't Coexist'." Fortune.com. Fortune Magazine. October 7, 2014. https://fortune.-com/2014/10/07/ibms-rometty-growth-and-comfort-dont-coexist/.

O'Shaughnessy, Lynn. 2022. "Federal Government Publishes More Complete Graduation Rate Data: Cappex." Cappex. 2022. https://www.cappex.-com/articles/blog/government-publishes-graduation-rate-data.

Patel, Sujan. 2015. "10 Examples of Companies with Fantastic Cultures." Entrepreneur. August 6, 2015. https://www.entrepreneur.com/article/249174.

Patel, Sujan. 2016. "How Fortune 500 Leaders Schedule Their Days." Startups.com. August 18, 2016. https://www.startups.com/library/expert-advice/how-fortune-500-leaders-schedule-their-days.

"Personally Disrupted: 14 CEOS Who Got Axed after Failing to Navigate Disruption." 2019. CB Insights Research. CB Information Services. July 17, 2019. https://www.cbinsights.com/research/ceo-disruption/#blackberry.

Peters, Kim, and Alex Haslam. 2018. "Research: To Be a Good Leader, Start by Being a Good Follower." Harvard Business Review. September 21, 2018. https://hbr.org/2018/08/research-to-be-a-good-leader-start-by-being-a-good-follower.

Pines, Giulia. 2018. "The OKR Origin Story: A Closer Look at the Man Who Invented Okrs." What Matters. June 4, 2018. https://www.whatmatters.com/articles/the-origin-story.

Pokorny, Kevin. 2015. "Coaching with Fast Feedback." Kevin Pokorny Consulting. April 9, 2015. https://pokornyconsulting.com/coaching-with-fast-feedback/.

Probasco, Jim. 2022. "Top LGBTQ+ CEOS." Edited by Vikki Velasquez. Investopedia. May 31, 2022. https://www.investopedia.com/top-lgbtq-ceos-5323561.

Prossack, Ashira. 2018. "This Year, Don't Set New Year's Resolutions." Forbes. Forbes Magazine. December 31, 2018. https://www.forbes.com/sites/ashiraprossack1/2018/12/31/goals-not-resolutions/?sh=4d85d633879a.

"Re:Work." 2022. Re:Work. Google. 2022. https://rework.withgoogle.com/print/guides/5721312655835136/.

"Re:Work." 2022. Re:Work. Google. 2022. https://rework.withgoogle.com/print/guides/6229207193485312/.

Reiners, Bailey. 2021. "57 Diversity in the Workplace Statistics You Should Know." Edited by Kal Hoss. Built In. October 21, 2021. https://builtin.com/diversity-inclusion/diversity-in-the-workplace-statistics.

Rella, Emily. 2022. "Google's CEO Is Asking Employees 3 Simple Questions to Boost Productivity." Entrepreneur. August 8, 2022. https://www.entrepreneur.com/article/432968.

Robinson, Kim. 2021. "Words Matter: Gender-Coded Language in Job Ads." Employers Council. May 27, 2021. https://www.employerscouncil.org/resources/words-matter-gender-coded-language-in-job-ads/.

"The ROI of Executive Coaching." 2022. American University. 2022. https://www.american.edu/provost/ogps/executive-education/executive-coaching/roi-of-executive-coaching.cfm.

Rozovsky, Julia. 2015. "Re:Work - the Five Keys to a Successful Google Team." Re:Work. Google. November 17, 2015. https://rework.withgoogle.com/blog/five-keys-to-a-successful-google-team/.

Ryba, Kristin. 2021. "What Is Employee Engagement? What, Why, and How to Improve It." Quantum Workplace. March 2, 2021. https://www.quantumworkplace.com/future-of-work/what-is-employee-engagement-definition.

Sanders, Ian. 2015. "17 Quotes on the Future of Technology from Davos 2015." World Economic Forum. January 22, 2015. https://www.weforum.org/agenda/2015/01/17-quotes-on-the-future-of-technology-from-davos-2015/?utm_content=buffer84cf1&utm_medium=social&utm_source=twitter.com&utm_campaign=buffer.

Schmidt, Eric, Alan Eagle, and Jonathan Rosenberg. 2020. *Trillion Dollar*

Coach: The Leadership Playbook of Silicon Valley's Bill Campbell. London: John Murray.

Schwartz, Karen. 1996. "Tangy Touch in the Sky." New Bedford Standard-Times. Standard-Times. November 16, 1996. https://www.southcoasttoday.com/story/business/1996/11/17/tangy-touch-in-sky/50619361007/.

"Senior Leader Demographics and Statistics in the US." 2020. Zippia. 2020. https://www.zippia.com/senior-leader-jobs/demographics/.

Sharkey, Mike. 2022. "The Four Types of Organizational Culture." Workplace. Meta. September 29, 2022. https://www.workplace.com/blog/organizational-culture.

Shashkevich, Alex. 2019. "Online Dating Is the Most Popular Way Couples Meet." Stanford News. Stanford University. August 21, 2019. https://news.stanford.edu/2019/08/21/online-dating-popular-way-u-s-couples-meet/.

Skillman, Peter. 2019. "The Design Challenge." Medium. April 14, 2019. https://medium.com/@peterskillman/the-design-challenge-also-called-spaghetti-tower-cda62685e15b.

Smith, Dominic. 2021. "Celebrating 50 Years of Email." Google Workspace. Google. October 29, 2021. https://workspace.google.com/blog/productivity-collaboration/celebrating-50-years-of-email.

Stanuch, Kamil. 2020. "My 11 Notes from 'Trillion Dollar Coach: The Leadership Playbook of Silicon Valley's Bill Campbell.'" Medium. June 1, 2020. https://kamilstanuch.medium.com/my-11-notes-from-trillion-dollar-coach-the-leadership-playbook-of-silicon-valleys-bill-campbell-606e7043ec49.

Statt, Nick. 2014. "Zuckerberg: 'Move Fast and Break Things' Isn't How Facebook Operates Anymore." CNET. April 30, 2014. https://www.cnet.com/tech/mobile/zuckerberg-move-fast-and-break-things-isnt-how-we-operate-anymore/.

"Status Dropout Rates." 2022. National Center for Education Statistics. U.S. Department of Education. 2022. https://nces.ed.gov/programs/coe/indicator/coj/status-dropout-rates.

Stempel, Jonathan. 2017. "21st Century Fox in $90 Million Settlement Tied to Sexual Harassment Scandal." Reuters. Thomson Reuters. November 20, 2017. https://www.reuters.com/article/us-fox-settlement/21st-century-fox-in-90-million-settlement-tied-to-sexual-harassment-scandal-idUSKBN1DK2NI.

Sull, Charles, Donald Sull, and Ben Zweig. 2022. "Toxic Culture Is Driving the Great Resignation." MIT Sloan Management Review. Massachusetts Institute of Technology. January 11, 2022. https://sloanreview.mit.edu/article/toxic-culture-is-driving-the-great-resignation/.

Sull, Don, and Charlie Sull. 2022. "MIT SMR's Culture 500." MIT Sloan

Management Review. Massachusetts Institute of Technology. 2022. https://sloanreview.mit.edu/culture500/research.

Sull, Donald, Charles Sull, and Andrew Chamberlain. 2019. "Measuring Culture in Leading Companies." MIT Sloan Management Review. June 24, 2019. https://sloanreview.mit.edu/projects/measuring-culture-in-leading-companies/.

Taylor, Ryan. 2021. "John F. Kennedy (JFK) Moon Speech Transcript: 'We Choose to Go to the Moon.'" Rev. Rev. August 30, 2021. https://www.rev.com/blog/transcripts/john-f-kennedy-jfk-moon-speech-transcript-we-choose-to-go-to-the-moon.

Thompson, Gregg. 2021. "The Top 10 Coaching Mistakes." Bluepoint Leadership Development. Simplify Compliance LLC. November 5, 2021. https://bluepointleadership.com/resource/the-top-10-coaching-mistakes/.

Tú , Minh. 2021. "What Is OKR? Characteristics of Okrs? How to Implement Okrs?" Hocmarketing.org. Cloudtek. August 29, 2021. https://en.hocmarketing.org/advanced-marketing/okr-model.

Ubl, Malte. 2020. "Design Docs at Google." Industrial Empathy. July 6, 2020. https://www.industrialempathy.com/posts/design-docs-at-google/.

"The Ultimate OKR Guide." 2022. Perdoo. August 16, 2022. https://www.perdoo.com/okr-guide/.

Varner, Ann. 2018. "Mrs., Miss, and Ms.: The Evolution of 'Ms.'." UMKC Womens Center. University of Missouri-Kansas City. September 5, 2018. https://info.umkc.edu/womenc/2018/09/05/mrs-miss-and-ms-the-evolution-of-ms/.

Vidojevic, Andjela. 2022. "Collaborative Leadership: Creating a Team-Centric Mindset." Pumble Blog. Pumble. July 7, 2022. https://pumble.com/blog/collaborative-leadership/.

Villafañe, Camila. 2018. "10 Steve Jobs Marketing Lessons and His Famous Marketing Quotes - Postcron." PostCron. 2018. https://postcron.com/en/blog/10-amazing-marketing-lessons-steve-jobs-taught-us/.

"What Is a Key Performance Indicator (KPI)? Guide & Examples." n.d. Qlik. Accessed October 19, 2022. https://www.qlik.com/us/kpi/.

"What Is Important Is Seldom Urgent and What Is Urgent Is Seldom Important." 2019. Quote Investigator. May 22, 2019. https://quoteinvestigator.com/2014/05/09/urgent/.

"What Is the Great Resignation? Definition, Causes & Impact." 2022. TheStreet. June 29, 2022. https://www.thestreet.com/dictionary/g/great-resignation-big-quit-great-reshuffle.

"Who Was Steve Jobs? See the Apple Founder's Career and More." 2022. Entrepreneur. May 25, 2022. https://www.entrepreneur.com/article/197538.

"Why Diversity Builds Better Products: Rainforest Qa." 2017. Rainforest QA.

June 19, 2017. https://www.rainforestqa.com/blog/2017-06-19-why-diversity-builds-better-products.

"Why Spanish Speakers in US Are Getting into Trouble." 2018. BBC News. BBC. May 22, 2018. https://www.bbc.com/news/world-us-canada-44201444.

Wiles, Jackie. 2019. "There Are 4 Manager Types and Not All Are Created Equal." Gartner. August 22, 2019. https://www.gartner.com/smarterwithgartner/what-type-of-manager-are-you.

Williams, Simon J. 2014. "Promoting Collaboration: 4 Lessons from Google." Redbooth. February 7, 2014. https://redbooth.com/blog/promoting-collaboration-br4-lessons-from-google.

Winters, Jeanette. 2020. "Employee Engagement - Owner versus Renter Mentality." HR Exchange Network. International Quality & Productivity Center. March 17, 2020. https://www.hrexchangenetwork.com/employee-engagement/columns/employee-engagement-owner-versus-renter-mentality.

Wissman, Barrett. 2018. "An Accountability Partner Makes You Vastly More Likely to Succeed." Entrepreneur. March 20, 2018. https://www.entrepreneur.com/article/310062.

Wolff, Adam, and Nick Dellamaggiore. 2019. "Creating a SEV Process That Scales with Robinhood." Robinhood Engineering. Medium. October 10, 2019. https://robinhood.engineering/creating-a-sev-process-that-scales-with-robinhood-4b433f9c439b.

Wood, Robert. 2008. "Standing Long Jump Test (Broad Jump)." Top End Sports. 2008. https://www.topendsports.com/testing/tests/longjump.htm.

Xu, Tammy. 2020. "Side Project Programs Can Have Major Benefits for Employers." Built In. July 4, 2020. https://builtin.com/software-engineering-perspectives/20-percent-time.

Zetlin, Minda. 2022. "In Just 3 Words, Google CEO Sundar Pichai Taught a Leadership Lesson to Every CEO." Inc.com. July 15, 2022. https://www.inc.com/minda-zetlin/google-ceo-sundar-pichai-memo-hiring-slowdown-inspiration.html.

ABOUT THE AUTHOR

Andrew Swerdlow is a pioneer in technology development, leading cutting-edge software projects across multiple disciplines. During his leadership at Google, Instagram, Facebook, and YouTube, he's been awarded more than thirty-five patents.

In addition to possessing deep experience building and leading globally-distributed software teams of 100-plus engineers, Swerdlow is known as a passionate leader with a knack for caring for his team members while unlocking team productivity. His team's work has reached billions of users across multiple products.

Swerdlow earned his BSc and MSc from University of Victoria, as well as another MSc from Drexel University along with SAPM certification from Stanford University.

Despite his multiple professional accomplishments, Swerdlow is most proud of his mentorship to the next generation of leaders, guidance to entrepreneurs and startups, cofounding of the San Francisco-based experiences incubator called The Laundry, and his family.

Connect with him at AndrewSwerdlow.net.